Multimedia in Action!

Linda Tway
Sapphire Pacific
La Jolla, CA

AP PROFESSIONAL

Boston San Diego New York
London Sydney Tokyo Toronto

AP PROFESSIONAL
1300 Boylston Street, Chestnut Hill, MA 02167

An Imprint of ACADEMIC PRESS, INC.
A Division of HARCOURT BRACE & COMPANY

United Kingdom Edition published by
ACADEMIC PRESS LIMITED
24–28 Oval Road, London NW1 7DX

Library of Congress Cataloging-in-Publication Data

Tway, Linda
    Multimedia in action! / Linda Tway
          p.   cm.
    Includes bibliographical references and index.
    ISBN 0-12-705250-X (pbk. : acid-free paper). --ISBN
0-12-705251-8 (CD-Rom)
    1. Multimedia systems. I. Title.
QA76.575.T88 1995
006.6--dc20   95-10182
                                                                   CIP

Printed in the United States of America
   95 96 97 98   ML   9 8 7 6 5 4 3 2 1

Contents

Acknowledgments   ix

Purpose of This Book   xv

Introduction to Profiles   xvii

1   Introduction   1

What Is Multimedia?   2   •   What Is Multimedia's Great
Appeal?   2   •   The "Media" in Multimedia   4   •   Multimedia
Arenas   6   •   Multimedia Platforms   9   •   What the Future Holds
for Multimedia   13   •   Summary   14   •   Further Reading   15   •

2   General Concerns of the Developer   17

Introduction   18   •   Copyrights and Other Legal Issues   18   •
Storage   22   •   Application Delivery   25   •   Summary   30   •
Further Reading   31

3   An Overview of Development Software and Hardware   33

Introduction   34   •   Text   34   •   Static (or Still)

Graphics 37 • Animation and Morphing 40 • Sound 42 •
Video 44 • Integration and Interactivity 47 • Multimedia
Database Software 51 • Cross-platform Compatibility 52 •
Summary 54 • Further Reading 55

4   Multimedia as Educator   57

Introduction 58 • Overview of Profiles 59 • Particles and
Prairies 60 • The Video Linguist 69 • Dinosaurs 74 •
Further Reading 82

5   The Multimedia Trainer   83

Introduction 84 • Overview of Profiles 85 • A.D.A.M.
(Animated Dissection of Anatomy for Medicine) 86 • Multimedia
Hazmat 99 • Further Reading 108

6   The Multimedia Reference Tool   111

Introduction 112 • Overview of Profiles 113 •
Encarta 113 • Novato Electronic City Hall 124 •
Further Reading 132

7   Marketing with Multimedia   133

Introduction 134 • Overview of Profiles 135 • Electronic
Business Card and Mary Chapin Carpenter 136 • Grow with Hawaii
into the Pacific Century 147 • Further Reading 154

8   That's Entertainment!   155

Introduction 156 • Overview of Profiles 157 • The Journeyman
Project and Buried in Time 158 • The 7th Guest and
The 11th Hour 172 • Further Reading 184

9   Adapting Books to Interact   185

Introduction 186 • Overview of Profiles 187 • Living
Books 188 • The Essential Frankenstein 197 • Further
Reading 207

10   Consulting in the Multimedia World   209

Introduction 210 • Overview of Profiles 211 • Imagix

Contents

Productions   212   •   Sapphire Pacific   221   •   Further Reading   231

Resource Directory   233

Magazines and Newsletters   234   •   Organizations   235   •
CD-ROM Sources   235   •   Software   236   •   Hardware
Peripherals   246   •   Glossary   251

Index   259

Acknowledgments

In the course of writing a book, it is inevitable that many other people play a role. In this book, an unusual number of people helped make the various pieces all come together. To accurately describe the development of the multimedia titles profiled in this book, I interviewed nearly 25 people from 16 companies and organizations. In addition, many others who work with them provided information and software, and served as liaisons, which greatly facilitated my interviews. In the interest of accuracy, I asked each person I interviewed to read and approve what I had written before I submitted it to my editor. Even the most conscientious efforts can result in occasional "glitches" in communication. And I must admit that a few people I interviewed relayed such humorous anecdotes that I wanted to be certain that I could pass those stories on to you. In addition, many companies provided demo versions of multimedia software for the accompanying CD-ROM.

Before I acknowledge all those who helped with this project, I must first thank my editor, Jenifer Niles. She showed extraordinary patience and understanding regarding the complexities of coordinating the various aspects of this project and made every effort to facilitate the completion of this book. I am also grateful to Mike Williams, Gnomi Gouldin, Karen Pratt, and Jacqui Young at APP for assisting with various aspects of the project.

For my profile of "Particles and Prairies," I thank Liz Quigg and Jim Shultz from Fermilab in Illinois and Pat Franzen who currently teaches at Germantown Hills Middle School in central Illinois. All were very enthusiastic about sharing their experiences regarding development of high-quality educational software and how it can be incorporated into a school's curriculum. I thank Patrick Nee from Cubic Media whose insights into the development of the "Video Linguist" illustrate how luck can play an important role in the success of a product. John Porcaro at Microsoft Corporation provided information on "Dinosaurs" and detailed how that company's concern for accuracy affected its development.

Greg Swayne of A.D.A.M. Software talked to me at length about the development of "A.D.A.M.," and I appreciate his permission to relay an embarrassing faux pax the firm made. I also thank Amy Woodward Parrish from A.D.A.M. for providing me with software and a good laugh from time to time. For my profile of "Multimedia Hazmat," I am grateful to Marie Burlinson of RJM Multimedia who shared her insights into the aspects of good training software, and to Jack Tyler and Paul Smith of the Fire Academy in British Columbia who discussed the resulting effectiveness of the program.

I thank Kathy Fiander and Jay Gibson at Microsoft for the information they provided on the development of "Encarta" and for explaining its uniqueness from other electronic encyclopedias. Richard Bennion of StudioGraphics shared his experiences in developing "Novato Electronic City Hall" and the various aspects involved in creating an effective kiosk. Jody Quinteros, also from StudioGraphics, coordinated the interview and facilitated my acquisition of software and company background information.

From West End Post Interactive, I am grateful to Carolyn Carmines and James Marzano, and I also thank Tim Smith from Red Sky Interactive. They provided a fascinating look at the challenges involved in packing the "Electronic Business Card" and other multimedia products onto a single floppy disk. I am also grateful to Faith Jackson from West End Post Interactive for her rapid responses to my requests for background information, software and screen grabs. David Teton-Landis from Tom Coffman Multimedia explained that firm's strategies in developing "Grow with Hawaii into the Pacific Century" using IBM's Ultimedia system.

For "The Journeyman Project" and its sequel "Buried in Time," I thank Michel Kripalani. He provided a fascinating look into the complexities involved in developing a photorealistic program while keeping costs down. I thank Graeme Devine and Rob Landeros of Trilobyte for a sometimes comical interview regarding the development of "The 7th Guest" and its sequel, "The 11th Hour," and for sharing details of the enormous challenges they had to overcome. I also thank Jane Le Feyve, also from Trilobyte, for her efforts in coordinating the interview and making sure I had the necessary software and company information.

From "Living Books," I am grateful to Mark Schlichting for a delightful conversation that allowed me to understand the different personalities that make the "Living Books" so much fun. Todd Power offered his insights into quality control, and Steve Linden pointed me in the right direction to get the interviews I needed. For "The Essential Frankenstein," Rachel Forrest from

Byron Preiss Multimedia provided valuable insights into the strategies needed to make an electronic version of a classic book such as *Frankenstein* and *Slaughterhouse Five* much more enriching than the original version.

And I thank Gary Chapman of Imagix Productions for sharing his experiences as a consultant developing multimedia applications for other companies. His associate Gary Holley also spent time explaining his role in the development process.

Numerous companies provided demo versions of multimedia development software to be included on the CD-ROM for this book, and I am grateful to all of them as well. These companies are Adobe Systems, Future Vision Multimedia, Gold Disk Software, Gryphon Software, HSC Software, Lenel Systems International, Macromedia, North Coast Software, and Turtle Beach Systems.

For assistance with the development of the program for the CD-ROM, I am grateful to John Slade of Knowledge Garden. Others who helped in various ways are Karen Cutler at NewMedia Magazine, Michelle Dollarhide from Waggener Edstrom, Bill Riedel from Scripps Institution of Oceanography, and Elizabeth Riedel from The Bishops School in La Jolla.

Finally I am very grateful to my family and friends for tolerating my "absence" for a number of months while offering their encouragement and support.

Purpose of This Book

Anyone embarking on a new enterprise is inevitably faced with a certain amount of ignorance—not from a lack of intelligence but from a lack of insight and experience. This is particularly true of an enterprise involving state-of-the-art and rapidly changing technology such as multimedia. Unfortunately, lack of insight and experience can undermine the success of that enterprise. Many savvy business people are convinced that it is not always best to be the "first," because this places the burden (which translates into cost) of research and development (R&D) on the leading-edge company. Although being "first" may preclude initial competition, it also involves a greater risk of making mistakes (and paying dearly for them).

Companies that "follow" are in the enviable position of learning from the efforts of pioneering companies, even though the follower may be taking on a large and successful competitor by the time it enters the race. Naturally, not all companies that have pioneered a technology are willing to divulge much information about their endeavors, but those who are can provide valuable guidance to companies launching similar projects.

I have some personal experience in the burden of R&D in the area of artificial intelligence (AI) a decade ago. At that time, AI software was not only very expensive ($5,000–$10,000 was not an unusual cost for software that fit onto a single medium-density $5\frac{1}{4}$ " disk—bugs and all), it was also pretty scarce and had a steep learning curve. Those companies from which one could purchase AI software were apt to go out of business very quickly. I was fortunate that my early tenure in R&D was spent with the University of California, and the projects on which I worked were funded through various research grants. Since the time I formed my own software development company in 1989 for AI and multimedia application development, I have become even more painfully aware of the cost of R&D (it comes out of my pocket now), and I am particularly grateful for the generous advice and guidance of others who have led the way through their own application development.

It is with this in mind that this book has been written. The drop in multimedia hardware costs and the greater availability and usability of multimedia software have made multimedia application development accessible to a wider audience of users than ever before. And multimedia itself is so captivating that many users see an immediate title that they would like to develop.

Although the potential developer may have access to the necessary hardware and software, there still exists a lack of inside knowledge about the unexpected pitfalls (and solutions) that the developer will encounter. This book is meant to fill that gap. Nearly all the titles profiled in this book have received major awards. And the companies that developed these titles have graciously agreed to share their own experiences in developing them—experiences that will help others with their own multimedia development.

Included in this book are interviews with some of the largest players in multimedia title development such as Microsoft, smaller entrepreneurial companies such as Presto Studios and Tom Coffman Multimedia, and educational development centers such as Friends of Fermilab. Each provides a unique experience and background, interesting anecdotes, and valuable advice to the potential multimedia developer.

It should be particularly heartening to the small developer to read the attempts of other small companies to develop multimedia products that were able to win major awards in competition against some of the largest software companies in the world. After all, multimedia is a new game in the computer industry—in many ways its production and "content" have more in parallel to the publishing industry than to traditional computer technology.

Perhaps most interesting is the unusual mixture of people involved in developing multimedia titles. Most have come to the technology from other careers: graphic arts, science, film production, and personnel training. They embraced multimedia as a way to augment and amplify what they had been trying to communicate to others. A graphic artist saw multimedia as a way to tell interactive stories to children and found immediate gratification from creating and viewing an animated sequence in a matter of hours instead of months. A science teacher became involved in multimedia when she saw how much easier it is to convey scientific principles to students using video and sound. Many others have similar stories to tell. I was particularly impressed by the candor (and sometimes humor) the various people relayed and learned a great deal that will help me in my own multimedia projects.

Because of the varied backgrounds of the people I spoke with, our interviews involved a much richer perspective of multimedia application development than stories that are purely technical or from a strictly computer programmer's viewpoint. As a result, this book will be of interest to a much wider audience and equally useful to those starting out in multimedia title development and those who already have experience.

Introduction to Profiles

The pages that follow provide a fascinating look into the development of multimedia titles in virtually every arena from education and training to entertainment and book adaptation. Each chapter includes a profile of two (or, in the case of education, three) multimedia titles. My goal when seeking the titles to include in each chapter was twofold. My first concern was that every title had been recognized as an example of an excellent multimedia product in terms of content, design, and interactivity; and all the titles profiled here have won major awards in very stiff competition.

My other objective for each chapter was to include titles that would provide different viewpoints in terms of the development process. This involved aspects such as content, the target audience, and the size of the company that developed it. For example, the chapter on education profiles three titles that were developed under very different circumstances and from very different perspectives. One titles was developed by a not-for-profit organization for middle school children, another title targets the adult learner and was developed by a small for-profit firm, and the third illustrates an edutainment title developed by the largest software company in the world. Each one of these profiles shows a distinct approach to creating a multimedia application, such as acquiring content, managing a project team, and targeting (and marketing to) a particular audience.

Every person I spoke with offered guidelines (and sometimes warnings) to those who are interested in developing a similar type of application and most of them also shared humorous anecdotes that occurred during development. Several of them expressed opposing viewpoints, such as the size of the team required to produce a multimedia application, but these differing perspectives are valuable in illustrating the various approaches used by different persons and organizations.

Finally, I would like to point out that it was not easy for me to decide which title to include in which chapter. Many of the titles lend themselves to being used in different areas, particularly education. For example, A.D.A.M. Software, although certainly a training program, could just as easily have been profiled as an educational title. The Living Books are included here with other book adaptations, but are very educational and have won awards in this category. And Encarta is certainly educational, although it is included here as a reference title. It is because of this that I encourage the reader to explore all the profiles in this book. Every one of them provides guidelines and information useful to the developer of any type of interactive multimedia title.

INTRODUCTION

· O N E ·

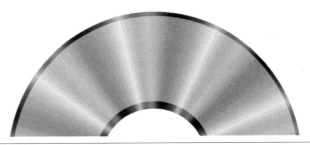

What Is Multimedia?

The word *multimedia* has been used by different industries to mean different things. Technically, the term refers to the use of more than one medium to convey information. This could mean using two slide projectors at one time (as was common years ago) or combining a narrative with a video to enhance a presentation. Music videos on MTV are a good example of "multimedia" in the music industry—video is used to provide visual impact to a soundtrack. There is no doubt that combining several means of communicating is much more effective, and the more media that are used, the greater the impact and amount of information that can be presented. Although we may enjoy listening to the music of *Swan Lake,* the visual impact of seeing the ballet performed at the same time not only enriches our enjoyment of the music, but it also allows us to better understand the story behind the music, especially if we are also able to read a program that explains the story.

In the computer industry, we tend to use the phrase *desktop multimedia* or *digital multimedia* to distinguish it from other meanings. However, even within the computer world, this may mean anything from the use of text and graphics to the additional use of sound, animation, and video (both digital and analog). More recently, multimedia (specifically *interactive multimedia*) has come to imply all of these elements combined in an interactive program so that the user has control over the information provided.

What Is Multimedia's Great Appeal?

The rapid growth of the multimedia industry is staggering. The market for consumer CD-ROM titles was $325 million in 1993 and is expected to grow to a $1 billion market by the end of 1996. Some recently opened software stores sell multimedia titles almost exclusively, and many bookstores now sell multi-media titles as electronic books. There is no doubt that multimedia is having an enormous impact on the way we use our computers.

To better appreciate the tremendous success multimedia is experiencing, it is interesting to take a look at another computer technology that in recent years promised to revolutionize the way people interact with computers: artificial intelligence (or AI). AI refers to a computer's ability to perform various tasks in the same way that humans do and encompasses such areas as "robotics," "expert systems," and "neural networks." Such tasks generally involve taking complex, interrelated information and putting it together to form a coherent "thought," resulting in a decision or action that closely reflects what a human would conclude or do given the same information.

For a time, the entire notion of AI was glamorized, not only by the media but also by those involved in AI. Perhaps because of the difficulty in explaining the concept in a nontechnical way, AI was portrayed in futuristic images of what would someday be possible using this technology. People expected that they would be having "normal" conversations with their computer and in general be interacting with it like a human, years before it would happen.

It is true that AI was slow to take off in the business arena. It got its start in research labs and academia, where funds and the impetus to bring it to commercialization were scarce or lacking. And those working in the field had difficulty in communicating to the layperson what it was all about and how it could benefit a business. In addition, the hardware required and the software available to develop AI applications were further obstacles. This all changed in a matter of a few years, but by then the layperson was already disillusioned (or frightened that a computer was going to replace him or her in the workplace).

Make no mistake—AI *did* take off and had a great impact on the computer industry. It is an integral part of most "intelligent" software and many products on the market today, whether for making complex financial analyses or for autofocusing your camera. Good AI technology should, after all, be invisible to the user. So, in the minds of most people, AI technology faded into something of little interest that they could not personally relate to, when what they had been expecting was a way to more personally interact with their computers.

Enter "multimedia," another technology that promised to change the way we use our computers. It is interesting how skeptical many were at first encountering multimedia, probably as a result of the perceived letdown of AI technology. Fortunately, most grasped its implications almost immediately. And for a very good reason—even a four-year-old child can understand it. There is no need to explain how it can benefit (or entertain) the user—the user can see it and, in some sense, feel it.

Multimedia is, in fact, the technology that made people feel as if they are interacting with their computers. Like a conversation with another person, interactive software allows you to lead the conversation into different directions, and if you do not understand something, you can interrupt and ask for more information (which may be "spoken" to you by the computer) or ask to see a picture. This element of guidance and interactivity is very appealing.

The "Media" in Multimedia

The effectiveness of a multimedia title is closely tied to the various media it contains. It is not my intention to provide detail in this book on the development of video and graphics, for example, but rather to provide an overview of their role, design, and basic requirements in terms of software and hardware. There are several good books that provide detailed guidelines for effective multimedia development (see Further Reading at the end of this chapter).

It is important to understand the various "media" that may be used in an interactive application, because each requires special software and hardware. In Chapter 3, we will look at each of these media in a little more detail.

Text

Text is the basic element of most multimedia titles. Exceptions to this include entertainment and children's titles. Text is of concern to the developer from two main standpoints. The first is the way in which text is presented to the user: it should be easy to read and well designed. This involves the consideration of font, color, and text size. Unless the application includes a great deal of reference material (such as an electronic encyclopedia or book adaptation), text should be kept to a minimum—the user will not read long displays of text. No matter what the application, text intended to instruct the user how to use the program should be brief.

The second main concern of the developer is what lies behind the text; that is, the interactive "links" that the user does not see but can activate to get to additional information. This *hypertext* or *hot text*, when clicked on, may bring up additional explanatory text, a photograph, video, or sound. The developer must pay close attention to the organization of these links, particularly in an application in which text plays a key role, such as an encyclopedia or training system.

Graphics

Graphics may include a drawing, a high-resolution photograph, or an icon. Graphics are perhaps the most important aspect of a multimedia title because they provide a great deal of information at a relatively low "cost" in terms of required storage. Graphics may also serve as hyperlinks to other types of information.

Animation and Morphing

An animated sequence is a set of graphic images that may be displayed quickly as a series of frames or a set of objects (or "characters"). Morphing is a type of animation in which interpolations between specified points on two or more images are used to create a transitional effect, such as the image of a cat changing into a dog.

Video

A few years ago, it was not practical for video (such as that recorded with a standard VCR) to be displayed on a modestly priced microcomputer. The hardware required was expensive, and the ability to store a number of video clip files took prohibitive amounts of storage. Now, however, due to falling hardware prices, larger storage capacities, and more advanced data compression techniques, video is increasingly commonplace. In fact, video playback capabilities are becoming standard on most new PCs that come with Windows. This, in turn, will drive the market toward software that incorporates video.

Sound

Sound may include a narrative, music, or special effects and, when properly integrated, greatly enhances a multimedia application. For example, a narration is a useful accompaniment to an animation to explain what is happening while the user is viewing the animation. Like video, high-quality sound files require a lot of storage, but the evolution of data compression techniques along with the drop in prices for large hard drives and CD-ROM drives has made sound an integral part of multimedia titles.

Interactivity

The real key to an effective and successful multimedia title is its interactive design, which allows the user to "navigate" through the program any way that he or she chooses. This is what makes the program feel more personal to the user. The interactive links may connect any one of the four types of media (that is, text, graphics, video, and sound) with each other.

Multimedia Arenas

An interesting phenomenon surrounding multimedia is that it is the first PC technology driven by the consumer market and not the business market. Although multimedia will continue to infiltrate all areas of computer use, education and entertainment (and a blend of the two, called *edutainment*) have been the largest arenas for multimedia titles. The home computer buyer purchased over 700,000 multimedia PCs and more than 500,000 multimedia upgrade kits in 1993 alone. These statistics are not hard to understand. It is now possible to purchase a multimedia computer complete with CD-ROM titles such as an interactive encyclopedia for the same price as an encyclopedia delivered in book format.

Although businesses have not been as inclined to upgrade to a multimedia computer just so they can play sound or video clips, the use of multimedia sales presentations and training programs has found an important niche in the business world. Many businesses find multimedia applications have greatly increased job productivity and reduced the cost to train new employees.

Some of the arenas in which multimedia titles have been most successfully exploited will now be explored.

Education

Educators claim to have been the first to recognize the power of multimedia and take advantage of the technology. Multimedia exposes students to multiple forms of information, thus reinforcing the learning process. More important, students may access information in a nonlinear way. Not only is this a more intuitive way to learn, but it also allows students to learn at their own pace. Less knowledgeable students may access explanatory information that more advanced students need not spend time on. This permits the beginner to move at a comfortable pace and allows advanced students to progress more rapidly (and avoid becoming bored). Another rapidly growing market involves "edutainment,"—multimedia software that provides educational material in an entertaining way, encouraging users to explore and learn while having fun.

Training

Like education, training has benefited tremendously from multimedia for many of the same reasons education has. Training programs frequently include tutorials or quizzes, which may involve expert system technology as well. Businesses and other professions (especially medicine) using multimedia training programs have experienced significant time savings in training new or inexperienced personnel.

Information Access

One of the first uses for CD-ROM was data storage. A CD-ROM disk holding 600 MB of data was a considerable breakthrough for those wanting to archive files. Eventually, other information found its way to CD-ROM such as large volumes of literary works, encyclopedias, and other reference books. Most of the early CD-ROMs were not very interactive: they allowed you to enter one or more keywords to search for a specific topic and presented the information in textual format. Graphics were rare or absent. Fortunately, information stored on CD-ROMs is now much more interactive. True multimedia-based references are commonplace and a great way to search for information, both quickly and comprehensively.

Sales and Marketing

Not very long ago, a business that wanted to create an impressive presentation including animation, sound and video had to rely on an outside firm to produce a videotape. The recent proliferation of presentation software has made this unnecessary in most cases. Now, any company may easily put together a striking multimedia demonstration that can be run on a portable computer or in a kiosk.

Entertainment

There is no doubt that the multimedia market has been driven by the consumer's voracity for entertainment. What began as Mario Brothers on the Nintendo has mushroomed into an enormous market for multimedia entertainment running on virtually every computer platform. Multimedia "games" cover the spectrum of entertainment for every age group and rely on technologies ranging from joy sticks to virtual reality headsets. Special virtual reality arcades have opened up that allow "users" to experience adventures truly beyond belief. Other entertainment is meant to have educational content, and this "edutainment" is a rapidly growing area of multimedia.

Book Adaptation

Imagine reading a novel in which you can control the plot and the character's actions and that may have a very different ending than the same novel read by your friend. Although it sounds futuristic, such "hyperfiction" is available now and will undoubtedly lead to an entirely different approach to writing novels in the future. Although most of the current hyperfiction involves an adaptation of a work that was previously written for a linear, paper-based format, an increasing number of titles are being written specifically for the interactive computer environment. Other than providing an interesting "twist" to a novel, multimedia is also a great way to learn more about the book you are reading. If you are reading about a character who lives in Algiers, and you'd like to know more about that location, a simple click on the word *Algiers* could display a map and pertinent background material. This can greatly enhance your understanding of the book you are reading.

It is probably apparent that many of these categories overlap to some degree. Edutainment is obviously a blend of education and entertainment. But where do you draw the line between a reference CD-ROM and one that is a book adaptation, or between education and training, or even education and information access or a book adaptation? Later chapters in this book focus on each category, and in many cases a title that is profiled within one chapter could be placed in a different chapter. But the very fact that multimedia titles affect people in many different ways means that they are useful in many different arenas.

Multimedia Platforms

There are many platforms on which one may develop and run multimedia titles. Although the ultimate goal is a single version of a title that can be run on any platform (e.g., Mac, Windows, IBM), a title is generally developed on one platform and different versions are then created to run on other platforms. If a title is small enough, more than one version of it may be placed on the same CD-ROM, allowing it to be run on more than one platform. This is becoming increasingly common with titles developed for Mac and Windows. However, with Director (an authoring software package), a developer may now create a single title that can be run both on a Mac and in Windows.

Here, we take a brief look at the most common platforms used to develop multimedia titles. It is not my intention to provide detail on specific hardware and software, in part because many books are available that focus on these topics and in part because the industry is changing so rapidly that specific information quickly becomes out of date.

Apple Macintosh (Mac)

Most Macintosh enthusiasts are quick to point out that the Mac was years ahead of the PC-compatible computer in terms of graphics and multimedia. Indeed, the first Macintosh computer (released in 1984) had built-in graphics and sound capabilities, something the PC did not acquire until much later. The easy-to–use graphical user interface (GUI) of the Mac introduced to the user the concept of windows, icons, menus and pointers (the first letters of which spell *wimp*, as many die-hard PC-enthusiasts liked to counter). Of course, the GUI interface has since swept the PC market as well, as is attested to by the popularity of Windows.

The Mac was also ahead of the PC with built-in CD-ROM drives and integrated digital signal processor (DSP) chips, which quickly process complex sound, graphics and video, thus greatly increasing real-time performance of the computer. This, of course, is crucial for multimedia applications. In addition, it is very easy to install additional hardware components to a Mac computer partly because of its use of a single SCSI interface to connect various peripherals and also because of the strict controls Apple has placed on all its hardware components.

Perhaps one of the most important aspects of the Mac is the standardized interface of every software program used on the Mac. This means that no matter what software the user installs, it will work essentially the same way, whether it is a word processor or a graphics package. Menu items and their operations are standardized, as are icons and file formats. The Mac comes with an easy-to-use authoring system called *HyperCard* as well as a graphics package called *QuickDraw* that supports both bitmapped and vector graphics. Using vector graphics, the developer can keep graphic file sizes to a minimum.

Multimedia developers have found Apple's QuickTime to be particularly valuable because it synchronizes audio and video tracks and keeps the two in sync even on computers running at different speeds. Because of its built-in graphics and sound capabilities, the Macintosh has been the computer of choice for graphics, desktop publishing, and music synthesis. It is also commonly used in primary and secondary schools. However, it has not been able to gain a foothold in the corporate world, which has so far been the largest market for microcomputers. Its relatively high price has also made it less popular with the home computer user who can purchase a PC-compatible system for much less.

PC-Compatible Systems

When the IBM-PC was introduced in 1981, it used an architecture called *ISA* (or industry standard architecture), which evolved into the EISA (extended industry standard architecture). The EISA architecture has been the standard architecture used by numerous PC clone manufacturers such as Compaq, Tandy, AST, Hewlett-Packard, and NEC. In 1987, IBM introduced a proprietary architecture called the micro channel architecture in an attempt to more effectively compete with the clone market (see the section on the IBM PS/2 platform).

Few standards have been set up for PC-compatibles. This is due, in part, to the number of different vendors producing PC-compatible clones and hardware peripherals. This can make it very difficult to install hardware devices, because there are frequently conflicts with other devices. In addition, there are no set standards for file formats. Graphics files may be formatted for .PCX, .BMP, .TIF, .DIB, .RLE, .TGA, and on and on. And the traditional operating system (MS-DOS) has been considered unfriendly by many users because of its command language interface. PC-compatible computers have no built-in sound capabilities or CD-ROM drives, although graphics are built into the motherboard in new systems.

In spite of these obstacles, the PC-compatible computer has done extremely well, especially in the corporate market. Although earlier PCs were not very graphically oriented, they were very powerful "number crunchers" and were especially useful for spreadsheet and database applications. The availability of business-related and statistical software for the PC has always exceeded that for the Macintosh. PCs have also gained a strong foothold in the consumer market because they are much cheaper than a Macintosh and because many people wanted to be able to work on files that they were using at work (where there was most likely a PC and not a Mac).

In recent years, the PC has gained momentum in terms of its graphical user interface. The introduction of Windows (which has shown considerable improvements over earlier versions) and the subsequent proliferation of Windows-based software has placed the PC in direct competition with the Macintosh in terms of graphics and multimedia capabilities. In fact, the recent growth of the multimedia market has resulted in the introduction of long-needed standards for PC-compatible computers—the MPC (or multimedia PC) standard.

In an attempt to overcome the problems encountered with the plethora of hardware and software products and the lack of strict standards, the Multimedia PC Marketing Council was formed in 1991. It established a set of standards to ensure compatibility among hardware devices and software used on computers, and it licenses a certification mark (MPC Multimedia PC) to be used on products conforming to those standards. These standards (now referred to as *MPC Level 1*) include 2 MB RAM, a 386SX 16 MHz CPU, a 30 MB hard drive, a CD-ROM with a transfer rate of 150 KB/sec and a seek time of 1 sec, 8-bit digital sound, graphics resolution of 640×480 with 16 colors, MIDI I/O, and a joystick.

The MPC Level 2 specification, established in 1993, is a considerable enhancement of the MPC Level 1 standards (see Table 1.1). MPC Level 2 calls for 4 MB RAM (although 8 MB is recommended), a 486-25 MHz CPU, a 160 MB hard drive, a double-speed CD-ROM (XA ready with multisession capability) drive with 300 KB/sec transfer rate and a maximum average seek time of 400 msec, 16-bit audio, 640×480 resolution with 65,536 colors, a MIDI I/O, and a joystick

As computer capabilities increase, the MPC standards will also continue to do so. The MPC "platform" is a major contender in the multimedia market.

Table 1.1 *Comparison of MPC standards for Level 1 and Level 2. Included are the minimum requirements as well as additional recommended capabilities.*

	System Requirements	MPC Level 1	MPC Level 2
MINIMUM	RAM	2 MB	4 MB
	Microprocessor	386SX–16MHz	486SX–25MHz
	Hard Drive	30 MB	160 MB
	CD-ROM Drive	150 KB/sec transfer rate; maximum average seek time 1 sec	300 KB/sec transfer rate; maximum average seek time 400 msec; CD-ROM XA ready, multisession capable
	Sound	8-bit digital sound; 8-note synthesizer; MIDI playback	16-bit digital sound; 8-note synthesizer; MIDI playback
	Graphics	640 × 480; 16 colors	640 × 480; 65,536 colors
	Ports	MIDI I/O; joystick	MIDI I/O; joystick
RECOMMENDED	RAM	8 MB	8 MB
	Microprocessor	386SX–33MHz or 486	
	CD-ROM Drive	64 KB onboard buffer	64 KB onboard buffer; CD-ROM XA audio; support of ADPCM
	Graphics	256 colors	Capability to deliver 1.2 megapixels/sec given 40% CPU bandwidth

IBM PS/2

The IBM PS/2 series of microcomputers uses more proprietary hardware than the PC-compatible computer. Higher end models in the series also use a proprietary architecture called *MCA* (or micro channel architecture). As a result of these features, the PS/2 is more difficult to clone, and it is easier to add various hardware components to the system. This is because the MCA bus configures itself to accept add-on peripherals so that the user does not need to set switches and jumpers (a major headache with PC-compatibles). The MCA architecture will not accept hardware devices used in EISA systems (i.e., PC compatibles). This is an important consideration when purchasing video capture boards and other hardware peripherals.

The PS/2 may use one of several operating systems—OS/2 (IBM's operating system), DOS, or Windows—allowing it to run most software developed for

PC compatibles. Although the IBM PS/2 does not have built-in multimedia capabilities (such as sound), IBM offers a wide range of hardware and software to develop multimedia (or "Ultimedia," as IBM refers to it).

Amiga

Introduced in 1985, the Commodore Amiga was certainly one of the earliest multimedia computers, with built-in chips dedicated to processing graphics and sound. Its DMA (direct memory access) allows for data transfer directly between memory and hardware peripherals, thus bypassing the microprocessor. Graphics and animation are displayed quickly and smoothly and may even be shown on an NTSC monitor. Most current Amiga systems come with authoring software called *AmigaVision*. The Amiga has always been fairly inexpensive, making it appealing to the consumer market.

Amiga uses a proprietary operating system that is not only multitasking but also "reentrant," which allows a process with priority (such as a screen refresh) to interrupt one with less priority (such as reading data from a disk). Both of these capabilities are essential in effective multimedia control.

In spite of its strong points, the Amiga falls behind other current multimedia platforms in terms of graphics and sound. Amiga's video-compatible output is probably its strongest feature, resulting in its widespread use as a Video Toaster engine for video production.

There are many other platforms I have not discussed (such as NeXT, IRIS Indigo, Tandy's VIS, CD-I, and Sega). My purpose here has been to focus on those that are not only the most common but also have played a significant role in multimedia's penetration in the marketplace. Nearly all of the software I will examine in the pages that follow were developed on (and are deliverable to) these platforms.

What the Future Holds
for Multimedia

There is no doubt that multimedia will continue to penetrate the market and find its way into virtually every microcomputer application. It is also being used to reinvent the ways we use familiar technologies, such as television.

In the not-too-distant future, cable television will allow home viewers to interact with their television to shop and access information the same way they do currently through various on-line services. Viewers will be able to compete with game show contestants and interactively select programs from a 500-channel cable network. Cable companies are working with America Online, CompuServe, and Prodigy to deliver interactive programming, and prototypes of interactive television are already being tested in some areas of the country.

Airline travelers will not be limited to watching the movie selected for that flight or to listening to eight channels of music. Multimedia systems will provide travelers with video games, e-mail, fax and voice services, CD audio with 20 or more channels, interactive video shopping and travel information. Major airline companies such as United and American, have signed contracts with computer firms to install multimedia systems on their aircraft in the near future. Northwest Airlines already provides an interactive service on its flights to Hawaii. Using such a system, travelers may select from CD audio, four to six movies, and ten games. It is expected that some airlines may even provide gambling through their interactive systems.

In terms of financial statistics, the growth in multimedia over the next few years is predicted to be tremendous sales of multimedia titles to the consumer market are estimated to be nearly $320 million in 1994 alone. The installed base of MPC units is expected to grow from 7 million in 1994 to nearly 30 million in 1998. And in 1998, the total multimedia market is estimated to be close to $30 billion!

Is it all hype? Perhaps, but multimedia is a technology driven by the consumer market. And the consumer market has driven CD audio, television, and other products that have been enormously successful. In fact multimedia's future is so promising, many predict that soon we will not even be talking about the "multimedia" capabilities of a computer or software. It simply will be assumed that this is the way we interact with our computers.

Summary

In this chapter, we have taken a look at the basics of multimedia technology. The following are the main points covered in Chapter 1:

- Interactive multimedia contains numerous methods of providing information, all combined in an interactive program in which the user may control the information presented at any one time. ·

- Multimedia provides a richer, more intuitive way to learn and interact with our computers. ▪

- The media that may be included in a multimedia title are text, graphics, animation, sound, and video. ▾

- Multimedia has been successfully used in education, training, information access, sales and marketing, entertainment, and book adaptation. ▪

- Probably the most successful arenas for multimedia have been education and entertainment, and a fusion of the two called *edutainment*.

- The computer platforms most commonly used include Macintosh, PC-compatible, IBM PS/2, and Amiga, although there are many other platforms as well.

- The Macintosh has been most commonly used for graphics, desktop publishing, and music synthesis, and it is commonly used in primary and secondary schools.

- The PC-compatible computer has the strongest foothold in the corporate and home-computer markets.

- The MPC standard has contributed to the penetration of multimedia in the PC-compatible marketplace.

- The IBM PS/2 uses a different architecture than PC-compatible computers. This MCA (micro channel architecture) makes it easier to add hardware components to the system.

- Although the Amiga is impressive in terms of its video capabilities, its sound and graphics fall behind other multimedia platforms currently used.

- Future predictions for the growth of multimedia are impressive: the total multimedia market is expected to be close to $30 billion in 1998.

Further Reading

Arnst, Katherine. 1993. "Multimedia: Joyful and Triumphant?" *Business Week* (December 6): 167.

Bergman, Robert, and Thomas Moore. 1990. *Managing Interactive Video/Multimedia Projects*. Englewood Cliffs, NJ: Educational Technology Publications.

Bunzel, Mark, and Sandra Morris. 1994. *Multimedia Applications Development*. New York: McGraw-Hill.

Burger, Jeff. 1993. *The Desktop Multimedia Bible*. Reading, MA: Addison Wesley.

Guglielmo, Connie. 1993. "Forecast 1994." *NewMedia Magazine* (December): 51.

"Multimedia at 42,000 Feet." 1993. *NewMedia Magazine* (November): 23.

Ochsenreiter, Glen. 1994. "The Multimedia PC: Here and Now in a World of Interactive Possibilities." *CD-ROM Professional* (March): 103.

Perlmutter, Martin. 1991. *Producer's Guide to Interactive Videodiscs*. White Plains: Knowledge Industry Publications.

Perry, Paul. 1994. *Multimedia Developer's Guide*. Indianapolis, IN: Sams Publishing.

Rosenthal, Steve. 1993. "Mega Channels." *NewMedia Magazine* (September): 36.

Tway, Linda. 1992. *Welcome to Multimedia*. New York: MIS:Press.

Vaughan, Tay. 1992. *Multimedia: Making it Work*. Berkeley, CA: Osborn/McGraw-Hill.

GENERAL CONCERNS
OF THE DEVELOPER

· T W O ·

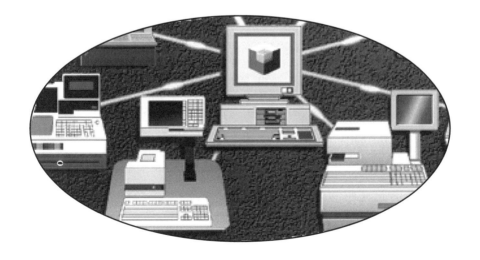

Introduction

In the next chapter, I will present the various media in more detail. Each requires specific hardware and software, which may or may not be of concern to you, depending on the type of title you plan to develop. However, certain issues affect anyone developing a multimedia title: legal issues, storage, and application delivery. These topics are the focus of this chapter.

Copyrights and Other Legal Issues

Before you embark on any multimedia project, you had better be familiar with copyright laws as they apply to the material you want to use. Copyright infringement is one of the main concerns of multimedia developers. Multimedia is a particularly sticky area because it usually involves the integration of material created by many different individuals or companies. Although it may be tempting to scan a photograph from a magazine or include a portion of a musical recording as background for your application, you may not do so without written permission from the owner of this material. In fact, even if you take your own photograph and include faces that are recognizable (not necessarily famous), you may be in for a lawsuit. On the other hand, you should be equally concerned about protecting your own material so that others may not make a profit at your expense. Let us take a brief look at some of the legal issues that concern the multimedia developer.

The United States Copyright Act

The U.S. Copyright Act protects what is called *intellectual property*. This refers to any idea or concept that has been put into some tangible form. A person may have some idea about a character, but this idea in itself is not protected by copyright law. However, if the person produces a drawing or written description of that character, it can be considered to be in a "tangible" form and protected by the Copyright Act. In addition, copyrights protect works of "creative art" rather than technological inventions (which are protected by patents, discussed later). Art may mean literary works, visual art, sound recordings or performing art. Copyright owners are entitled to control what is done with their material.

There is a limit to the amount of time that material is protected. In general, any material published on or after January 1, 1978, may not be used without written permission by anyone other than the owner during the lifetime of the creator plus a period of 50 years following the death of the creator. Work for hire or anonymous work is generally protected for 100 years following its date of creation or 75 years after its publication. Work for hire is considered to be under the ownership of the person who hired the creator of the work, not the actual creator. After the period of protection has expired, the material becomes in the public domain and may be used by anyone without permission.

Exceptions to Copyright Protection

There are some exceptions to copyright protection, such as the "fair use" doctrine, which allows a person to copy material without permission with consideration of the following:

- Whether its use is for commercial or nonprofit educational purposes,
- The nature of the work to be copied,
- The relative amount and substantiality of the portion to be copied,
- The effect of the copy's use upon the potential market for or value of the copyrighted work

Another exception involves the use of material that is altered to the point that it is no longer recognizable. However, simply distorting or manipulating an image, for example, does not protect you from copyright infringement. The problem in these times of easy electronic manipulation is that virtually anyone can alter an image or sound file. If you have any doubts, you should either seek the advice of a copyright attorney or avoid using the material altogether without written permission.

Publications or data produced by the federal government are considered to be public domain. Many developers download federal regulations and other material available on bulletin board systems for use in a multimedia application. Be aware, however, that state governments do claim copyright protection over their material, so be sure that what you are using is truly in the public domain.

Avoiding Copyright Infringement

Infringing a copyright may not only cost you a fine (from $500–$20,000 for unintentional violation to $100,000 for intentional infringement), but it also could result in other financial losses, such as the expense of creating another image, logo, or associated tune. A good example is the lawsuit against "Barney," the purple dinosaur who delighted a huge audience of children with his song "I love you … " Unfortunately, the tune to this song is "This Old Man." Barney's trademark and much of his identity were built around this tune, and even though his lyrics were different, it has been argued that this was in violation of copyrights.

A more subtle example involves a photograph of people on the street. Although you may have taken the photo, and clearly own the right to its use, you may not use the photo if the faces of the people are recognizable and you have not obtained their written permission to use their images. Or perhaps you have put together a sales presentation to be shown to a dozen people in your office. Some of the screens display photos taken from a published source. This is also technically illegal, even if you have no intention of selling this presentation as a product.

At some point, most multimedia developers encounter the need to use material that is copyright protected. This need not be a big or expensive obstacle. Sometimes it simply involves a letter of permission from the copyright owner giving you the right to use the work, with a small fee or even no fee at all. Publishers frequently give permission to use their material with no fee; a credit suffices in many cases. A straight fee is the cleanest way to proceed, but many times, you may have to pay the author a royalty fee. This can add up when you are seeking material from multiple authors, so you may want to consult with an attorney to determine the most cost-effective way to proceed.

No matter what you do, be sure you have the agreement in writing from the copyright holder, and that it clearly defines what rights you have to the material. Just because the author has agreed to allow the use of his or her material in a videotape does not mean that you may also use it in digital format on a CD-ROM.

Many companies sell royalty-free material such as videos, music clips, and graphic images that may be incorporated into a multimedia application. In general, the only stipulation is that you may not resell these as "clips," but use them only to support a multimedia title.

Creating and Protecting Your Own Work

Because of the complications and costs that are often involved in using copyrighted material, it is advisable to create as much of your own images, sound, and video as possible. Certainly you will want to also copyright your multimedia title. No matter what you have created, you should, at the very least, use the copyright symbol with the name of your work or product just as soon as you begin using that name. A safer approach is to register your work with the Copyright Office (Publications and Information Section, Library of Congress, Washington, D.C. 20559) because this may be used as legal evidence of your ownership. (Be aware, however, that a patent may be an even better approach, as will be discussed.)

An unexpected (and tragic) situation developed for many authors whose photographs or other material were published in journals or magazines and who did not retain the copyright to that material. A decade or so ago, it was not apparent that this would present a problem. But now many of these authors would like to incorporate their photographs in a multimedia application (such as an electronic catalog) only to find that they cannot use their own published material without permission because the publisher holds the copyright. I mention this as a warning to artists, scientists and other professionals whose work is regularly published. Be sure that you retain the right to use anything that you may want to use at a later time.

So what do you do if you discover that someone has infringed on your copyright? The first thing you should do is contact the copyright holder. If you hold the copyright, seek out a good copyright attorney. Generally the first legal step is to send a written "cease and desist" letter to the party violating your copyright. You will likely be able to obtain a preliminary injunction that will prevent the violator from using your material. Many cases are settled out of court, but if you do go to trial, you may be entitled to actual damages, a portion of the infringer's profits, attorney's fees, and "statutory" damages (the $500 to $100,000 mentioned earlier).

Patents

Some argue that registering for a copyright may, in fact, put you at more risk of someone stealing your idea because in doing so, you must provide a description of your creative idea. This *description* may not be used by others, but it does not prevent them from using something that was developed based on that description. A patent, on the other hand, protects a technological innovation or invention, such as a new machine or a new process for doing something. A patent protects its owner for 17 years. To apply for a patent, you must contact the U.S. Patent and Trademark Office (Commissioner of Patents, Washington, D.C. 20231).

When Compton's NewMedia announced in November 1993 that it had been awarded a patent for technology to perform basic multimedia search and retrieval, developers were not only surprised but concerned. Such a patent, if upheld, could mean that developers of *any* multimedia title could be forced to pay a percentage of their profits to Compton's, since they would be licensing this technology from Compton's. Many argued that this type of multimedia search and retrieval technology (such as HyperCard) had been around for quite some time, thus representing "prior art," and was not the sole invention (nor intellectual property) of Compton's.

The furor over the patent award and its far-reaching implications prompted the U.S. Patent and Trademark Office to reexamine Compton's patent claim, leading to a reversal in its decision (in March 1994) regarding all 41 of Compton's claims to patent protection. At the time of this writing, Compton's has appealed the rejection and filed another application to protect the more narrowly defined area of interactive multimedia encyclopedias. There is no doubt that even this will stir controversy and concern.

Certainly, the growth of multimedia almost guarantees that the legal issues surrounding the industry will continue to escalate, in both frequency and dollar amount. Refer to the books by McIntosh and by Brinson and Radcliffe (listed at the end of this chapter) for more complete information on copyrights and multimedia development.

Storage

Graphics, sound, animation and video files have enormous storage requirements (see Table 2.1 on page 23). A 256-color image with a resolution 640×480 uses about a third of a MB of storage. A 1-minute, 16-bit sound clip with a sample rate of 44.1 KHz (CD audio quality) will use over 10 MB of space, and broadcast-quality video gobbles up 1 MB of space per frame. Because of this, storage space is of major concern to the multimedia developer.

Table 2.1 *Comparison of sizes of the various types of files used in a multimedia title.*

Text	No. Pages		File Size (bytes)	
	100		240,000	

Graphics	Dimensions (pixels)	No. Colors	Format	File Size (bytes)
	250 × 250	256	.PCX	4,000
	250 × 250	256	.BMP	64,000
	640 × 480	256	.PCX	12,000
	640 × 480	256	.BMP	308,000

Sound	Sample Size	Sample Rate	Channel	File Size (MB/min)
	8 bits	22 KHz	1	1.32
	8 bits	22 KHz	2	2.62
	16 bits	44.1 KHz	1	5.29
	16 bits	44.1 KHz	2	10.58

Animation	No. Frames	Format	File Size (bytes)	
	20	.FLC	8,600	
	20	.FLI	46,000	

Video	No. Frames	Format	File Size (MB)	
	32	.AVI	1.06	
	40	.AVI	1.38	

(Data compression is also very important, particularly with video files, and is discussed in Chapter 3.)

In general, you should have *at least* twice the hard disk space available to develop an application as the required space to run it (and this is a modest estimate). (*Note:* This does *not* include the amount of storage you need to archive and back up your data!) So if you are planning a title to be delivered on a CD-ROM and expect that the files will take most of that space, you had better have a hard drive or other storage device with at least a gigabyte or so of available storage for development purposes. However, many titles do not require all of the space on a CD-ROM—your title may require only 50–100 MB of space. Several options are available for data storage as you develop your application. The following are the main ones you should consider.

Fixed Hard Disk Storage

This is the best option if you can afford it. Data access is much faster using a hard disk than with other options, and this will save you valuable development time. As a rule of thumb, get the largest hard drive you can possibly afford. Multimedia files quickly use up all available space. You should also be careful to archive earlier versions of files as you go—it is cheapest to archive them to tape. That way, the files will still be available should you need them at a later time, but they will not use up valuable hard disk space. Most developers have multiple hard disk drives, either internal or external, with multiple gigabytes of available storage.

Removable Cartridges

Removable magnetic cartridges, such as those made by SyQuest and Bernoulli, are one of the best ways for the developer to incrementally increase the storage capacity of his or her computer as needs grow. And removable storage has the added advantage of being a useful way to back up your hard disk.

Magnetic cartridge drives work on the same principle as the usual fixed hard drive, but the platter (which is encased in a protective cartridge) can be removed from the drive containing the electronics and the read/write heads. Because the environments in which they operate are not sealed, as they are with a fixed disk, there is a greater possibility of small dust particles entering. Therefore, the read/write heads must be kept further from the platter. This means that data must be stored at a lower density than in fixed hard drives. Most removable 5¼" cartridges can accommodate 44–230 MB.

The Bernoulli drive, although a type of magnetic cartridge drive, uses a different technology. Rather than a rigid platter, the Bernoulli disk is flexible like a floppy disk. The distinctive feature of the Bernoulli drive is that it takes advantage of the difference in air pressures between one side of the spinning disk and the other side near the read/write head. This causes the surface of the flexible disk to approach the head more closely, enabling data to be written more densely. This technology also makes the Bernoulli disk less susceptible to damage. In conventional hard drives a power failure or a jolt can cause the read/write head to touch the disk, resulting in a disastrous disk crash. In a Bernoulli drive, on the other hand, a powered-down state causes the flexible disk to move away from the read/write head, thus greatly reducing the chances of a disk crash.

Removable cartridges are highly adaptable, useful both for expanding your main storage and for backup. Removable cartridges currently have capacities ranging from 44–230 MB and can even be used with both a PC and a Macintosh computer. They are an ideal means of developing multimedia titles, particularly those that are not very large.

Magneto-Optical Disks

Magneto-optical, or MO, drives utilize an optical technology that enables high-density storage on a durable medium. When data are to be written to a disk, a laser beam heats its surface to the temperature at which it loses its magnetic structure (almost 200°C), and the write head writes the zero bits to the disk. This magnetic polarity is retained as the disk cools. Then the write head makes a second pass to reverse the magnetic polarity to write the one bits. The read/write head remains at a safe distance from the disk surface, eliminating both the possibility of a disk crash and the wear to which floppy disks are susceptible. Magneto-optical is sometimes called *erasable optical* because the disks can be rewritten. Storage capacities of the most popular magneto-optical disks currently range from 128–650 MB. The drives connect to your computer through a SCSI port. The technology may soon overtake the magnetic cartridge drives.

Application Delivery

The main concern regarding the medium used for application delivery is how widespread that medium is in the marketplace. Although it is possible to deliver a small title on several floptical disks (each capable of holding 21 MB of data) or on a Bernoulli or SyQuest cartridge, most users do not have the hardware necessary to read these media. The media used most commonly to deliver a multimedia application reflect the type of hardware that has penetrated the market most successfully, floppy disks (for small titles), compact discs, and videodiscs. Some guidelines regarding these delivery options follow.

Floppy Disks

The only real advantage that floppy disks hold over optical media is their widespread deliverability. Virtually anyone with a microcomputer has access to a floppy disk drive. However, multiple floppy disks are feasible only for titles that are very small or for demo versions. As multimedia titles become increasingly large, floppy disks are becoming more obsolete. Mass-produced CD-ROM disks currently cost only pennies more to manufacture than a single floppy disk, which holds only 1/600th the amount of data. In addition, floppy disks are susceptible to erasure because they are a type of magnetic medium.

Compact Discs

Compact discs (or CDs) are an optical storage medium in which a laser beam is used to encode data. (In general, *disk* refers to a magnetic medium and *disc* refers to an optical medium.) The disc itself is made of a refractive transparent material, either glass in the case of a "master" or plastic in mass-produced discs. The disc contains "pits" that are etched (or "burned") onto its surface by a laser beam. These pits scatter light in a nonreflective way, indicating an off state. Nonpitted areas or "lands" are reflective and represent an on state. These off/on states are the basis for storing digital data. The surface of the CD is covered with a thin coat of aluminum to increase its reflective properties and finally with a protective plastic coating and a label. A laser beam reads the data from the side of the disc opposite the label.

All compact discs have certain physical features in common: they are all 120 mm in diameter with a central hole measuring 15 mm across. In addition, they have a uniform thickness of 1.2 mm. These standard properties allow them to be placed into any compact disc drive.

Compact discs were first regarded strictly as a mass-storage device for very large databases, reference material, and archived data. They hold a great deal of information: currently about 600 MB or the equivalent of over 400 high-density 3½" floppy disks or 250,000 pages of text. The next generation of CD will hold even more data (multi-gigabyte CDs are on the way). Because of this, CDs are ideally suited to the huge storage requirements of interactive multimedia titles, especially with the advent of faster double-, triple-, and quad-speed drives that provide much smoother animation and video.

Compact discs are perhaps the greatest driving force behind the multimedia industry, which in turn is driving the CD market. Another driving force behind CDs is the widespread use of audio CDs. This means that the consumer market is already familiar with the technology to some extent, and the large audio CD market has driven down the price for CD technology in general. An added advantage of compact discs is that they are quite durable and cannot be erased by exposure to magnetic fields as hard disks and floppies can.

Although compact discs share the same physical specifications, the way they encode and format digital data may differ, requiring specific hardware for the various formats. For example, some compact discs run on a special computer system or "player" (much like a VCR player) that uses a television monitor instead of a computer monitor. Examples include CD-I, Photo CDs, and Tandy's VIS format. These are commonly used for entertainment. Other formats, such as CD-ROM, CD-ROM XA, and CD-R use a standard computer system and monitor (although the CD hardware is an add-on feature).

In an attempt to maintain standards for encoding digital data on compact discs, Philips and Sony developed certain specifications (designated by the different colors of the documents containing the specifications) to provide a foundation for compatibility across platforms. Each of the formats discussed here (and summarized in Table 2.2) adheres to various sets of these specifications.

CD-DA (Compact Disc–Digital Audio)

CD-DA refers to standard audio CDs that adhere to the Red Book specification, allowing them to be played on any audio CD player. Digital sound or music is stored as 16-bit stereo with a sampling rate of 44.1 KHz. Audio CDs may be played on standard CD-ROM drives used with computer systems.

Table 2.2   *Comparison of formats used for compact discs.*

CD Type	Usage	Readable by ...	Specification	Special Features
CD-DA	Audio CD playback	• Audio CD player • CD-ROM drive	Red Book	• Provide high-quality digital sound
CD-ROM	• Data storage • Software delivery	• CD-ROM drive • CD-ROM XA drive • Some Photo CD drives	Yellow Book (Mode 1)	• Greater performance than CD-DA • Provides way to encode and access data
CD-ROM XA	Synchronous playback of mixed media	• CD-ROM drive with ADPCM audio	Yellow Book (Mode 2)	• High performance • Provides synchronous playback • Provides bridge to CD-I technology
CD-I	Developed for real-time multimedia applications	• Dedicated player with Motorola 68000 micro-processor and RTOS	Green Book	• Real-time operating system provides more efficient synchronization of mixed media
CD-R	Recording CD-ROM discs	• CD-ROM drive • CD-ROM XA drive • Audio CD player	Orange Book	• Multisession capability permits multiple recording sessions
Photo CD	Storing photographic images	• Photo CD player • CD-ROM XA drive • Philips CD-I drive	Orange Book	• Special type of CD-ROM XA bridge disc with multisession capabilities

CD-ROM
(Compact Disc–Read-Only Memory)

The CD-ROM is quickly becoming the major delivery medium for multimedia. The CD-ROM software business was estimated to be more than $3 billion in 1993 and is growing at an annual rate of more than 40%. CD-ROMs use the Yellow Book specification, which is built on the Red Book standard. However, the Yellow Book standards require higher performance specifications and special methods for encoding, organizing, and accessing data on the disc.

Within the CD-ROM Yellow Book standard are several formats. One of the most popular of these is the ISO 9660 format (also known as *Mode 1*), which uses standard methods of handling the disc's volume table of contents (or VTOC) and permits faster file access. Any ISO 9660 CD-ROM disc can be read by any operating system having the ISO 9660 software driver, thus greatly increasing CD-ROM compatibility.

CD-ROM XA
(CD-ROM Extended Architecture)

One of the problems with the standard CD-ROM is the way in which it treats mixed media, such as video and sound. At any one time, the computer's microprocessor can transfer only one type of data, such as video or sound. In a typical scenario, the graphics data is first transferred as a discrete chunk, and then audio data is transferred as another chunk. This can result in asynchronous playback, causing a video clip to look like a foreign movie in which the lip movements are not synchronized with the vocalization.

The extended architecture of CD-ROM XA uses an extension of the Yellow Book specification (sometimes referred to as *Mode 2*) and provides for synchronous playback by interleaving different data types when they are stored. In addition, the XA drive includes a special ADCPM (adaptive differential code pulse modulation) translator that allows high-quality audio files to be greatly compressed. The CD-ROM XA drive takes over the task of decoding, decompressing and playing high-quality audio signals (a job normally done by the microprocessor), resulting in smoother playbacks. It also bridges the gap with CD-I, to a limited extent. CD-ROM XA "bridge" discs may be read also by CD-I and other dedicated players (although the reverse is not yet possible). An example of this is the Photo CD, discussed later.

CD-I
(Compact Disc-Interactive)

CD-I technology requires a special player that is usually connected to a television set, although a color monitor may be used as well. The player is capable of reading not only CD-I discs but also CD-DA, Photo CDs, and several other

CD formats as well. A CD-I player has a Motorola 68000 microprocessor, a special real-time operating system (or RTOS), and specific audio and video hardware. Its operating system allows for much easier synchronization of mixed media and is therefore an ideal technology for multimedia. CD-I uses the Green Book specifications, which are an extension of the Red Book and Yellow Book standards.

CD-R
(Compact Disc-Recordable)
Optical discs such as compact discs and videodiscs (discussed later) are generally recorded or "burned" in a single session. Once the disc has been written to a single time, it cannot be written to again. Although this makes it a very safe medium from the standpoint of safety (it cannot be erased like magnetic media), it also makes it inconvenient from the standpoint of the user who would like to archive data but needs to do so incrementally. Fortunately, there is another alternative: CD-recordable.

Now, just about anyone can "burn" his or her own CD-ROM disc using a CD-recordable system. Although they were quite expensive a few years ago (about $20,000), you may now purchase a CD-recordable system for less than $3,000 (most currently cost about $6,000–7,000). The Orange Book standard was developed specifically for CD-R technology, the main feature of which is its "multisession" capability. This permits you to write data to different parts of the disk in multiple sessions. You cannot rewrite on the disc, but for certain applications this is a decided advantage over single session CD-ROM recording. The resulting discs may be recorded for use with CD-ROM, CD-ROM XA, and CD-DA drives. Although most systems are used currently for work-related archiving, I have heard of family history enthusiasts who have purchased a system for their home computer to develop an interactive record of their "roots," including photos, narratives and even videos.

Photo CD
Photo CDs, developed by Eastman Kodak, are used to store photographic images to be viewed on a television screen. They may be played on a dedicated Photo CD player or a Philips CD-I player connected to a television or by a CD-ROM XA drive. They use the CD-R multisession technology, but unlike CD-R in which the disc is recorded by the individual user, Photo CDs are "mastered" at specified Kodak locations where the user takes a set of photos to be burned onto the CD-ROM. It generally takes multiple sessions to fill the CD-ROM disc, and costs about $1 per photo. Kodak has announced that its Photo CDs will soon be able to incorporate narration, music, and other effects.

Videodiscs

The videodisc (or laserdisc) is another type of optical medium involving the use of a laser beam to read pits and lands on the surface of a disc. However, the size of the pits may vary on a videodisc, affording it analog storage capabilities. Several years ago laserdiscs went head-to-head against videotapes for the video media market, but in spite of the superior quality of laserdiscs, the videotape industry prevailed. No doubt, part of this was due to the consumer's greater familiarity with "tapes" such as reel-to-reel and cassette and the consumer's unfamiliarity with videodiscs. However, in terms of multimedia application delivery, videodiscs (with their large analog storage capabilities) have done quite well, particularly in the areas of education and training that rely heavily on the incorporation of video.

Two videodisc technologies currently are used: CAV (constant angular velocity) and CLV (constant linear velocity). With CAV technology, the disc rotates at the same speed, no matter which track it is reading. This permits NTSC standard video of 30 frames per second across the 12" disc, resulting in 30 minutes of full motion video per side (or 1 hour per disc). The advantage of CAV technology is that it provides the ability to quickly search for and freeze any frame of video on the disc, and the speed of video playback can be closely controlled by the user.

With CLV technology, the disk rotates at different speeds depending on which track is being read. Because of this, there is no direct correlation between the tracks and frames, making it difficult to access specific information on the disc and control playback options. However, CLV allows about twice as much data to be stored on an individual disc (the equivalent of about 2 GB of storage per side).

Obviously, the choice of media used to deliver a multimedia title depends on the size of the title, the degree of interactivity of the title, and the intended market's hardware capabilities. All of these need to be evaluated before development begins.

Summary

This chapter has presented a discussion of the issues of general concern to the multimedia developer—legal issues, storage, and delivery of a title. The main points presented are as follows:

- Any "creative art," such as literary works or visual, audio, and performing art, is protected by the U.S. Copyright Act. Any multimedia developer must be sure that he or she does not infringe on an owner's copyright protection.
- Patents protect technological innovations and inventions (vs. creative art) and provide greater protection than copyrights.
- Storage is of major concern to the multimedia developer due to the tremendous storage requirements of graphics, sound, and video files used in multimedia titles.
- Although fixed hard disk storage is the preferred option for the developer, other options, such as removable and magneto-optical storage, provide the developer with essentially infinite storage capacities.
- Multimedia applications are most commonly delivered via floppy disks, compact discs, and videodiscs.
- Compact discs have driven the multimedia market due to the public's familiarity with them and their relatively low cost.
- Several formats are used by compact discs, including CD-DA, CD-ROM, CD-I, CD-R and Photo CDs. Each format is based on certain specifications and are readable by certain drives (or players).
- Videodiscs have been used quite frequently in applications involving training and education due to their large storage capacity, providing an ideal medium for the delivery of large video files.

Further Reading

Bowers, Richard. 1994. "Welcome to the Second Computer Revolution: A Beginner's Guide to CD-ROM." *CD-ROM Professional* (January): 20.

Bowers, Richard. 1994. "Does the Whole Multimedia Game Belong to Compton's?" *CD-ROM Professional* (March): 40.

Brinson, Diane, and Mark Radcliffe. 1994. *Multimedia Law Handbook*. Ladera Press.

Carlton, Tom. 1994. "Doing It Yourself: Archiving and Desktop Publishing with CD-Recordable." *CD-ROM Professional* (January): 68.

Crawford, Tad. 1990. *Legal Guide for the Visual Artist*. New York: Allworth Press.

Fishman, Stephen. 1993. *The Software Developer's Legal Guide*. Berkeley, CA: Nolo Press.

Jeff Angus Review Board. 1994. "CD-R: Out of the Oven and Piping Hot." *InfoWorld* (June 6): 70.

Lediaev, Lucy, and Lex van Sonderen. 1994. "Using and Developing with CD-Interactive." *CD-ROM Professional* (March): 83.

McIntosh, Stephen Ian. 1990. *The Multimedia Producer's Legal Survival Guide.* Multimedia Computing.

Pohlmann, Ken. 1992. *The Compact Disc Handbook.* Madison, WI: A&R Editions.

Rodarmor, William. 1993. "Rights of Passage." *NewMedia Magazine* (September): 49.

Sherman, Christopher (ed.). 1994. "Compton's Files Patent Appeal, Narrows Scope to Encyclopedias." *Multimedia Wire* (June 24).

Spanbauer, Scott. 1993. "CD-Recordable: The Write Stuff." *NewMedia Magazine* (October): 62.

Vaughan, Tay. 1994. "Who Owns Multimedia?" *NewMedia Magazine* (January): 22.

Wilson, Lee. 1990. *Make it Legal.* New York: Allworth Press.

Young, Andrew. 1994. "Cutting Gold: A Guide to In-House CD-ROM Production." *CD-ROM Professional* (January): 100.

An Overview of Development Software and Hardware

• THREE •

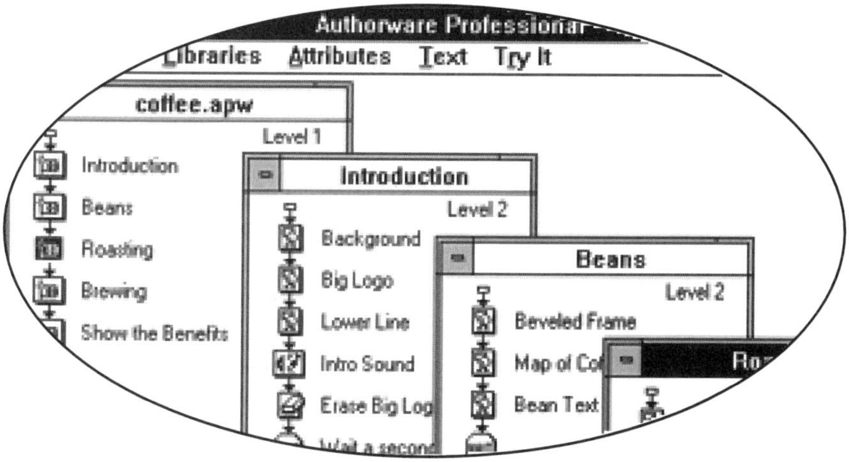

Introduction

The last chapter focused on issues of concern to any multimedia developer, whether for education, sales presentations, or entertainment. In this chapter, we will take a closer look at the various media included in multimedia titles and the software and hardware required for each. Depending on the type of title, some of these media are of more importance than others. For example, reference and information access titles require sophisticated text linking and searching capabilities, while entertainment relies heavily on sound and animation. Most sales presentations also require sophisticated animation techniques, and training titles frequently utilize full motion video and are delivered on videodisc. Demonstration versions of many of the development software tools discussed and illustrated in this chapter are included on the CD-ROM accompanying this book.

Text

Text is the main element of many multimedia titles and is certainly the type of computer-based communication most familiar to users. Nearly all multimedia titles use text to provide instructions on using the program. Wherever possible, this text should be kept to a minimum—the user will not read long lines of instructional text. Text may also serve as a label on an illustration, which may be linked to additional information, accessible by clicking on the label (see, for example, Microsoft Dinosaurs, which uses "hot" labels quite extensively). Multimedia applications involving information access or reference, such as Microsoft Encarta, generally include large amounts of text and may use narration and animation to augment the text display.

No matter how the text is intended to be used, it must be clearly readable to the user. Selection of font, color, and size is very important, as is the relative

Figure 3.1 *Examples of sans serif and serif fonts. Sans serif fonts are generally more readable on a computer monitor.*

Sans Serif Fonts:

Helvetica **Avant Garde** Stone Sans

Serif Fonts:

Sabon   Times   Palatino

balance of text with other types of information such as illustrations or animation. Although it may be desirable to use a font that is in keeping with the type of application, it is generally wise to use sans serif fonts wherever possible because they are easier to read, particularly on a computer screen. Figure 3.1 illustrates some serif and sans serif fonts. In addition, text style should be consistent throughout the application.

Hypertext (i.e., text linked to additional information) is an important aspect in reference titles. Such words may be set off from other text so it is obvious to the reader that additional information is associated with those words. This requires "tagging" or marking those words by the application developer. Some software supports "auto" hypertext, in which the user may click on any word in the display, and any associated information is automatically displayed. Such a feature can be a time saver to the developer because specific words do not have to be marked, but this can be frustrating to the user because there is no indication which words are linked to other information and which are not.

For those applications requiring extensive text, the developer is often faced with the task of converting paper-based text into electronic format. Retyping the text is labor intensive, time consuming, and may require considerable proofreading (depending on the proficiency of the typist). However, this option is available to anyone with a word processor. A much better option involves the use of a scanner (preferably a flat-bed scanner that can scan an entire page at one time) and OCR (optical character recognition) software that translates the various shapes into textual characters (see Figure 3.2). This

Figure 3.2   *Illustration of text being read and interpreted by OCR software. The left window shows a graphical representation resulting from scanning in text, while the right window contains the interpreted textual characters. Courtesy of MindWorks, Inc.*

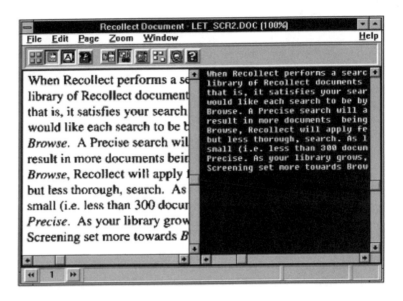

saves considerable labor and time, but does require some proofreading since OCR software is not 100% accurate. It is well worth the extra money to purchase OCR software that is as accurate as possible: it should be at least 95% accurate, preferably closer to 99%. Part of the accuracy will depend on the quality of the document being scanned, as well the typeface style and size. Symbols are notoriously difficult for OCR software to translate correctly, although you can "teach" the software to recognize various characters.

Some textual information may be downloaded from a bulletin board system (BBS) using a standard modem, particularly many government documents that are public domain. Examples include Federal Regulations, which may be incorporated into an environmental application. Such text may need to be reformatted, but should not require extensive proofreading. In addition, you may be able to transfer text from CD-ROM discs containing public domain information. These are becoming increasingly common, particularly for government information.

Static (or Still) Graphics

Perhaps the most important component of multimedia applications is graphics. Visual representations are generally much more effective at conveying information than text. Graphics include illustrations (such as line drawings) and photographs, and these may be displayed in rapid succession to produce animation or "movies" (as discussed in the next section). Although graphics files require more storage than text, they use far less than sound and video files and as such can provide a tremendous impact with relatively little "cost" in terms of storage. Graphics may be created using various graphics software or scanned in and edited or modified using the same type of software. Also, many vendors provide graphics libraries (such as detailed drawings or high-resolution photographs) on CD-ROM that may be used royalty free in multimedia applications.

Raster vs. Vector Graphics

Graphics may be stored as either "raster" (also called bitmapped) images or "vector" images. Each has its advantages and results in different storage and display requirements. Raster graphics store images using pixels (or picture elements) and are particularly useful for displaying illustrations involving detail and subtle changes in color and shading such as photographs. Because bitmapped graphics involve a pixel-by-pixel representation of an image, they generally result in larger files than raster graphics, particularly with images that are large and contain many colors. However, they retain the minute detail contained in photographs and display relatively quickly, although they do not retain the same image quality when resized (see Figure 3.3).

Vector graphics, on the other hand, store images as a set of instructions for re-creating the image as an object consisting of geometric elements such as lines, circles, arcs, and angles. These instructions require relatively little storage and result in smaller graphic file sizes. However, complex images may take a long time to display (and require a faster processor) because the image is actually reconstructed as it is being displayed, based on the instruction set. The real advantage with vector graphics, however, is that the same image may be resized, moved, or rotated while maintaining its original quality and proportions. This is particularly important for three-dimensional graphics and is commonly used for maps (which may be readily enlarged to view more detail) and for CAD/CAM and design work, in which an object or structure can be rotated to display different views.

Figure 3.3   *(a) Objects created using a bitmapped graphics package. Note that when enlarged, the circle loses its original quality. (b) Objects created using a vector graphics package. Not only is the original, small circle of higher quality than the one produced by the bitmapped software, it retains its high quality when enlarged.*

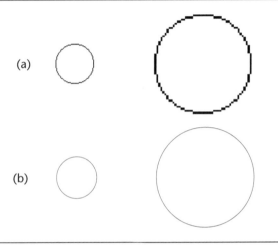

(a)

(b)

Bitmapped graphics are more commonly used in multimedia titles (especially on the PC) and provide exceptional detail, and the software for creating them is readily available to most users. Windows has a built-in graphics program (called Paintbrush), though there are many more versatile packages for creating or modifying bitmapped graphics. Software such as Adobe Photoshop and PhotoFinish (see Figure 3.4) provide very sophisticated tools to create and edit bitmapped graphics. Using such software, one is able to add special effects, use various filtering techniques, modify hue and saturation, and convert images to many different formats. Most also provide scanning capabilities, the usual way in which photographs and other graphics are captured for the computer. Another way to create graphics that is becoming increasingly common is to capture and digitize images from videos using special video capture equipment.

Resolution and File Size

Resolution is determined by the number of pixels that can be displayed on a screen. Although most current multimedia titles use a resolution of 640×480 pixels with 256 colors, the SVGA (Super VGA) standard of the MPC Level 2 computer is capable of displaying the same resolution with 65,536 colors, or

Figure 3.4 *Graphics software provide sophisticated editing tools for filtering and color separations. Courtesy of Softkey International Inc.*

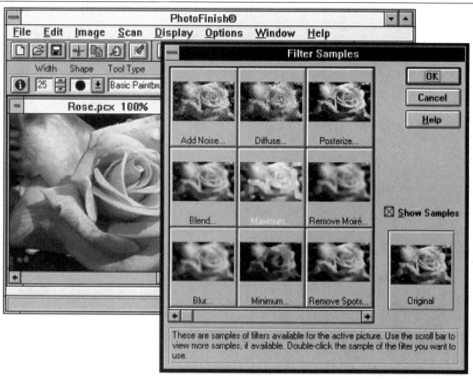

images with a resolution of up to 1024× 768 pixels with 256 colors or 1280×1024 pixels using 16 colors. The size of a bitmap file is determined by the resolution and number of colors contained in the image. File size can be calculated using the following formula:

(width × height × bits) / 8 = number of bytes in file

where the width and height refer to the number of pixels and the bits are the number of bits of color. So, for example, an image that is 320×200 pixels with 8-bit color (i.e., 256 colors) will result in a file size of 64,000 bytes; that is (320×200×8)/8 = 64,000). A full-screen image of 640×480 with 8-bit color will be 307,200 bytes. Table 2.1 on page 23 showed some examples of file sizes based on resolution and the number of colors.

The size of a graphics file is important to the developer. Large files not only have greater storage requirements, but they also take longer to display. As computer systems and CD-ROM drives continue to get faster, the time it takes to display a large image will continue to decrease.

Animation and Morphing

Several types of animation are commonly used in multimedia titles, and though similar to morphing, there are some differences as are discussed.

2-D Animation

The most commonly used animation technique is to create a series of images that are displayed in rapid succession. Such "frame-based" animation involves a different image, or "frame," for each view and works like a filmstrip. Photographs that are displayed this way can give the appearance of movies, although full-motion video (discussed later) is of higher quality and is becoming increasingly common in multimedia applications. Another common type of animation is "cast-based" animation in which the background image remains the same, but individual objects appearing on that background are given "instructions" to move across the background. Both techniques are also called 2-D animation, because they involve the appearance of flat images moving on the screen. Software such as Animation Works Interactive and Autodesk Animator provide the developer with sophisticated tools to create impressive animations.

3-D Animation

Another type of animation frequently used for virtual reality is 3-D animation, in which three-dimensional objects are created using a mathematical model. Thus, each object may be shown in various views, giving the user a realistic sense of a third dimension. In creating 3-D animation, the developer must first create a "model." This involves drawing the object in several views according to specified coordinates along x, y, and z axes. The model is then made to look more realistic by adding shading and "rendering" the image, which involves blending the background, model, light sources, and textures to make cohesive frame transitions.

Like 2-D cast-based animation, objects are given paths of movement, but 3-D animation differs greatly because objects may turn and tilt, retaining a three-dimensional look. In addition, each frame in between a major change in orientation does not need to be drawn. This difference is due to the mathematical model, which interpolates how the object should appear in various positions and orientations. The complexity of 3-D animation requires computers with fast CPU speed, especially for full-screen animation. Special software (such as Autodesk 3-D Studio) is required to create 3-D animation that provides modeling and rendering capabilities.

Many entertainment titles (such as The 7th Guest and The Journeyman Project, both profiled in this book) make effective use of 3-D animation to give the illusion of walking through a house or museum or traveling through space.

Morphing

Morphing is a technique that takes two or more images and blends them to give the illusion that the first image is changing into the last one. An example of morphing is the "chameloid" in Star Trek VI who convincingly changed from an adult female, to a child, and to a hairy beast. Like frame-based animation, morphing involves two or more images, or "frames." But in morphing, key coordinates that are "equivalent" on the two images are indicated, and these permit the morphing algorithm to create a smooth, seamless transition from one image to the next.

Figure 3.5 shows the last two butterflies that are part of a morphing transition involving four butterflies. Note at the bottom of the screen display the storyboard that shows the sequence of the morphing to take place. In Figure 3.6, equivalent points on each of the butterflies are marked and linked together, such as positions on the wings and body. Marking many points results in smoother transitions. Once this is done, the morphing algorithm interpolates the transitions necessary to go from specified points on the starting image to those on the ending one. Morphing software (such as PhotoMorph and Morph) also provide other transitional effects such as warping and distortion in which a single image may be changed, such as the shape of a head or the expression on a face.

Figure 3.5 *The butterflies are part of a morphing transition involving those shown in the story-board at the bottom of the screen. Courtesy of North Coast Software Inc.*

Sound

One of the most important components of multimedia is sound, whether it is in the form of music, narration to accompany text or to explain content, or special sound effects to enhance the action being displayed on the screen. Sound is especially important in entertainment titles. The most common type of sound files incorporated into a multimedia application is "digital sound," which is created by converting analog sound using an analog-to-digital converter (or

Figure 3.6 *Equivalent points on each butterfly are marked along their wings and bodies to create a smoother morphing transition. Courtesy of North Coast Software Inc.*

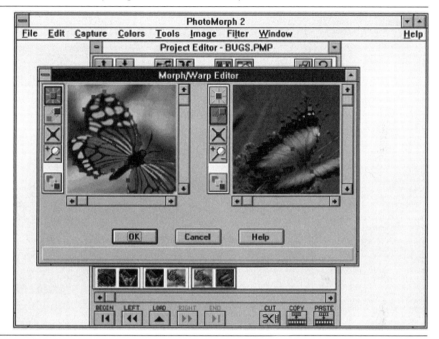

ADC). To play back this signal the computer's sound card translates the digital information back into analog sound using a digital-to-analog converter (or DAC).

Digital audio sound involves varying degrees of quality, similar to graphics resolution. This quality is related to the number of channels recorded, sampling size and sampling rate. Mono sound is recorded on a single channel whereas stereo sound is recorded using two channels (right and left). The latter results in much better quality but requires twice as much storage space as mono sound. Sampling size refers to the amount of information, or the range of sound adjustment, made during the recording. Examples are 8-, 12-, and 16-bit sampling sizes. The MPC Level 2 standard requires a sound card capable of playing 16-bit sound. Finally, the sampling rate refers to the speed (or the number of sound samples per second) at which the sound is recorded. Sampling rates are measured in KHz, and examples include 11, 22, and 44.1 KHz sound rates. Increasing all of these variables—that is the number of channels, sampling size and sampling rate—results in higher quality sound. Audio CDs use digital sound recorded in 16-bit stereo with a 44.1 KHz sampling rate to produce exceptional musical quality. Most currently produced multimedia titles use this same digital quality for sound. As with graphics, the higher the resolution of the sound, the greater the storage requirements. Table 2.1 compared sound quality with the resulting file sizes.

As with graphics and animation, it is possible to purchase CD-ROMs with sound libraries containing music and special effects, or you can record your own sound using a microphone, sound board, and special sound software such as Wave for Windows and SoundTrak (see Figure 3.7). This software allows you to record sound using different sampling size and rates, add special effects such as echo and fade, and mix multiple sound files such as voice and music.

MIDI (or musical instrument digital interface) is an international standard that allows electronic musical instruments to interface with digital computers. The standard involves universal hardware, cabling, and communications protocols, allowing different brands and types of electronic equipment to communicate with each other. The MPC standard requires a sound board with a MIDI interface, allowing an MPC computer to communicate with an electronic instrument to record and play back music. MIDI is capable of transferring many different types of information through 16 channels. For example, MIDI may simultaneously record information on the notes being played, as well as the volume, duration, and speed of each note. The resulting quality is far superior to magnetic recordings and requires much less disk space. For example, 1 minute of high-quality music requires about $10\frac{1}{2}$MB of storage when saved in .WAV format and only about 15 KB when saved as a MIDI file. The way in MIDI stores information about sound is analogous to the "mapping" of a vector graphic. Rather than storing a complete representation of the sound, information about the sound is stored instead, resulting in less storage requirements. MIDI files use a different format (.MID) than wave (.WAV) files and require special editing software such as Studio 3.1.

Video

Video is without doubt the most effective way to convey information in a multimedia title. Its appeal and impact parallels that of television: sight, sound,

Figure 3.7 *Sound editing software such as SoundTrak allows the user to edit a sound file to add effects, mix multiple sound files, and control audio resolution. Courtesy of Animotion Development Corp.*

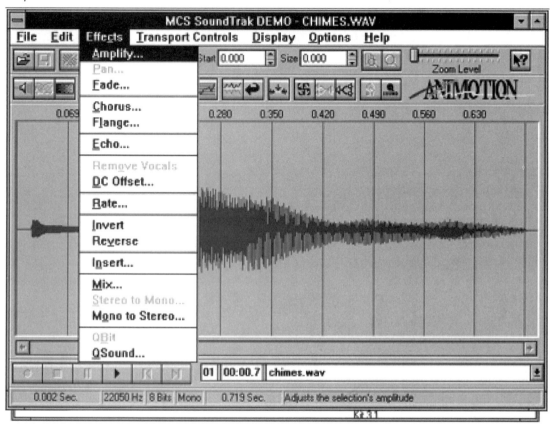

and motion all converge to attract and maintain one's attention. Video also presents the greatest challenge to the developer due to the tremendous amount of storage it requires. A 1 second video clip displayed at 30 frames per second (fps) takes up approximately 30 MB of uncompressed storage. The two main types of video used in multimedia are analog and digital. Analog video is recorded and stored on videocassettes and laserdiscs (discussed in Chapter 2). Videodiscs have large analog storage capacities and are particularly well suited to long videos commonly used in educational and training multimedia. (Particles and Prairies, profiled in Chapter 4, uses videodisc technology.)

Digital video is by far the most commonly used in multimedia titles for the consumer market. However, even with the larger capacity and lower cost of current hard disks, video clips have presented a major obstacle in the multimedia industry and have led to various data compression and decompression (or codec) techniques and standards. This compression and decompression can be accomplished using either software or hardware.

Software codecs include Intel's Indeo, IBM's PhotoMotion, Cinepak, QuickTime and Video for Windows (which is an extension of the Widows environment), and they result in different file formats (such as .AVI and .MOV). All users with a 386 PC (or higher CPU) can play video on their computers, making software-based video much more attractive to the developer in terms of the size of the market already equipped to play back video. This is the major advantage of software-based video: it requires no special boards to play video. However, a disadvantage is that it does not provide the same quality as television or VCR video. Its resolution and frame rates are less than those using special video hardware.

Most hardware-based video compression is currently based on two industry standards, JPEG and MPEG. Established by the Joint Photographic Experts Group and the Motion Picture Experts Group, respectively, these codecs require a special add-in card for encoding and playback. One of the main differences between the two codecs is that JPEG compresses every frame in the video, whereas MPEG compresses key frames and only the changes that occur between those frames. Thus, if the background remains the same from frame to frame and the only changes involve the movement of an object across the background, MPEG records only the changes of that object. MPEG provides much higher compression ratio (up to 200:1 versus 100:1 for JPEG), and the quality of the video is far superior to that resulting from JPEG compression.

Many developers consider hardware-based codecs to be a disadvantage because they require the user to have special add-in cards. However, it does provide video of higher resolution and frame rates than software-based video, making it desirable to those requiring TV-quality video.

No matter what type of video is being produced, the developer must have a special video capture board, a video camera (unless the video is being acquired from another source), and video editing software, such as D/Vision's Cineworks (see Figure 3.8). Such software allows you to control such elements as resolution, playback speed, and transitions. Although it is possible to acquire video from other sources rather than produce it yourself, many developers find that video recorded for other purposes may not convey the information necessary for the multimedia title being developed. In most cases, the developer must record some, if not most, of the video to be used in a title.

Figure 3.8　　*Video files require special editing software to control resolution, playback speed, and transitions. Courtesy of Touch Vision Systems Inc.*

Integration and Interactivity

Of course, the real key to an effective multimedia application is its interactivity, and this is accomplished by linking all of the multimedia components—that is, text, graphics, animation, sound, and video—into a cohesive interactive application. Links must be made that allow the user to navigate through the program in many different ways, and yet a structure must be maintained so that the user does not get lost in "hyperspace" while navigating. The software used to tie together all the multimedia components includes presentation and authoring/production software. Although each provides an environment best suited for certain types of multimedia development, the boundaries separating them are becoming increasingly vague as software packages become more comprehensive and powerful.

Presentation software (such as Compel and Astound) is useful in building slide shows for presentations, allowing you to incorporate effective animation and sound. Many presentation packages allow you to access data from a database or spreadsheet to produce effective charts and other diagrams used in the slide show (see Figure 3.9) and may provide the user with some amount of interactivity (such as going to an adjacent screen or accessing additional information). Software used to produce presentations is easy to learn and does not require the developer to program "code." However, it does not provide as much power and flexibility as authoring software and therefore is not as well suited to create a more complex multimedia title.

Figure 3.9   *Some presentation software provides a link to databases and spreadsheets to automatically produce a chart based on the data. Courtesy of Gold Disk Software.*

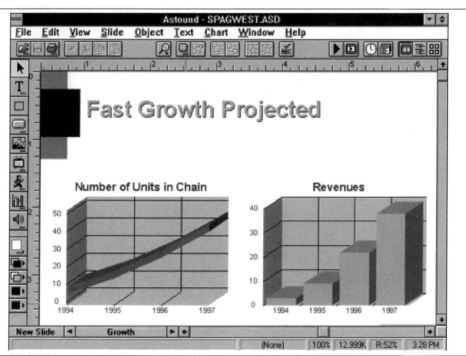

Authoring software is best suited for developing titles that allow the user to intricately control the navigation and information that is presented at any given time. This is much more complicated than a sequential slide show used in presentations. (Production software is essentially authoring software with enhanced controls over the synchronization of various media.) Most authoring software provides an easy-to-use screen design interface that allows the user to create objects such as buttons and graphics using a set of tools. By clicking on a specific tool, the user can create an object by "drawing" it on the screen using a mouse. Figure 3.10 shows several objects (for example, text, buttons, and a window with animated fish) created in this way, using Multimedia Tool-Book, as well as the "tool palette" used to create the objects.

Figure 3.10   *Screen designers allow the developer to quickly draw objects such as text windows, buttons, and graphic objects, such as animation. Courtesy of Asymetrix Corp.*

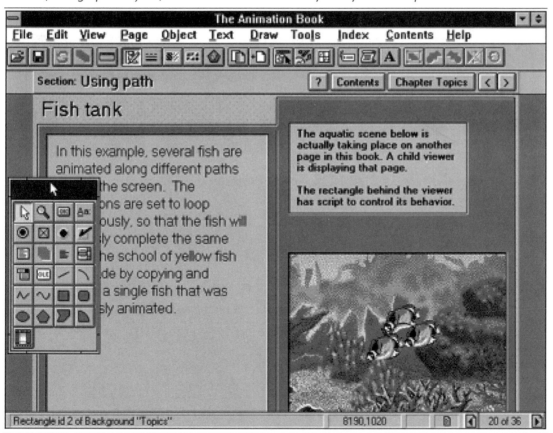

Although screen designers allow the developer to rapidly design the user interface and prototype an application, higher levels of control are required for most multimedia applications. This involves the use of some type of programming environment. Two main types of programming are used in authoring software: script based and icon based. Script based environments require that the developer type in lines of code, similar to any other programming languages that evolved from the command language interface. Figure 3.11 shows the script in Multimedia Toolbook to control the animation of the fish shown in Figure 3.10. Although this is a high-level language and very English oriented, it still requires that the developer understand the syntax and enter code—a more difficult learning task than that required by a screen designer.

Icon based programming environments, on the other hand, are more similar to screen designers, in that the user selects from a set of icons, each containing a set of commands telling the computer what to do. They also frequently are hierarchical in nature, with several levels extending from the main program (see Figure 3.12). These tend to be easier to learn than scripting languages because they are more intuitive and do not involve learning special syntax.

Figure 3.11 *Example of the scripting language used in Multimedia ToolBook to control animation. Courtesy of Asymetrix Corp.*

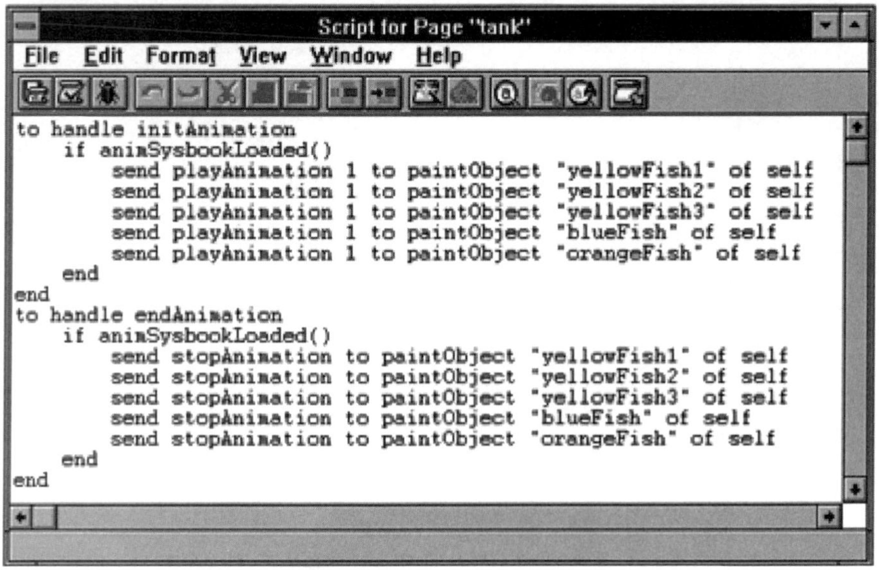
Script for Page "tank"
File Edit Format View Window Help
to handle initAnimation
if animSysbookLoaded()
send playAnimation 1 to paintObject "yellowFish1" of self
send playAnimation 1 to paintObject "yellowFish2" of self
send playAnimation 1 to paintObject "yellowFish3" of self
send playAnimation 1 to paintObject "blueFish" of self
send playAnimation 1 to paintObject "orangeFish" of self
end
end
to handle endAnimation
if animSysbookLoaded()
send stopAnimation to paintObject "yellowFish1" of self
send stopAnimation to paintObject "yellowFish2" of self
send stopAnimation to paintObject "yellowFish3" of self
send stopAnimation to paintObject "blueFish" of self
send stopAnimation to paintObject "orangeFish" of self
end
end

Figure 3.12 *Example of an icon-based authoring package. Note the set of icons on the left, that are used instead of a script to control the program's actions. Courtesy of Macromedia, Inc.*

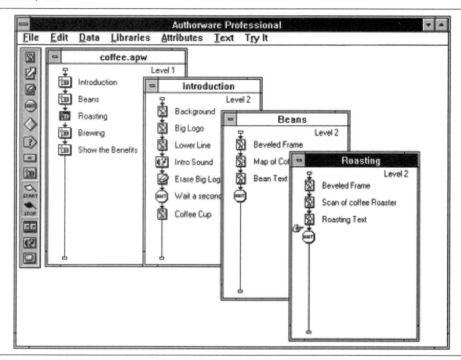

In addition to providing an environment to tie the various elements together with interactivity, most presentation and authoring software also contain a set of libraries with clip art, music, sound effects, and animation. The majority also have a runtime module that allows the developer to create an application and distribute it without any requirements that the user have any special software to run the program.

Multimedia Database Software

As you develop a multimedia application, it will quickly become clear that you will require some means of organizing the hundreds or even thousands of files you will create. Not only will you be inundated with various types of files, such as graphics and video clips, and different file formats, such as .TGA, .TIF and .BMP, you will also have several versions of each file, resulting from numerous modifications. Even the most organized person can have trouble recalling which subdirectory, drive, or even storage device contains a particular file.

A multimedia database can save you from the frustration of misplacing files on your hard drive, and can even help you locate and control off-line media such as CD-ROM and videodisc players. Multimedia databases differ from standard databases in that they store thumbnail representations of files and pointers that indicate where the files are stored. This not only reduces the size of the catalog, but it also reduces the time needed to locate files. Once a file has been located, you may view various information such as file size, format, and keywords (see Figure 3.13) and look at a thumbnail representation of on-line or off-line files (see Figure 3.14), and either view graphics in greater detail or listen to sound files.

Most multimedia database packages also allow you to edit a designated file by clicking on its thumbnail image to launch the appropriate editing software. For example, by clicking on a thumbnail of a sound file, you could immediately launch your sound editing software (such as Wave for Windows), edit the file, save it, and even paste it into another application. Other multimedia database packages provide their own editing tools. A multimedia database may also be used to develop a database application with multimedia capabilities.

Whether you purchase a multimedia database package that is programmable or not depends on your needs. Databases without programming capabilities limit the user to predefined fields including information such as filename, type, size, date, and keywords. And most support a limited number of file formats. However, these are generally sufficient capabilities for most modest multimedia projects. Some multimedia database software (such as MediaDB) provide a programming language that permits the user greater control over field definition, network capabilities, and cross-platform access.

Cross-platform Compatibility

Finally, if you plan to develop a multimedia title that you want to run on more than one platform, you need to carefully consider both the hardware and software

Figure 3.13 *Multimedia database software store information about text, sound, graphics, and video files. Courtesy of Lenel Systems International Inc.*

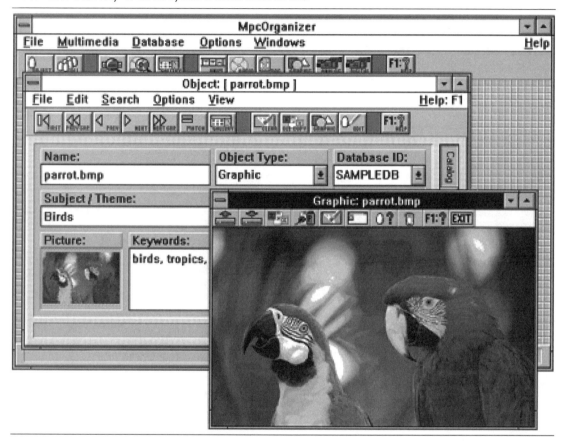

you will use. Although the Mac provides a more standardized environment for multimedia development, the Windows environment has a far greater installation base in the consumer market—the market in which multimedia is making its greatest impact. Until very recently, many multimedia titles that were deliverable to both a Mac and Windows platform were provided on a CD-ROM disk in two different versions, Mac and Windows. Now, however, developers may use Macromedia's Director to reach both platforms, because any title produced using Director is readable by both a Mac and Windows. This will greatly facilitate the development process.

Figure 3.14   *Multimedia files may be viewed as thumbnail images using multimedia database packages. Courtesy of Lenel Systems International Inc.*

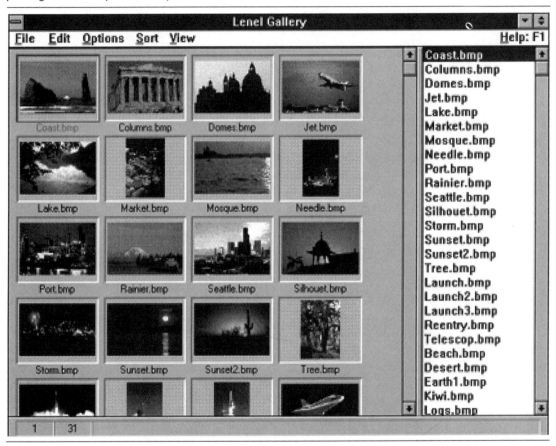

Summary

This chapter has provided an overview of the types of software and hardware involved in multimedia application development. Your requirements will depend on the type of application you intend to produce. The following are the main points covered in this chapter:

- Text is a key component in most multimedia titles, although it should be kept to a minimum unless the application involves information access or reference.
- Still graphics are perhaps the most important component in multimedia titles, providing a tremendous amount of impact with very little "cost" in terms of storage.
- Raster or bitmapped graphics are the type of graphics most commonly used in multimedia titles. They retain minute detail and display quickly, but they require more storage space than vector graphics and cannot be resized without some distortion.
- Animation generally involves the use of multiple still graphic images and displays them in rapid sequence to give the illusion of movement.
- Digital audio sound files may require large amounts of storage, especially if they are of high quality. MIDI, though of very high quality, requires much less storage space than wave audio files.
- Video is the most effective medium for conveying information in a multimedia title. However, it requires tremendous amounts of storage as well as sophisticated compression techniques.
- Authoring software is used to tie together all the various media into a cohesive, interactive application that allows the user to navigate through the program.
- The programming environment in authoring software provides much greater flexibility and control in developing an application. The programming may be script based or icon based.
- Multimedia database software is useful in keeping track of information on the various types of files used in multimedia application development.
- Cross-platform compatibility is crucial to those wanting to develop an application to run on more than one platform. Development software such as Director now allow a multimedia application to be run both on a Mac and under Windows.

Further Reading

Bishop, Phillip. 1994. "Multimedia Developers Get Message Across Platforms." *MacWEEK* (April 25): 49.

Brown, Michael. 1994. "Multimedia Databases Manage All Media." *NewMedia Magazine* (July): 65.

Churbuck, David. "Lights! Camera! Manual! (In-House Production of Multimedia CD-ROM Business Presentations)" *Forbes* (January 17): 92.

Corcoran, Cate. 1994. "Standard Interface for MPEG, Windows Is OM1 Group's Goal." *InfoWorld* (February 28): 14

Desmarais, Norman. *Multimedia on the PC: A Guide for Information Professionals.* New York: McGraw-Hill, Inc.

Doyle, Bob. 1994. "Crunch Time for Digital Video." *NewMedia Magazine* (March): 47.

Doyle, Bob. 1994. "How Codecs Work." *NewMedia Magazine* (March): 52.

Holsinger, Eric. 1994. *How Multimedia Works.* Emeryville, CA: Ziff-Davis Press.

Hudson, Barry. "Soup to Nuts CD-ROM Creation: Hard Lessons Learned in Cross-Platform Development." 1994. *CD-ROM Professional* (March): 65.

Lockwood, Russ. 1994. "Video Acceleration in the Fast Lane." *Byte* (April): 28.

Pepper, Jon. 1994. "Music to Your Ears (Improved Sound Effects in Multimedia Software a Boon to Business Users)." *Nation's Business* (May): 52.

Rosebush, Judson. 1994. "Digital Video: Future Predictions." *CD-ROM Professional* (March): 127.

Shaddoc, Philip. 1994. "It's a 3-D World." *Multimedia World* (September): 94.

MULTIMEDIA AS
EDUCATOR

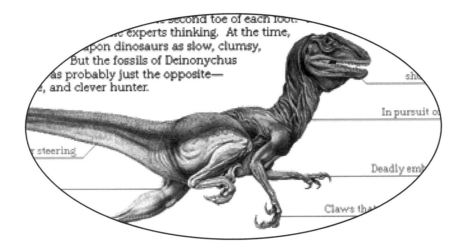

Introduction

One of the areas in which multimedia has had its greatest impact is education. Surveys have shown that people retain about 10% of the material represented in text alone, but with the addition of other media, such as interactive sound, graphics, and video, that retention level jumps to nearly 50%. If the same information is looked at several times, it has been estimated by some that the retention level may be as high as 80%. Many educators report a raise in test scores by as much as 90%. Although educational software may be targeted at very different audiences in terms of age and subject matter, all effective educational software must have good and accurate content. Software used in the classroom has additional requirements because of the teacher's involvement and the nature of the environment in which the software is used.

The use of technology in the classroom has been plagued with problems. Schools are notoriously short of funds, and the decision to purchase computer equipment is a major one. Until recently, computer systems have been used very traditionally: to simply convey, in the same way, the linear format of the material the teacher was presenting verbally. Students have been given computer exercises in rote memory and have not been given the chance to think creatively and learn problem solving for a variety of situations. Many teachers are computer phobic and really lack the necessary skills to teach the students how to effectively use this new technology. Even those who have made the effort to learn computer skills have been forced to use unimaginative computer programs geared to teaching in the traditional way. In most cases, the computer has been used as an electronic replica of the teacher.

Multimedia offers an excellent alternative to traditional teaching. By allowing students to explore and learn at different paces, every student has the opportunity to learn to his or her full potential. Interactive programs allow the student to solve problems in a more realistic environment (after all, the real world does not operate in a linear way) and to explore how a given situation relates to other situations and other disciplines.

But it is not as simple as it sounds. The advent of multimedia will not suddenly transform the classroom into an ideal environment of interactive learning. Several criteria determine the effectiveness of interactive learning: the quality of the multimedia title(s), the teacher's ability to use multimedia effectively, and the environment in which students are exposed to multimedia.

The quality of a multimedia title depends on its content, interactivity, and program design. To be effective in a classroom, though, the teacher must be involved and be willing to relearn the way she or he teaches. The nonlinearity of multimedia is oftentimes overwhelming to those who are accustomed to teaching in a very structured, linear way. And the environment in which the students use the software is also very important. Although students may learn from a multimedia title when left alone to explore it on their own, the learning process is greatly enhanced when certain goals or requirements are made clear prior to the student's accessing the program. Just as a student wandering aimlessly through a library may end up learning something, he or she will learn much more if given a specific learning objective, one that perhaps results in a classroom discussion or report.

The classroom is not the only place in which multimedia can play an important role in education. Increasingly, titles are coming out that focus on the adult learner, making effective use of sound and video to convey information that is not possible in a different format. And perhaps one of the fastest growing markets for educational (and edutainment) software is to general consumers who want access to information that will enhance their children's (and their own) learning experience, using their home computer.

Overview of Profiles

Three titles are profiled in this chapter that illustrate a range of educational software.

Particles and Prairies is a multimedia title targeted at middle school children, and one that illustrates how an interactive program can be put to use most effectively by including excellent content, teacher involvement, and the right environment to motivate and entice students to learn.

The Video Linguist is an interactive program used to teach a foreign language to the adult learner who already has some experience in that language. It makes unique use of video and sound to immerse the student in the culture of the language being taught.

Finally, Microsoft's Dinosaurs is included as a good example of a title that might be called *edutainment*, combining all the elements needed for a high-quality educational title for all ages, as well as some entertaining elements to appeal to a younger audience.

Particles and Prairies

Many readers have undoubtedly heard of Fermilab, the Fermi National Accelerator Laboratory, in Batavia, Illinois. This laboratory is renowned for its research in high-energy particle physics. In order to assist Fermilab's efforts at enhancing science education, the Friends of Fermilab, a not-for-profit organization, was founded in 1983 to develop programs for precollege teachers and students. In partnership with Friends of Fermilab, Fermilab's precollege programs are funded by Federal, state, and private sources. The Leon M. Lederman Science Education Center, a facility dedicated to Fermilab's precollege science education programs, opened in 1992 and currently offers over 40 programs in science and mathematics.

What many may not know about Fermilab is its extensive prairie restoration project, which has been ongoing for many years. Set in the tallgrass prairies of Illinois (see Figure 4.1 on page 61), Fermilab is the site of extensive environmental research and an effort to restore the fragile habitat of this disappearing ecosystem. Perhaps one of the most interesting school programs offered at the Lederman Science Center is Particles and Prairies, which teaches middle school students about the natural habitat surrounding Fermilab. The program is divided into three parts. Previsit activities take place in the classroom, where students learn basic information and skills to allow them to participate in field activities at the lab. On-site activities involve the actual field work itself, during which students visit Fermilab to gather data, make field observations, and do lab work. The postvisit activities may include any number of projects from group discussions to written assignments.

One of the most important components of the three-part program is an interactive multimedia system, called Particles and Prairies Interactive Multimedia Program (or simply Particles and Prairies), developed and produced by Liz Quigg, a multimedia developer at Fermilab. Liz worked in close collaboration with Jim Shultz and Fred Ullrich of Fermilab's Visual Media Services, as well as the Fermilab staff, local scientists, and a number of science teachers,

Figure 4.1   *Fermilab's facility is set in the tallgrass prairies of Illinois and has an extensive prairie research program. Courtesy of Fermilab.*

who helped with the content and curriculum development. Particles and Prairies won two major awards in NewMedia's INVISION Multimedia Awards Competition—the Award of Excellence, and the Gold Award for K–12 education.

The content of the title involves four main themes: restoration of the prairie, history, the ecosystem, and the outdoor lab (see Figure 4.2 on page 62). Says Liz, "We have a lot of video on restoration, because that's one of the things Fermilab is very proud of. This was one of the first large-scale prairie restoration projects using farming techniques."

The program includes databases containing information on birds and plants that are stored in HyperCard stacks. From each card, students have access to slides of all the plants and birds as well as bird calls from the videodisc. The accompanying videodisc also stores large amounts of other audio and visual data such as narratives, still photos, animations, and video clips. Many of the video clips provide experiences that the student would not have on a field trip,

Figure 4.2   *Illustration showing the information content of Particles and Prairies. Courtesy of Fermilab.*

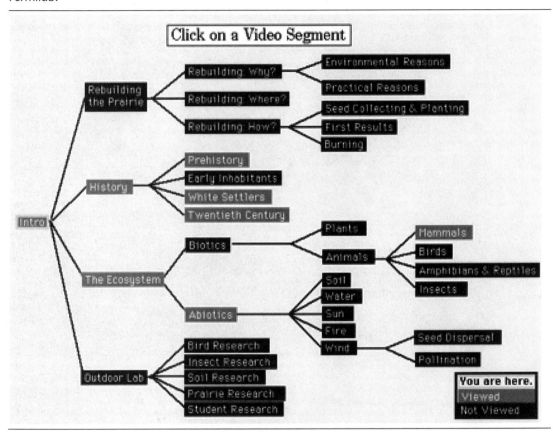

such as the burning of the prairie (called Burning the Prairie) and time lapse sequences of seasonal changes (called Our Changing Prairie). Other features included in the program are games that teach the children more about the prairie. One of the most popular of these is the Bird Call game, which is so effective that when the students are out in the field, they are able to recognize many of the bird calls they hear.

The complete multimedia workstation available at the Lederman Science Center runs on a Macintosh IIfx with 8 MB of RAM and a 120 MB hard disk drive, a 13" high resolution computer monitor, a 20" color video monitor, a Videologic DVA 4000/Mac video board, a Pioneer Laserdisc Player (LDV-8000), a Radio Shack audio mixer, and Yamaha speakers. The software used includes Aldus SuperCard, Claris HyperCard, and Voyager Videostack. This

Figure 4.3   *Screen display from program used at the Lederman Science Center's multimedia station. Courtesy of Fermilab and Eugene C. Brehm.*

multimedia station complements the hands-on exhibits at the science center and allows the student to view full-motion video on the same screen displaying the program (see Figure 4.3).

The program is also offered for classroom use to teachers on a budget that precludes such high-end hardware. A low-end version of the program is available that requires only a Mac SE with simple black-and-white HyperCard stacks and makes use of two monitors: one to display the program, and another to display the video (see Figure 4.4 on page 64). Teachers with a videodisc player may access all the photos and video clips on the videodisc using a barcode reader. The videodisc and guide are offered to teachers for $50, and

Figure 4.4   *Particles and Prairies may be used in the classroom equipped with a computer monitor and a video monitor. Courtesy of Fermilab.*

the HyperCard stack costs them an additional $5. Liz is quick to point out that their ability to offer the program at such a low cost is because they are a not-for-profit organization and received much of their funding to develop the program from the U.S. Department of Energy and the Illinois State Board of Education. It is also quite apparent that this cost has allowed more schools to be able to purchase the program.

Developed on a Macintosh, the program took approximately two years to complete. Liz Quigg was the project manager and programmer, and Jim Shultz and Fred Ullrich worked on the video production and editing. The visual and audio media include a total of 28 minutes of video clips, 750 color slides, and 11 bird calls. Although there was a lot of in-house video already available at Fermilab due to the numerous research projects conducted there, some additional footage was shot for Particles and Prairies. Jim explains, "We have a 2,000 reel library of archived footage from the lab including a lot concerning prairie research. So our actual production time was a little bit less than it might have been if we had had to shoot everything from scratch." But because of the slant of the software, some new shoots were required. "Since it was targeted toward middle school children, it was decided that we would use people of their age as much as possible in the video segments, and Liz selected middle school children to do the narrations," says Jim.

Jim spent a concentrated one to two months shooting and editing video for the project. He found the process of producing video for an interactive program to be a new challenge. Not only was he limited to 30 minutes of video on the disc, but he found the editing process to be completely different from the linear editing he had always used in previous projects. "Because it was interactive, it really involves a different editing approach—you have to break out of the mold of a linear editor. I had to look at the project as packaging segments," says Jim. "But there were some advantages because I didn't have to worry about transitions between segments. That was taken care of in the interactive program."

Jim also points out how important it is to keep the video clips short. Unlike linear videos in which there is more time to let things "develop," interactive videos clips require that the editor capture the information in as short a period as possible. "People want to explore at their leisure, and when they get bored, they want to jump back out of it to explore something else." Jim sees such "quick cutting" as a general trend in videos used in other genre, such as MTV and even documentaries. "People have come to expect fast-paced videos." Jim likens the new technology to creating "knowledge bites." "Just as we have worked with music bites and sound bites, multimedia involves the creation of 'knowledge bites' which encompass so much more information." A luxury Jim had to work with in shooting video for the historical portion of Particles and Prairies was a nearby historical town where a pioneer village has been recreated. Jim was able to shoot many "period" scenes such as farmers tilling the soil with horse-drawn plows, and he feels this enhanced the program quite a bit.

To transfer the numerous slides to video, Liz worked closely with Video Impressions, a video production company that also created some of the animation. Transferring the slides to video was painstaking because sometimes they wanted to shoot a part of a slide or to align a set of slides exactly the same. This latter technique was used to make the Changing Prairie sequences that included photos of the same area of prairie at two week to one month intervals through a time period of three years. This involved laying four frames per slide because sometimes laying individual frames can result in strange effects with the fields from neighboring frames. The use of four frames gave them some assurance that one of the four frames would be displayed properly.

Some of the visual and audio material used in Particles and Prairies was provided by outside sources such as the Kansas Department of Wildlife and Parks, the Cornell Laboratory of Ornithology, Morton Arboretum, and the Chicago Academy of Sciences. "People were very generous about contributing to the project," Liz recalls. "But when I asked for the material, I made it very clear that it was for an educational, not-for-profit project for Illinois school kids." This helped significantly in avoiding copyright issues, although they had to pay for some of the material. An example is an illustration of life in the soil which they acquired from National Geographic.

Many of the staff at Fermilab and local scientists were also involved in the project. Their expertise was invaluable in providing content and input into the development of Particles and Prairies. Liz points out, "One of Fermilab's strengths in developing educational programs is our access to experts." Some of those from Fermilab who contributed significantly were staff photographer Reidar Hahn, ecologist Rod Walton, amateur ornithologist Peter Kasper (who is a high-energy physicist) and amateur prairie specialists Mitchell Adamus and Finley Markley. The Education Office staff at Fermilab also contributed to the development of the program. Local scientists who also provided guidance were prairie restoration specialist Dr. Robert Betz from Northeastern Illinois University and Dr. Julie Jastrow, a soil scientist from Argonne National Laboratory.

Besides the efforts of Liz and Jim, there was also the effort of several science schoolteachers who had been developing guides for the field trips at the lab and for pre-visit and post-visit activities. Their work was supported by a grant from the Illinois State Board of Education. It was this material that provided the content for Particles and Prairies. The main contributor in this effort was Pat Franzen, then a teacher at Madison Junior High School in nearby Naperville, Illinois. In fact, it was Pat's eighth grade students who provided the narration for the program. Liz and Pat were very careful to work closely with children throughout the project. Not only did children provide the narrations, they also provided valuable input into the content of the program. If the narratives did not sound comfortable to the students they were encouraged to say so and to offer alternative ways of saying the same thing so that their contemporaries would find it more relevant and understandable.

Like Jim, Pat had to adjust to the interactive nature of the program. She worked closely with Liz to set up the content and structure, but its nonlinearity was quite new to her. "When Liz first described how the program was going to work I didn't have a clue what she was talking about," Pat is able to laugh now. "She told me it was not going to be a linear piece in which you go from beginning to end. I had a terrible time trying to figure out what she was talking about. But when we got into it, I was fascinated! I recognized then how it would allow the kids to explore and direct the learning toward their own areas of interest."

Pat says that as a teacher, perhaps the most valuable aspect of Particles and Prairies is that it is highly integratable and is equally useful across many curricula, such as science, history, and math. Teachers using the program are given suggestions on how to best use the program across the various curricula to effectively encourage students to explore other subjects. One of the program's features that stimulates this is what Pat and Liz call *teasers*. For example, while the student is exploring in the area of history, there may be a narration that alludes to some other topic such as animals, and the student jumps to that section of the program to learn about the animals. Says Pat, "Once a student has touched on the surface of a topic, they want to explore more. The program makes the kids excited about the learning process and makes them want to learn more about many different subjects."

Besides being an educator, Pat has also participated in a Fermilab cosponsored program called *Expanding Your Horizons,* which is designed to help middle school girls develop positive attitudes towards math and science. I asked Pat if there was any conscious effort to balance the genders of children depicted (and narrating) in Particles and Prairies. Pat says, "Yes, Liz and I talked about this and felt it was very important to have an equal distribution, and one of the researchers mentioned in the program is a well-known female scientist. We had an ethnic and racial mix of children involved in the program as well."

An interesting insight that Pat provided from the teacher's perspective is the difficulties some students have with different modalities. "Multimedia lends itself to the auditory learner, the visual learner, and—because of the interactivity—the hands-on learner as well. It's going to captivate more kids." And she adds, "A good teacher is able to deliver information via a number of different modalities so they can reach as many children as possible. But not every teacher has the capability to teach to all those different modalities. A multimedia station can."

I asked Liz for her advice to others developing an educational title such as Particles and Prairies, and she offered the following from her experience.

First, it takes a lot of time and work to put together the necessary photos, videos, and content and to get the permission needed to use them. They were fortunate to be not-for-profit and were buffered from some of the more difficult aspects of copyrights.

Second, from the very beginning the developer should consider all possibilities for the use of the product and understand any legal restrictions associated with the funding. When they began developing Particles and Prairies, they had no intention of making a commercial product. Once it won the NewMedia awards, they realized they would have a big job sorting out ownership and copyright issues if they were to move it to the commercial market.

Finally, she wishes they had had a graphic artist render an illustration similar to the one they obtained from National Geographic. Although the arrangement was generous, each time they want to press more videodiscs, they need to renegotiate their contract with National Geographic, which is time consuming and requires an attorney—something they would not have needed otherwise.

Liz also cautions that the developer does not always know what lies ahead when trying to acquire content for the project. In searching for visual material for the program, Liz contacted the Herpetological Society in Chicago in the hope they could provide photos of amphibians and reptiles. Two members (a husband and wife) who lived in Chicago invited her to their apartment where they could show her their collection of slides from which Liz could choose those she wanted to use. While sitting in their living room, Liz found herself literally surrounded by snakes. "I don't really like snakes, and it took all my self control to patiently wait until they showed me all their slides. As they did, they bought out snakes, one after the other, for me to admire. Actually I was surprised how well I handled it—it was more than I had bargained for. But I got my slides."

Particles and Prairies is a good example of a program that incorporates all the elements of a good educational multimedia title and one that is put to use in the classroom as effectively as possible. Teachers are trained how to use the program across many curricula, and the software itself is part of a larger project involving field work, classroom discussions, and written reports. It also points out that the efforts of a small team of developers can produce a top-notch program worthy of competing and winning against titles put together by some of the largest for-profit software companies. "When I think of the project, I sort of think of it like baking home-made chocolate-chip cookies," recalls Liz. "We were so small, it was so personal to us, and we won! There was this dream of multimedia going out to the masses and being embraced by the masses, and we were an example of that."

The Video Linguist

Multimedia titles targeting adult education are becoming increasingly common. One good example is The Video Linguist, a foreign language instructional title developed by Cubic Media in New York and the recipient of NewMedia's INVISION Award of Merit. Whereas most programs that teach a foreign language focus on beginning grammar and writing, The Video Linguist teaches more advanced conversational language by making very effective use of video and sound. Because of this, it is targeted at the person who has studied a foreign language for at least a year. Anyone who has taken a foreign language, even for a number of years, is aware that one is generally not proficient enough to converse when placed in a country where that language is spoken. In fact it was this experience that led Patrick Nee, the founder and CEO of Cubic Media, to develop The Video Linguist.

Patrick holds a Bachelor of Science degree in Mechanical Engineering from the Massachusetts Institute of Technology (MIT), where he worked in their Artificial Intelligence Laboratory, helping to develop robots for manufacturing. While at MIT, Patrick studied Japanese quite extensively, believing that knowledge of the Japanese language would be important because of Japan's increasing influence on emerging technologies. In 1989, Patrick went to Japan's Tokyo Institute of Technology to begin work on a Master of Science degree in Mechanical Engineering, which he earned in 1992. In order to do so, he had to complete his advanced studies in Japanese. However, when Patrick first arrived in Japan, he was struck by his inability to converse comfortably in the Japanese language. "In spite of all my years of studying Japanese, I couldn't carry on a conversation when I got to Japan," Patrick recalls.

And so began the germination of an idea for an instructional system that would teach the intermediate to advanced user to converse fluently in a foreign language rather than a beginning program targeted at grammar and the written language. "Once I became immersed in the Japanese culture and learned to speak fluently in their language, I knew I wanted to put that learning experience into a product that would teach others as though they were actually in that country."

And multimedia provided the ideal vehicle to accomplish that goal. With the added components of video and sound, The Video Linguist literally immerses the student into the culture of the language being taught. Currently available in versions to teach French and Spanish to the English-speaking student, the program plays actual television segments from that country. The student may choose from several categories including art, culture, sports, travel, weather, food, and wine (see Figure 4.5 on page 71), making it very appealing to a broad spectrum of users. It allows the student to display the text that is being spoken in the video segments, both in the original language being taught and in the student's native language (see Figure 4.6 on page 72).

Many other features are included as well. For example, the student may slow down the speech with the click of a button. The same phrases are spoken, but much more slowly, allowing the more novice students the opportunity to learn conversational language at a pace more in keeping with their own skills. The students may also choose to record their own voices, and play them back to compare their pronunciation with that contained in the video. The user may also click on any word displayed in the original language text to access an explanation of that word (see Figure 4.7 on page 73) These words and their meanings are stored during a session and may be printed out to reinforce the student's learning process.

Patrick began working on the product's concept in 1992 with an English language instruction system. After developing a business plan, he hired the necessary experts to create a prototype, and founded Cubic Media in 1993. Private investors provided most of the initial capital to develop the program. The program was developed on the Mac using QuickTime and C++, and versions are available for Windows as well. It also uses patented tools that uniquely handle the data and hyperlinks in a way that does not tax the CPU as it is displaying video. This allows the software to run smoothly even on low-end machines. Other proprietary tools they developed enable the close synchronization of video and text display in various playback speeds.

In order to develop the first two versions of The Video Linguist (i.e., French and Spanish), Patrick coordinated a team of approximately 16 people, most of whom were freelance and worked on the project part-time. Five to six language experts made up each of two teams (for the two languages) and provided assistance with translation and narration. In addition, there were several programmers and designers who worked on both languages. It took about a year-and-a-half to complete the first two versions of the product. Much of this time was spent developing their proprietary tools. Patrick estimates that future versions can be produced in about six months because now they can use the same engine and simply replace existing data with new data.

Figure 4.5　　*Opening screen of The Video Linguist showing the various topics the user may select. Courtesy of Cubic Media, Inc.*

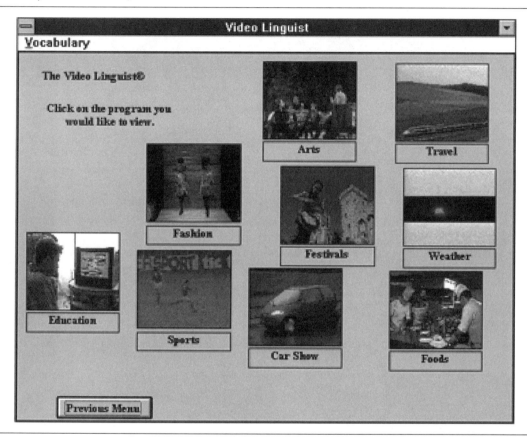

Patrick feels that one of the major things that helped them avoid any glitches in getting the product to market was their plan from day one to make this a cross-platform product. "Everything we did had to be feasible and doable on the other platform. That drove our choice to use QuickTime for video and C++ rather than authoring software." Because they knew speed would be a major issue, C++ was the obvious choice. "Some authoring software has decent speed on one platform and horrible speed on the other. Knowing we wanted a cross-platform product helped us avoid some speedbumps in the end that other developers have to contend with."

Perhaps the most effective and unique feature of The Video Linguist is its use of television segments to expose the student to the type of conversations they would encounter if actually visiting a country. Patrick recalls that the

Figure 4.6   *Throughout the program, the user may see a text display of the original language being spoken in the video, as well as corresponding native language text. Courtesy of Cubic Media, Inc.*

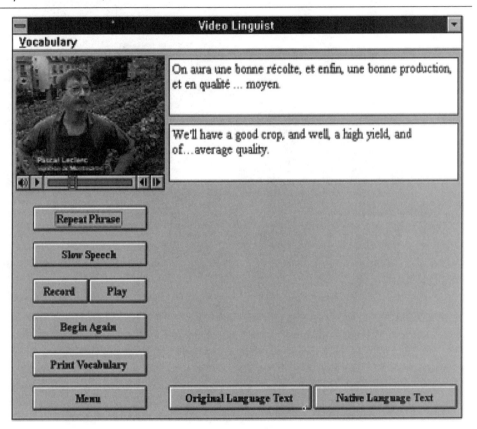

entire project would never have come about if it were not for a lot of luck in obtaining those segments. He had been working on the project for a couple of months and knew that the key element to the program was the video. After trying futilely to get to the right people at a number of companies that owned video material, he heard of an international television industry convention being held in France. The annual convention is attended by various broadcasting companies that want to buy television programs and segments from other countries. He knew this could be the source of the "in country" learning experience he wanted to capture in the instructional program he had in mind.

After checking into the cost of the conference, he flew to Europe, only to find upon arriving that the cost for admission was $2000—quite a bit more

Figure 4.7   *Any of the words displayed in the original language may be clicked on to see an explanation of that word. Courtesy of Cubic Media, Inc.*

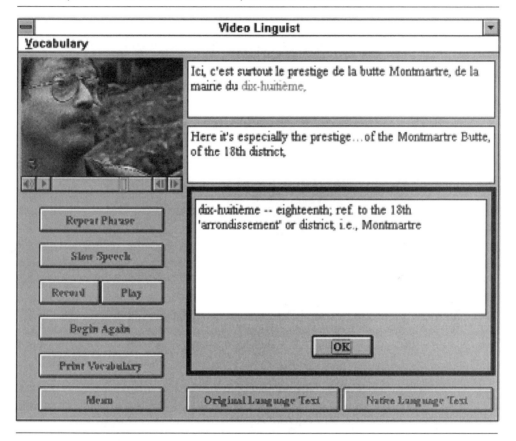

than he had been told. Patrick was shocked. "I complained and begged and asked to speak to the person in charge, and was told by the woman I was talking to that SHE was in charge, and that I couldn't speak to anyone else." Discouraged, he was about to fly back to the states, but before doing so, he made a call home to leave word he was returning. He had a message from a friend whose company just happened to have a booth at the conference. When he called the friend, he was told to contact someone in the booth to see if he could get a free pass. He did, and was admitted for free. "I was VERY lucky. If I had left the show before calling home to check in, or if my friend had called and left a message a day later, I would have missed the whole show and that was critical to getting all the materials," Patrick says. "At the show, I was able to sit down in one day and talk to the necessary contacts at the six or seven major companies I had been trying to reach for months." Without this stroke of luck, Patrick would not have been able to acquire the necessary television footage (some of it royalty free), and he doubts that the product would have been completed.

The unique nature of The Video Linguist dictates Cubic Media's marketing strategy. Patrick admits that one of his early misconceptions as a developer was that building a purely better product would ensure product sales. He now knows that not to be true, in part due to the abundance of CD-ROM products, and believes that the developer should carefully plan on how he or she is going to market the product. Although The Video Linguist is selling through traditional outlets, it can also be sold through more direct means of marketing. Because it is targeted at the intermediate to advanced language student, it is used extensively in universities and colleges. Patrick points out, "We can identify who language teachers are and do some targeted marketing. A lot of other products out there have to sit on the shelves at Egghead and hope they grab somebody's attention. I think in that sense, we're at an advantage."

The product is marketed to educators through direct mail. Cubic Media also has an agreement with a large publisher to distribute the product to the college market. Students who purchase a particular textbook may purchase The Video Linguist at a substantial discount—beyond the educational discount frequently offered by software vendors. Future plans include versions for Italian, German and Japanese as well as an instructional program to teach English as a second language to Japanese. They are also planning to release a product that targets the beginning student.

Patrick expressed a concern that many other developers have—namely, the glut of poorly produced CD-ROM software on the market. "I would certainly like to see more thoughtful products out there. I don't think making a quality interactive CD-ROM is as easy as it seems to many people. The existence of poor quality CD-ROM titles cheapens all of them. When people find that 80% of the CD-ROMS they buy aren't worth buying, they're just going to stop buying everything. And that's everyone's fear."

Dinosaurs

Of all the titles profiled in this book, Dinosaurs perhaps fits into the area of edutainment more closely than any other. It fills the requirement of good educational software, while providing some entertaining elements to make the program fun to use and explore. Dinosaurs has versions for both the Mac and Windows and has won numerous awards, including the Best Software Award (Gold Seal Category) from "Oppenheim Toy Portfolio" and it was cited as a Top 100 title in "CD-ROMs for Schools." Developed as part of the Exploration Series of titles produced by Microsoft Corporation, Dinosaurs is appealing to young and old alike. Unlike the other titles profiled in this chapter, which were developed by small firms, Dinosaurs illustrates an educational title developed by the world's largest software company. Because of this, different issues came into play—from the standpoint of acquiring content and program development.

Founded by Bill Gates in 1975, Microsoft Corporation (headquartered in Seattle) currently employs more than 15,000 people and showed revenues of $4.65 billion for the 1994 fiscal year. Initially focused on PC operating system software, Microsoft has branched into every area of the software industry. There are currently more than 8,000 Windows-based applications. Its enormous financial resources and development experience make Microsoft a formidable competitor to any company developing any type of software. One of the most recently formed divisions at Microsoft is the consumer division, headed by Patty Stonesifer, which is responsible for the development of interactive CD-ROM titles. So far, the 600 employees in the consumer division have produced more than 100 titles, and this is expected to more than double in the next year.

Because successful multimedia titles rely so heavily on content, Microsoft is building partnerships with various publishing companies in order to acquire content. One of Microsoft's advantages in this regard is its imposing reputation. Many publishers have chosen Microsoft to produce electronic versions of their books because they feel comfortable that the resulting product will be as technologically advanced as possible. And Microsoft also has a clear advantage over other companies in its distribution power throughout the world.

The consumer division produces several series of multimedia titles. One of these is the Exploration Series, which includes Musical Instruments, Ancient Lands, Dangerous Creatures and Dinosaurs. Although all have been quite successful, Dinosaurs has captivated an audience enthralled by prehistoric creatures and *Jurassic Park*. The program has a very easy-to-use interface, allowing the user to view more than 1,000 high-quality color illustrations with accompanying articles, and it contains hundreds of narrations and sound effects.

From the main Contents page (see Figure 4.8), the users may explore the world of dinosaurs through several options. For example, they may click on

Figure 4.8   *Contents screen for Dinosaurs. The user may explore the world of dinosaurs by clicking on the various icons such as Atlas and Timeline. Courtesy of Microsoft Corp.*

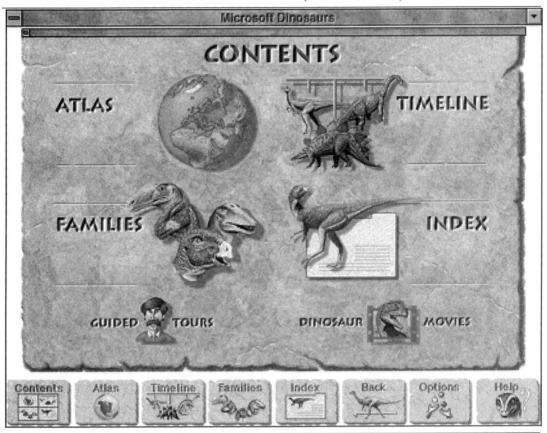

the Atlas icon to see where certain dinosaurs have been found (see Figure 4.9). From a display of the selected region, the user may click on any of the species names to find out more about that dinosaur. To look up specific dinosaurs the user may click on either the Families or Index icons on the contents screen. The screen displaying each dinosaur (see Figure 4.10) is full of "hot" labels that provide more detailed information on the creature and the way it lived. The user may also click on an icon to have the name pronounced or to go to another related topic. When the program jumps to the related topic, a narrative explains how the dinosaur is related to the topic about to be displayed. This greatly enhances the understanding as the user navigates through the program. And a timeline (see Figure 4.11) may be accessed to give the user an

Figure 4.9 *Various regions of the world may be explored in more detail to see where the various dinosaurs lived. Courtesy of Microsoft Corp.*

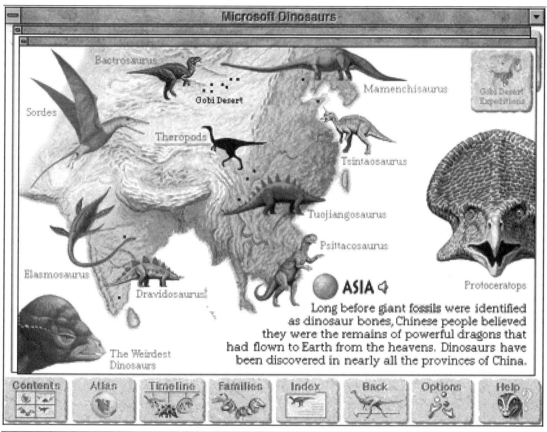

understanding of the relative times in which the different dinosaurs lived. Each of the time periods may be clicked on for more detailed information. In addition, the user may select from a number of Guided Tours and dinosaur movies taken from the PBS series *The Dinosaurs!*

John Porcaro is the Product Manager of the Exploration Series as well as a number of other projects that have been done externally such as Isaac Asimov's The Ultimate Robot and The Ultimate Frank Lloyd Wright (done in collaboration with Byron Preiss Multimedia, profiled in Chapter 9). When he first joined the consumer division there were fewer than 100 people, and he watched it quickly grow to 600 in a matter of a few years. The teams working on all the projects involve people with very diverse backgrounds—writers, edi-

Figure 4.10   *Each "page" displaying a dinosaur has "hot" labels that provide additional information. The screen layout was carefully designed to ensure that text wraps around the main image and that there is plenty of light space. Courtesy of Microsoft Corp.*

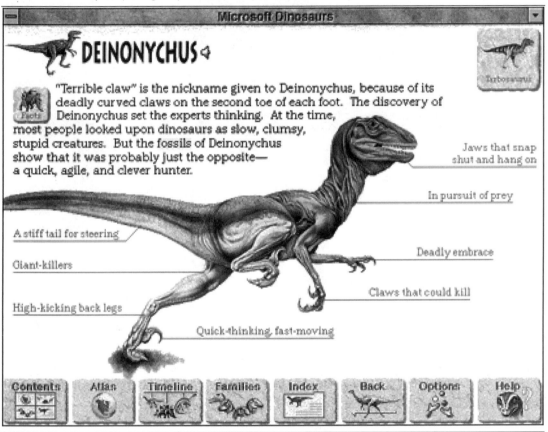

tors, designers, artists, teachers, cartographers, acquisition specialists, and of course, programmers. In general, each project has a core team (made up, for example, of writers and designers) that focuses on a particular project from beginning to end. Additional team members (such as sound engineers) may work on several titles at one time, and they generally come and go during the development of a project.

"Dinosaurs was not an easy thing to develop," John says. Although unable to provide specifics, he indicates that it involved a "pretty big" team and certainly took more than a few months to complete. Developed using a Mac for much of the design work, and a PC for the programming effort, the

Figure 4.11 *A timeline illustrates the relative time periods in which the dinosaurs lived. Such a timeline is provided in all the titles in the Exploration Series. Courtesy of Microsoft Corp.*

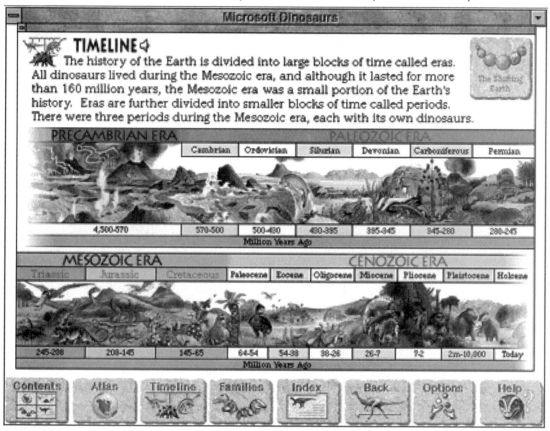

interface was written in a proprietary C code engine. This provided a hypertext-like environment with bitmapped pages and hot spots. Although other Microsoft multimedia titles have been developed using Microsoft Viewer, John points out that this was not the engine of choice to handle the rich visual content of Dinosaurs. "Viewer's main strength is dealing with lots of textual information, with visual content of secondary importance," he explains. "We came from the complete opposite place when developing the Exploration Series. We were most concerned about the images and graphical layout. The text database wasn't as important as the sound or the videos or the pictures."

When developing a title, they use different models and tools depending on content and the desired interface. Encarta and Cinemania were developed using Viewer, while Visual Basic was used for titles in the Composer Series. All the titles within the Exploration Series were developed using the proprietary engine mentioned above. As John points out, "We use a lot of the same elements across products where it makes sense. If you look at Dinosaurs, Dangerous Creatures, Musical Instruments or Ancient Lands, they all have the same interface and use similar elements such as a timeline, a graphical index, and hot boxes with more information, and all have a similar set of buttons at the bottom of the screen. You definitely know you're in the same series when you are in one of these products."

In developing Dinosaurs they wanted to be sure that it was visually appealing and had excellent content. Special care was given to screen design to ensure that the text wraps around the images, that there is plenty of light space to avoid detracting from the main image, and that text is displayed in bite-sized chunks rather than showing windows with scrolling text. For the main content of Dinosaurs (and some other titles in the Exploration Series), Microsoft collaborated with London-based publishing company Dorling Kindersley, which has published some 1100 books. All are highly illustrated, instructional, and appropriate for readers of various ages. Microsoft owns approximately 20–25% of Dorling Kindersley, and although this gives Microsoft access to a good deal of the publishing company's images and text, royalty fees are still paid for the use of such content. In addition, Dorling Kindersley does not necessarily own the copyrights to this content—many belong to the authors and artists who created the work. In some cases, Microsoft had to go to the individual authors to get permission to use the material. "Working with the publishing industry can get very complicated," John points out.

They also worked closely with the Dinosaur Society and its founder, Don Lessem. Don provided the scripts for the Guided Tours used in Dinosaurs (although an actor read the scripts), and he also served as a consultant for some of the content. Microsoft initially contacted the Dinosaur Society for general guidance in development and marketing and soon found out that the society was helping Steven Spielberg with a film called *Jurassic Park*. As John recalls, "We had no idea a movie was planned when we started the project—we just knew that kids liked dinosaurs and that it's been an interesting scientific topic for a long time. We lucked out with the timing of the movie. I think it helped the sales of the software." Similarly, their recently released Dangerous Creatures was ideally timed with the movie *The Lion King* which has stimulated children's interest in African animals. "We always try to keep our ear to the ground and figure out what the market is doing. We do a lot of research up front to find out what topics are going to be interesting to people. And we've been ahead of the curve a couple of times. It's been pretty interesting."

Because of the dynamics of scientific research, many of the articles were updated at the last minute to provide the most current information and theories regarding dinosaurs. Don Lessem was particularly impressed in working with the consumer division, because of their commitment and extra work to make the product as accurate as possible. He was also struck by their attempts to help out the Dinosaur Society by producing copies of its newsletter and including it with the software and by participating in a dinosaur exhibit the society has been taking around the country. All of this, says Don, helps the society in promoting and supporting dinosaur research.

Another important contributor to the project was David Weishampel, a leading dinosaur researcher at Johns Hopkins University, who critically reviewed the thousands of pages of material in Dinosaurs. Don Lessem believes Dinosaurs to be the best of the dinosaur products in its ability to get kids involved and in terms of its scientific accuracy. However, including scientifically accurate sound was somewhat problematic to the team because no one really knows what dinosaurs sounded like. Some of the developers worked with the Dinosaur Society for advice on how they might have sounded based on bone reconstructions. Although this provided some guidance regarding what sounds some of the dinosaurs may have made, paleontologists have no idea what most of them sounded like. And this is where creativity came into play.

"One of the important things our teams deal with is developing creativity as much as possible. We try to give each of the developers, writers and artists as much leeway as we can," says John. It is this creative liberty that can help when tackling a problem like sound effects. "We let the guys go a little crazy and decide in their minds what they thought the dinosaurs should have sounded like." Other sound effects resulted from unusual ways of recording everyday sounds. "We did these environments where rain is falling and one of the developers got some water in a bathtub and was splashing around. The sound engineer took the recording into the sound studio and transformed and enhanced it," John says. "He worked very hard to get this fun sound that worked really well, but it wasn't what you'd call scientific."

John emphasizes the importance of usability testing, and Microsoft has a very large lab set up for such testing. After developing a prototype, they put it in front of customers. "We're not afraid to get a group together and have them trash our ideas, so all along we're continually making sure this is what the market wants." They also continue to do research as they develop the product, which John admits is something a big company has the luxury of doing. Some of their usability testing involves taking the product to local schools where they let the kids play with the product and try to get the teachers to advise them on how they could use it in the classroom. "Making sure that the interface works is very important to us," says John. As an example, they spent a lot of time in deciding what labels to put on the buttons—Contents vs. Main or Back vs. Go Back—and they made choices based on what feels most comfortable to the customer.

"A lot of people think they can throw this stuff together in their garage, but the only ones who have been successful are those who have spent a lot of money and put a lot of care into the project," John cautions. "Microsoft obviously cares not only about making sure the information is accurate, but we put a lot of emphasis on the model itself and how easy the software is to use."

The success of Dinosaurs has exceeded their expectations. Microsoft met its first year projections within the first two months of its release. The enormous success of educational titles targeted at the consumer market, coupled with Microsoft's reputation for producing quality titles, is the reason why the consumer division is one of the fastest growing divisions at Microsoft.

Further Reading

Heier, Jeffrey L., Van Cooley, and Ray Reitz. 1993. "America School 2000 Project: Westfield's Technology Initiative." *T.H.E. Journal* (May): 83.

Howles, Les, and Connie Pettengill. 1993. "Designing Instructional Multimedia Presentations: A Seven-Step Process." *T.H.E. Journal* (June): 58.

Lim, Ellen. 1994. "DOS Multimedia Madness: Ten Commonly Asked Questions." *Multimedia Schools* (May–June): 38.

McKell, Lynn J., and Kenneth B. McKell. 1994. "High-End Audio for Multimedia Environments." *T.H.E. Journal* (September): 83.

Rohrer, Barbara L. 1994. "The Holmes Technology Center and Its Teaching Wall." *Multimedia Schools* (May–June): 34.

Sammons, Martha C. 1994. "Motivating Faculty to Use Multimedia as a Lecture Tool." *T.H.E. Journal* (February): 88.

Smith, Jerome J. 1993. "The SPICE Project: Comparing Passive to Interactive Approaches in a Videodisc-Based Course." *T.H.E. Journal* (August): 62.

Solomon, Martin B. 1994. "What's Wrong with Multimedia in Higher Education?" *T.H.E. Journal* (February): 81.

Stansberry, Domenic. 1993. "K–12 Takes the Plunge." *NewMedia Magazine* (February): 30.

THE MULTIMEDIA TRAINER

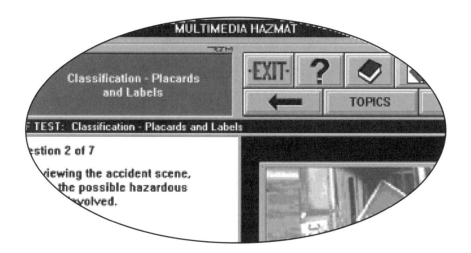

Introduction

It is estimated that corporations in the United States will spend over $300 million in 1996 just to train employees. Part of the reason for this astounding figure is the trend in downsizing, which has caused companies to rely heavily on part-time employees or outside contractors who may not have the necessary knowledge or skills to adequately perform the work. Training is essential to get these workers up and running fast. Ironically, full-time employees also are faced with training because they are expected to learn jobs that others may have performed within the company. This downsizing trend is accompanied by rapidly changing technologies and the need for employees to understand increasingly complex information.

Unfortunately, training is very expensive. It frequently involves sending an employee to another location, requiring the employer to pay for travel, lodging, and meals in addition to the actual training costs. When the employee being trained is also being paid salary while absent from the job, it becomes even more costly for the company. And the absence of an employee for some jobs (such as firefighting) that involve public safety can even result in the loss of life.

Other disadvantages are involved in traditional training in addition to corporate costs. One of these is that it tends to be structured to a linear format. After all, the roots of training is teaching, and in the last chapter I discussed the problems with traditional teaching. It does not afford the learner an opportunity to skip familiar topics and explore fully those with which he or she is less familiar. The ratio of trainer to trainee is generally low, and the learner may be forced to take the training when other circumstances (such as sickness) preclude an optimal learning experience.

It is little wonder that interactive training is one of the fastest growing categories of CD-ROM titles, and although videodiscs have been commonly used for training, CD-ROM-based training is becoming a much more practical route for most organizations because CD-ROM drives are much cheaper than videodisc hardware. CD-ROMs are also cheaper to produce and are quickly becoming a standard for application delivery. One of the reasons for the rapid growth in interactive training is that it is more cost effective than traditional training methods, and it also provides an ideal learning environment in which the person may use self-paced modules and exercises. The learner has a complete one-on-one interaction with the instructor (the program) and may explore whatever areas he or she needs to for the most effective learning. In addition, multimedia training allows the person to go through the training at the job site and coordinate the training with job duties that must be done at a given time (such as fighting a fire).

Interactive training can also be used to simulate certain circumstances or procedures that are difficult to do in a traditional, linear training environment. For example, in a medical school, a student may unexpectedly ask what would happen during the progression of a lesion. In a traditional training environment, the instructor would have to be prepared to stop, load an animated film (or a series of slides) and play it back to immediately reinforce the learning process. With an interactive program, the click of a button provides the same information, but with much greater effectiveness because of its rapid accessibility.

Because most training applications are targeted at the adult learner, the environment in which the training takes place is not as essential as it is for school-aged children. However, most everyone agrees that when combined with other training methods such as lectures, books, tests and interaction with an instructor, the training is much more effective. The people I interviewed for this chapter felt strongly that multimedia cannot replace traditional training or teaching methods. As they said, both methods have their strengths and weaknesses. The key is to recognize them and make the most of both methods to effectively train people.

Overview of Profiles

I interviewed people at two companies that have developed award-winning training programs. Each provides a different perspective on development because of the very different topics they address and the vastly different challenges involved in their development.

A.D.A.M. could just as easily have been included in Chapter 4 because it is certainly as much an educational title as a training one. However, because it is used extensively to train medical students about surgical procedures, I felt it would be a good title to bridge the gap between education and training. Certainly it is used in medical schools for both purposes.

Multimedia Hazmat is a training application used to teach emergency response personnel how to respond to a dangerous incident such as fire containment or handling hazardous material. It is used throughout the United States and Canada to certify employees according to standards set forth by the National Fire Protection Association.

A.D.A.M. (Animated Dissection of Anatomy for Medicine)

I must admit to a certain amount of personal interest when choosing A.D.A.M. for this book. When A.D.A.M. was first released, I was collaborating with a research scientist at the University of California in San Diego. We were trying to develop an interactive program that would allow the user to "expose" successive layers or cross-sections of microfossils in great detail, and A.D.A.M. was the first thing we saw on the market that paralleled our own efforts. At that time I contacted the technical people at A.D.A.M. to ask for suggestions and guidance regarding the work we were doing. I was struck by their eagerness to advise me and to help in any way they could, even though my request of their time could have been perceived as a burden. There seems to be a tendency for many multimedia developers to help out each other, recognizing that this is the best way to get the industry headed in a direction that is in everyone's best interest, developer and consumer alike.

A.D.A.M. (see Figure 5.1 on page 87) is a sophisticated medical training program that is used in a number of ways. Medical schools use it to teach anatomy and train students how to perform surgery. By peeling back successive layers of tissue (see Figures 5.2 on page 88 and 5.3 on page 89), students are able to display every structure of the human body in great detail (see Figure 5.4 on page 90). Rather than dissecting an actual cadaver to learn gross anatomy, the student uses A.D.A.M. to expose hundreds of layers of the body in four views—anterior, posterior, lateral (see Figure 5.5 on page 91) and medial. And the advantage is that with A.D.A.M., the student may replace a layer that has been removed—something that's not possible with a real

Figure 5.1 *Opening screen of A.D.A.M. Courtesy of A.D.A.M. Software, Inc.*

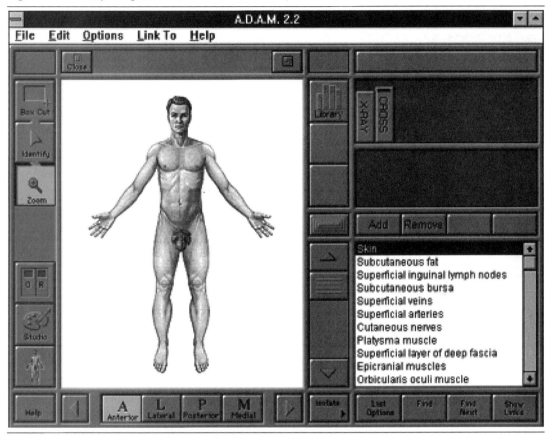

cadaver. As a surgical "flight simulator," A.D.A.M. has tools that allow the student to sterilize the surgical site, inject an anesthetic into the proper areas, and use an animated scalpel to cut through successive layers of skin, fatty tissue, and muscles. This allows students to practice surgical procedures before actually performing one in the operating room.

Physicians also find A.D.A.M. to be invaluable in explaining certain medical procedures to patients. For example, a patient requiring knee surgery may be shown a detailed illustration of the knee with torn ligaments and a video clip that will show how the surgical procedure will repair the ligament. As the patient asks questions about the surgery, the physician can provide additional illustrations, different views of the knee, and be sure that the patient is thoroughly informed about the prospective surgery. The patient may also be given

Figure 5.2   *Display of A.D.A.M. as user begins to "peel" away superficial layers of tissue. Courtesy of A.D.A.M. Software, Inc.*

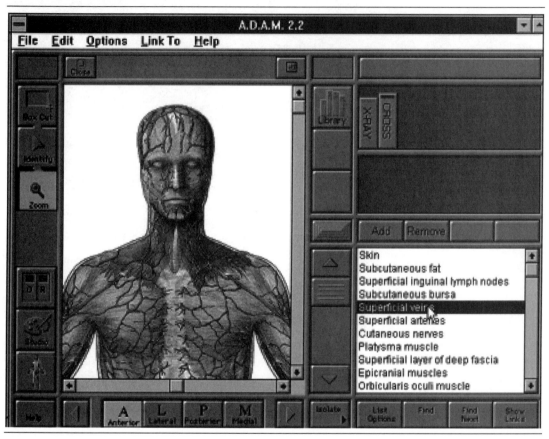

color printouts of the ligament before and after surgery to study further. This also allows him or her to discuss the procedure with others before deciding to go through with the operation. In this way, the patient is better able to sign the necessary informed-consent documents and is less apt to sue the doctor because of not understanding what the surgery entailed. Physicians find that using A.D.A.M. to explain the surgery has the effect of reducing the patient's fear. One of the features that makes A.D.A.M. even more effective in this role is that one may choose the sex and race of the displayed body.

A.D.A.M. has won numerous awards including NewMedia's INVISION awards of Best of Show, Silver (for health care and medical training), and Gold (for higher education application), the Best of Show award in the New York

Figure 5.3 *Display of A.D.A.M. as deeper layers are exposed. Courtesy of A.D.A.M. Software, Inc.*

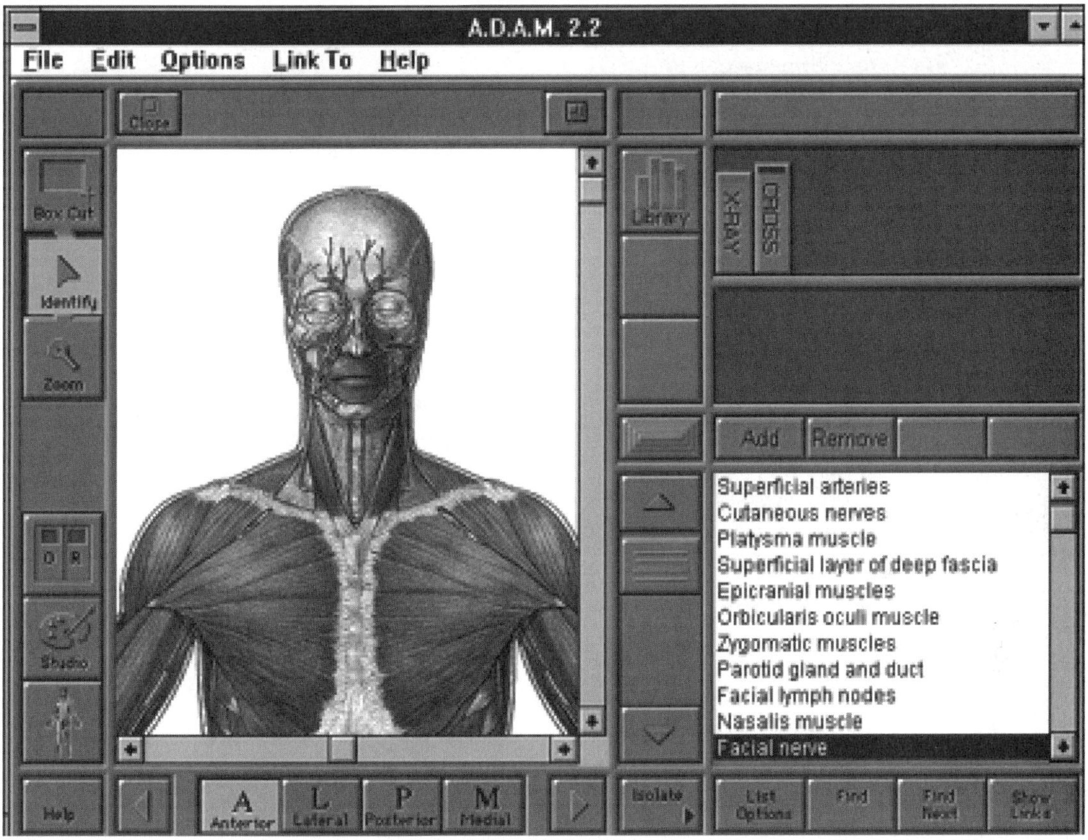

Festival for Multimedia, and many more. Actually there are several versions of A.D.A.M. ranging from the introductory (called A.D.A.M. Essentials, which costs $295) to the advanced (called A.D.A.M. Comprehensive, which retails for $2,295). The creators of A.D.A.M. have recently begun to also develop lower end consumer products such as A.D.A.M. The Inside Story, which is already considered one of the hottest home health care CD-ROMs on the market.

The database behind A.D.A.M. is enormous. It contains more than 3500 detailed color illustrations showing hundreds of layers and some 20,000 anatomic structures. In addition, it also has a collection of interactive textbooks, treatises, lecture notes, and bibliographies. To assist in training, there are also automated quizzes and self-paced training modules. Videos illustrate surgical

Figure 5.4   *The user may examine every structure of the body in great detail. Courtesy of A.D.A.M. Software, Inc.*

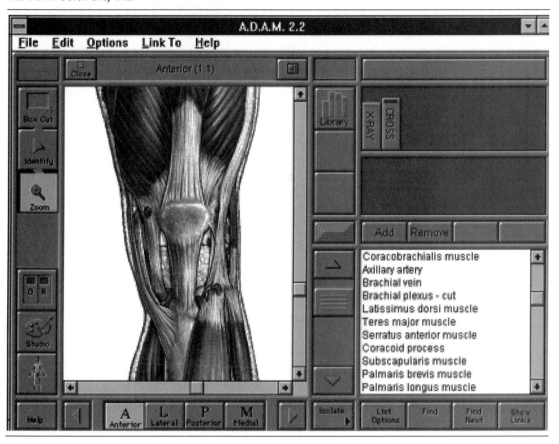

procedures and animations simulate progressive pathologies such as the development of a cancerous lesion. Users may even record their own surgical procedures using A.D.A.M. and save them for later playback.

It took three and a half years to create A.D.A.M. and it was a much larger task than was initially anticipated by its creators. Gregory Swayne is the President of A.D.A.M. Software, Inc., which was founded in 1990. Based in Atlanta, Georgia, A.D.A.M. Software currently has 86 employees, most of whom are medical and commercial illustrators, but there are also a number of programmers and other professionals who assist in sales, marketing and other business operations. Gregory explains that the company is rooted in medical illustration. Gregory himself was a professional medical illustrator, which

Figure 5.5 *Lateral view of A.D.A.M. Courtesy of A.D.A.M. Software, Inc.*

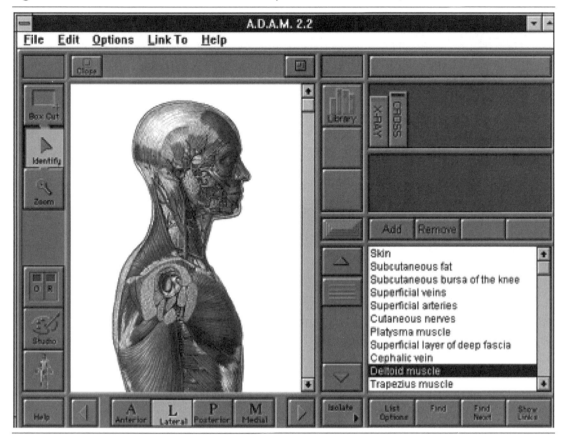

required him to attend medical school and take the same classes as those who planned to become physicians and surgeons. This meant he was required to learn surgical techniques and create detailed illustrations while in the operating room.

After graduating from medical school, Gregory began to freelance as a medical illustrator for various publishing companies. His work soon led him to provide illustrations to attorneys to be used in the courtroom for personal injury cases. This proved to be a fairly lucrative business and allowed Gregory to grow as a business and to hire seven additional illustrators. His first company, called Medical Legal Illustrations, is still the number one provider of courtroom exhibits for lawyers in the country. During the time they were providing medical illustrations to the legal profession, they began to notice a trend. As Gregory says, "A lot of doctors were getting sued by patients who claimed that if they had understood beforehand what was going to happen to them during surgery, they probably wouldn't have had the operation to begin with. The doctors were not communicating to the patient what was going to happen. So we thought, 'What if doctors had a communication tool that they could use to sit down with the patient and almost simulate the surgical procedure?' This would give the patient the opportunity for true informed consent. It was this thought that made us decide to create A.D.A.M."

Gregory continues, "The idea came to me when I was looking at a medical encyclopedia in which you could flip through a series of transparencies and peel away layers of tissues and structures. The idea of the encyclopedia was very simple because it involved only five to six layers. But we wondered if we could take every single structure in the human body from four views and illustrate it on separate layers from head to toe and allow the user to peel those off one at a time—all the way from skin to bone in those four views."

Fortunately, Gregory's legal illustration business was thriving and was able to provide the means to begin creating A.D.A.M. in terms of the revenues needed for initial development as well as a team of experienced medical illustrators. What they didn't have, however, was the realization of the enormity of the task they were about to undertake. Using a team of four illustrators, they began with a fairly simple structure—the hand. Gregory says, "This is the body part we used to validate the notion that this could even be done. The hand is very flat—not very deep. So in a way we sort of set ourselves up because it wasn't very representative of some of the real challenges that lay ahead. We found the hand to be fairly easy to create. There were a finite number of structures and they seemed to lay nicely together, and we thought 'Well, this is not so bad—let's just go ahead and do the whole body.' So we started over."

They didn't use that initial hand in the final body, but it served to teach them how to proceed with the project. They chose the foot as the starting point and worked from the foot all the way up the body to the head. Beginning with the deepest layer—the bone—they proceded to add one structure of the anatomy at a time, until they finished with the skin. When they started working on the foot, there were four illustrators—each one worked on all the layers in a single view. So for example, one illustrator drew all the layers of the foot in the anterior view, while another worked on all of them in the posterior view. That person would render everything such as bone, muscle, nerves, arteries, veins, skin, and fascia. After the initial sketches were drawn, they were reviewed by anatomists. Once approved, the drawings were colorized and rendered and then scanned into the computer. There they were rebuilt to appear as though they had all been drawn by the same illustrator. To help with this, they all worked with the same color "recipes," each of which was used for the various tissues and structures such as muscles, nerves, and veins.

The foot took approximately three months to complete using four illustrators. When they calculated how many structures there were in the foot as opposed to other parts of the body such as the head, neck, thorax, and pelvis, they realized that at that rate, it would take them six and a half years to complete A.D.A.M. Even though they had all their "recipes" and basic processes down, they knew they needed many more illustrators working on the project. Gregory immediately quadrupled the number of illustrators, resulting in four teams with four people in each—two medical and two color illustrators. Each team worked on all the body structures in a single view (such as anterior or posterior). Soon other people were added to the project who worked on cross-sections and MRIs (magnetic resonance images) and the multimedia programming. One of the greatest challenges involved the fact that there is not a one-to-one relationship between all the structures in the body. The foot has 18 structures, the knee has about 36, while the thigh has about 65. So additional structures had to be added as they moved up the body.

Gregory recalls, "The amount of blending and manipulation that had to be done once the illustrations were scanned in was really an incredible job. It all had to match and it all had to flow. It was like a gigantic jigsaw puzzle with 20,000 pieces that all had to fit together. It was a huge undertaking and we really didn't have any idea what we were getting into." He points to this as one of their greatest engineering challenges. "The drawings themselves had to be created in such a way that they blended together. Many of them were created months apart, and yet when they were put together, you couldn't notice the seams in the body. This seamless database is one of the things that's so elegant about the program. But it was tough to deal with."

They began with a single programmer, but as the project grew in complexity, others were added. The initial programming was done using SuperCard on the Mac. Bill Appleton, who developed SuperCard, was even brought in to help with some of the technical difficulties. The various Mac-based programs in the A.D.A.M. series have been or are currently being rewritten in C++ to improve speed and performance, although the Windows versions were all initially written in C++. The animations were created using Director. Users may even create their own animations and plug them into A.D.A.M.

Other than the engineering challenges, I asked Gregory if they hit any snags during development. He laughed and said, "All the time—every day as a matter of fact. This business is measured more in terms of whether you are able to overcome all the potholes in the road. The ones that survive are the ones that are innovative and can work around those things. One of the main difficulties we run into is the lack of good standards for the Windows environment. That's very frustrating to me because they are obstacles that we don't have any control over. I don't mind being creative when solving our own problems, but to deal with those that aren't under our control is frustrating."

Perhaps the biggest unexpected problem they encountered was that of being able to scroll through the completed body. Because their drawings were life-size, they ended up with an image that was 5'10" tall with literally hundreds of layers. The way the program initially worked was that the user would jump to the various body parts. But Gregory felt strongly that instead, the user should be able to smoothly scroll through the body so that there would be a continuity of structures. "To scroll through this enormous graphic took so long that it just wasn't feasible to allow the user to do it. And yet without this feature I felt that a lot of the understanding of the body's structures would be lost. So we labored about this for quite some time trying to figure out a solution around it. Finally, we had Bill Appleton, the developer of SuperCard, come in and see if he could figure any way around the problem. When Bill looked at the image and the problem with scrolling, he suggested that we treat the image as lines on the screen rather than as .PICT images. Using this method, we were able to write an algorithm that would allow the user to quickly scroll throughout the complete body. That was certainly the biggest hurdle we ran into," recalls Gregory.

The innovative thinking that went into the development of A.D.A.M. was also at work in acquiring the necessary funds to create it. Part of the money was "siphoned" from Gregory's legal illustration company. However, as the project grew, Gregory knew he would have to seek other funds. When they built the foot, they took the program to potential investors, primarily physicians, in the area. Gregory points out, "They immediately understood the potential impact of a product like A.D.A.M. in the health care market." It was by selling stock in the company that they were able to generate more funds to move ahead with the project. But I was most struck by their clever marketing strategy to sell what Gregory humorously refers to as "body parts." "When we finished the foot module, for example, we began selling that as a product to the podiatry market. And then when we finished the knee and lower leg, we were able to sell that product to the orthopedic surgery market. They were complete products as far as those markets were concerned. We had to be creative in terms of selling in order to raise money."

They even took their "body part" modules to schools and were surprised that they were eager to buy the products as well. In some cases they would prepay for the entire body because they were so eager to have it. "I have a tremendous amount of respect and loyalty for those early customers because

A.D.A.M. was essentially vaporware at the time." Especially enthusiastic and supportive were Dr. Naomi Broering (Director of the Learning Resources Center) at Georgetown University and Dr. Michael Altman (Dean of Medical Informatics) at Northwestern University. Georgetown University currently has about 30 copies of A.D.A.M. that they use to train medical students. As Gregory says, "These people really went out on a limb to support us, but they saw something that really sparked their imagination and they could see the application."

Gregory feels strongly about the responsibility of developers to spend extra time, effort and money in order to provide the customer with a quality product. He warns, "We, in the industry, have some damage control to do. The honeymoon is over and people are not going to be forgiving of paying $49 for something to find that they've been duped. If you are willing to invest in quality, the public will pay you back." One of the problems, as Gregory points out, is that currently there is no good mechanism for the buyer to select a CD-ROM title. "We don't yet have the advantage of radio which is a wonderful 'try-before-you-buy' model for music. When you walk into a music store, you generally know what you're buying. How is someone supposed to sort through the sea of CD-ROM titles without the benefit of having tried or experienced the products? And they cost $49.95. So they look at the box and have to make their decision based on that." Gregory sees the Internet as a possible solution to this problem. He points to the tremendous success of Doom, whose developers uploaded a limited version of the game onto the Internet, making it available to potential buyers free of charge. Once users tried it out, they could buy the full version if they liked it. And people liked what they experienced. Doom has been enormously successful as a result. But as Gregory points out, "You really have to believe in the quality of your product to do something like that. A lot of people don't want to do that because they know they couldn't survive. But I believe that the Internet will be the ultimate distribution channel."

Gregory is very supportive of the small entrepreneur. "I have a lot of faith in the young developers. The best ones are really those that are working out of their garage and are untethered. That is when the best things seem to happen. That's how we were when we first started and I hope we've maintained that. Even though we've grown, we still have that basic entrepreneurial spirit." He advises any developer to carefully research the market before beginning an application to be sure there is a need for it. Because of the plethora of CD-ROM titles currently available, he cautions that any new title coming out must offer something unique that other titles don't have.

He also stresses that any truly good product must be innovative and influence multimedia technology in some way. "If your product is new and innova-

Figure 5.6   *A.D.A.M. The Inside Story teaches the consumer about basic human anatomy. Courtesy of A.D.A.M. Software, Inc.*

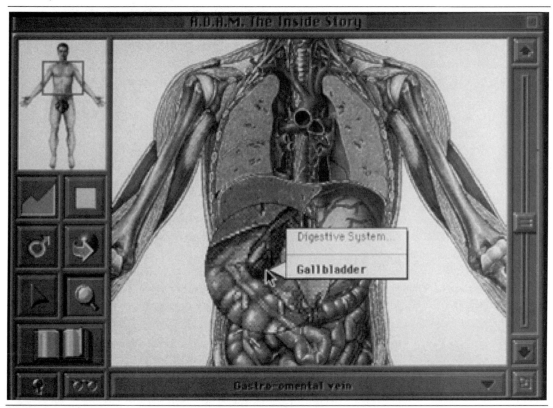

tive, you're also going to help define what multimedia is." This, he says, should be every developer's goal—to continually elevate the quality of multimedia on the market. "This is one of the reasons we wanted to get into the consumer game—we wanted to lift the quality of consumer multimedia titles. I've known for a long time that A.D.A.M. would make an impact there." A.D.A.M. Software is now developing several low-end products for the consumer market, such as one on pregnancy, and the previously mentioned A.D.A.M. The Inside Story, which is their first edutainment product, bringing to life the characters of "Adam" and "Eve." It not only teaches the user about the basics of human anatomy (see Figure 5.6), but it also has segments that show what happens when someone is stung by a bee or burned (see Figures 5.7 on page 97 and 5.8 on page 98).

Figure 5.7 *A screen display from A.D.A.M. The Inside Story explains to the user what happens when a person is stung by a bee. Courtesy of A.D.A.M. Software, Inc.*

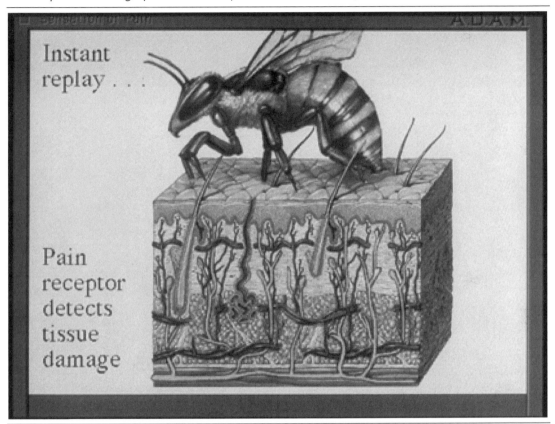

But they are expanding in the higher education market as well. They're currently working with Benjamin/Cummings Publishing to develop a CD-ROM to accompany Elaine Marieb's *Human Anatomy and Physiology,* the number-one selling physiology book for undergraduates. "We've taken the twelve most difficult concepts in cardiovascular medicine and created interactive simulations that let the students control the variables that would affect the heart rate and blood pressure. Through these simulation activities, the students can really begin to understand these concepts. The text and the interactive CD-ROM (called A.D.A.M. Interactive Physiology) are married to each other and to A.D.A.M. and will provide the best of all three worlds." Gregory feels strongly that multimedia should not try to replace books, nor can books

Figure 5.8   *The body's impulses that occur as a result of a burn are illustrated in A.D.A.M. The Inside Story. Courtesy of A.D.A.M. Software, Inc.*

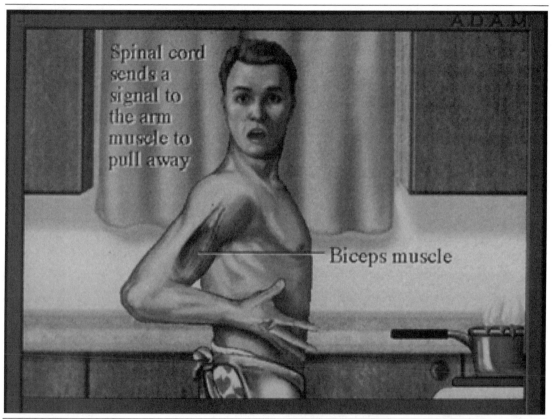

replace multimedia because they cannot communicate processes nearly as dynamically as interactive software can. "We're building a bridge. We're letting them keep their books and we're adding value to the book. Over time they'll figure out that they can use both."

A.D.A.M. is widely regarded as one of those unique titles that has elevated the definition of multimedia. The extra effort and time that went into its development is apparent in its rich interactive design and illustrative detail. One of those who has recognized the power of A.D.A.M. for training new medical students is C. Everett Koop, the former U.S. Surgeon General. In a recent speech, Koop said that over the next few years "A.D.A.M. will become the primary anatomical reference." And he added, "A medical school that doesn't turn out computer-literate graduates will be guilty of providing poor education." He compared computer-shy instructors to "a grade-school teacher not letting her kids use pencils a hundred years ago."

But not even the best titles make it to market without a "glitch" or two. Gregory admits to one that got past them when they released the first version of A.D.A.M. "We had the program set up so that after you installed it, the first thing that you would see when you opened it up was a close-up of A.D.A.M.'s head. The way we'd set up that default was we would center the program on his head, and then close the program. This meant that after installation, the program would always open up on his head. Well, we had the program mastered and mass produced, and sent it out to everyone. The idea was that when the user opened up A.D.A.M., the first thing they would see was A.D.A.M.'s head. Well, whether it was on purpose or whether it was an accident, one of our people lined up A.D.A.M. over the groin area without the fig leaf on. This is what got mastered and sent out on that version," Gregory laughs. "Anyway that view was what everyone saw the first time they opened the program. Ah boy, I remember that one. That was quite a laugh. We thought about redoing the master, but we had so many people calling and laughing about it that we decided to leave it on there for a while."

Multimedia Hazmat

As I discussed in the introduction to this chapter, one of the major problems with traditional training is the cost involved, especially if personnel must travel a long distance to receive that training. And yet when training is essential to saving lives, it becomes imperative in spite of the cost. Ironically, in order to receive that training, the employee is often unavailable to assist with life-threatening situations. Examples include fire containment and the handling of hazardous materials which both involve very specialized skills and a certification program in order to effectively deal with very dangerous situations. This is where interactive training programs can prove to be invaluable. They are a much more cost effective way to train employees, and because they can be used on-site the employee is still available to perform their normal duties.

RJM Multimedia, headquartered in Bellingham, Washington, and founded by Marie Burlinson, has been developing interactive training software since the early 1980s. Some of their early programs included a software simulator used to train people to use various software and an expert system that taught personnel in a telecommunications company how to troubleshoot various problems. Although their earlier work involved the development of customized software for very large Fortune 500 companies, they have recently begun to develop products. One of these is Multimedia Hazmat, an interactive training program for emergency response personnel. It has already won two major awards: one from the Society of Technical Communications, and NewMedia's INVISION Bronze Award for End User Applications. For the Society of Technical Communications award, they were competing with other companies in the Puget Sound Chapter such as Aldus and Microsoft.

In order to better understand the value of Multimedia Hazmat it is important to understand the circumstances that led to its development. The province of British Columbia in Canada is enormous—equivalent to the size of California, Oregon, and Washington combined. Much of the province is very isolated, and although there are fire stations spread throughout the region, the task of training some 13,500 firefighters as well as other emergency response personnel is very costly. For each trainee, there is the expense of travel to the lower mainland of British Columbia, hotel, meals, and the training course itself. There are also the risks involved by not having one or more people available on-site when an emergency occurs. And yet training is vital to their ability to do their job.

Paul Smith, Directory of the Fire Academy in British Columbia, explains "We do a lot of long-distance training. Even though we've made great strides, there was still the element of the actual hands-on training that was missing. And when people take an exam following training, they need to see the results immediately to see how they can improve. That element was also missing." Interactive training was the obvious solution to their dilemma. When Paul saw some of the software RJM Multimedia had been developing for one of the ministries in Vancouver, he was immediately eager to have them build a training system for the academy. Their three-year collaboration led to the development of Multimedia Hazmat.

Currently there are two versions of the program. The "awareness" level (see Figure 5.9 on page 101) trains a person to recognize a hazardous incident and to contact the right people to deal with it. The user learns placard classifications (involving color, numbers, and symbols—see Figure 5.10 on page 102), basic information on hazardous materials, how to use the *Emergency Response Guidebook*, and how to respond to a hazardous situation (see Figure 5.11 on page 103). Built-in tests (see Figure 5.12 on page 104) reinforce the information presented. The program is used not only by new trainees but also by those needing a refresher course, which is required on a yearly basis due to changes in the regulations. The "operations" level program trains those who

Figure 5.9   *Opening Screen of Multimedia Hazmat. Courtesy of RJM Multimedia Inc.*

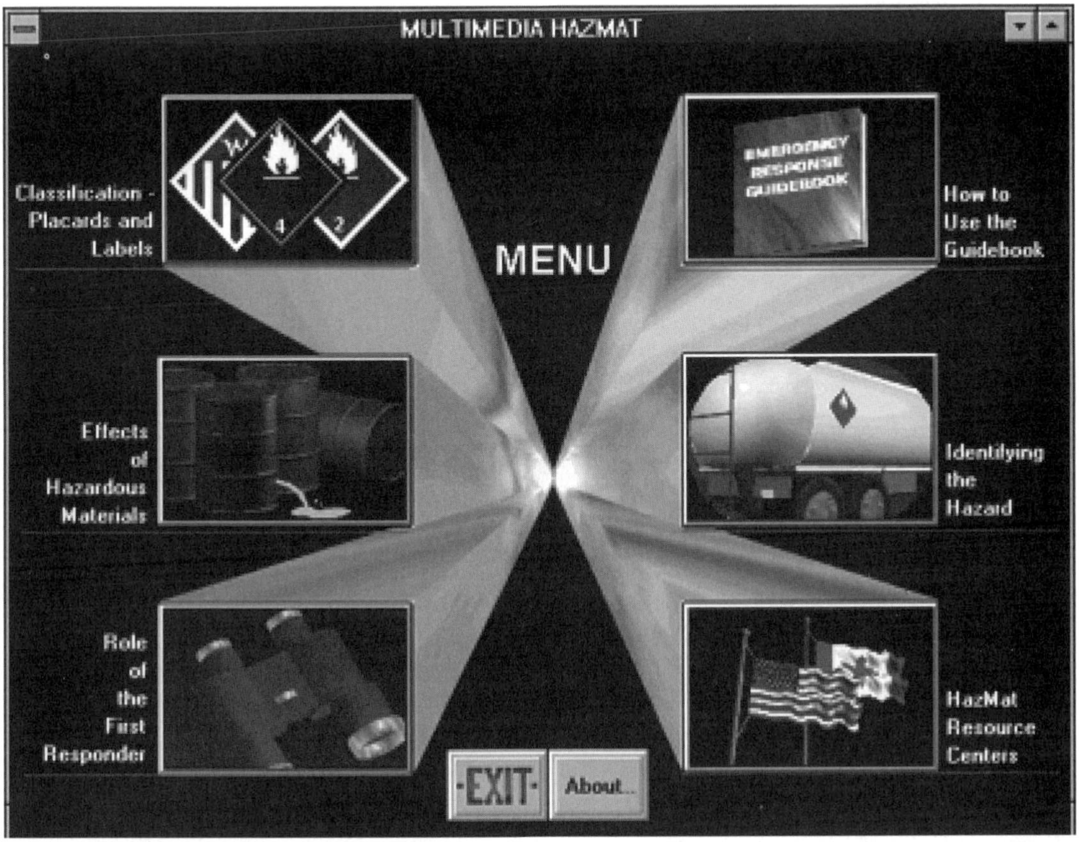

are responsible to carry out some defensive action and requires a higher level of understanding.

Both versions are based on the National Fire Protection Association Standard 472, a federal standard that dictates how a hazardous incident should be handled. Both also track the user's progress and have an assessment kit to test their knowledge upon completion of the computerized training. The test indicates the areas in which the user is weak, and if he or she is not skilled enough, the training is repeated with emphasis on those areas. This training/testing cycle continues until the user is completely skilled. Marie says, "Because we deal with safety training, we want people to be as prepared as possible to be on the job. We don't want them getting hurt when they are on the job. So we keep them in that training/testing cycle until they meet the training standard."

Figure 5.10   *Segments of Multimedia Hazmat teach the user about placard identification. Courtesy of RJM Multimedia Inc.*

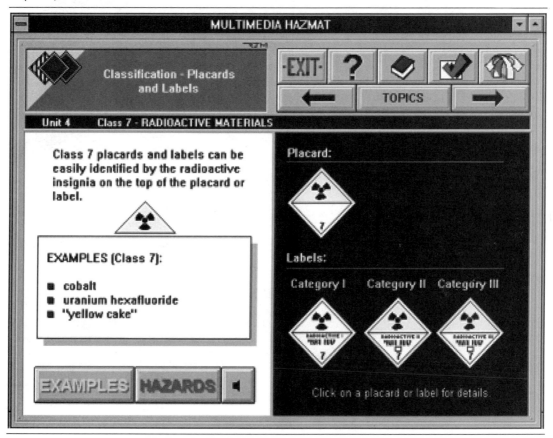

Perhaps the most powerful part of the program that monitors the user's skills is the Course Manager, a shell that can be used with a number of different training programs. The Course Manager keeps a permanent record of the user's progress as he or she goes through the computerized training (see Figure 5.13 on page 106). It monitors which portions the user has completed, generates tests, and assesses his or her skills. Each time the user retrains, a different test is generated so that the user is being evaluated based on standards rather than how well he or she has learned to take a particular test.

Besides providing enormous cost savings to train emergency response personnel located in remote areas, it also saves money in more populated areas because the same program may be used by any number of people. And one of

Figure 5.11 *Throughout the program, trainees are taught how to handle hazardous materials. Courtesy of RJM Multimedia Inc.*

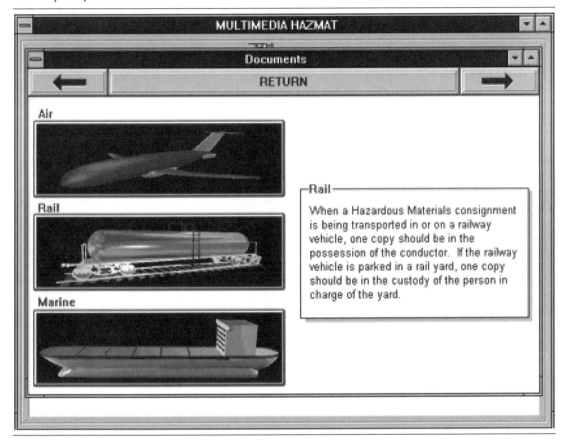

its real advantages over traditional training courses is that the person may use it to go through the training according to the user's own schedule. As an example, firefighters experience long periods of inactivity in between emergencies. They may use this time to train, but are immediately available when an emergency arises. They may then continue where they left off in the training course when they return to the fire station. As Paul Smith points out, "The person can access it when they want to and when they are in a learning mood. That's very important in terms of their retention level."

Much of the software used to develop Multimedia Hazmat involved proprietary tools developed by Marie and other programmers at RJM Multimedia over a number of years. Although Marie has a Master's Degree in Computer

Figure 5.12   *Built-in tests provide the users with an indication of their progress, thereby telling them areas in which they need more training. Courtesy of RJM Multimedia Inc.*

Science from Johns Hopkins University, she has taught extensively and thinks of herself as an educator. It is her experience in instructional design that led her to develop training software. She says, "The teaching methodologies that are possible with technology have fascinated me since the 70s, but the hardware wasn't there. So I've been waiting all this time for the hardware, and now it's here."

The proprietary tools used for Multimedia Hazmat link to existing authoring software and provide much greater flexibility and control. Because they are coded in C, C++, and Visual Basic, they provide much greater speed as well. Although the company currently has 14 employees, there were 6–7 people on the team that developed Multimedia Hazmat, including instructional designers, graphics designers, writers, and programmers. Most of the video production was done in collaboration with another company, although Marie says they are working now to bring more of that in-house. Because they are not content experts, all of their work requires extensive collaboration. The Fire Academy provided the content for the program and Paul Smith and others in the academy worked closely with the project team, particularly during the early phases of development. Marie emphasizes the importance of the validation process—especially with a program involving safety. The academy personnel were involved throughout the duration of program development to help with the validation process.

Part of the content provided by the Fire Academy was sound and video, although Marie estimates that they had to reshoot two thirds of the video used in Multimedia Hazmat. "We originally thought we had all the video we needed, but it didn't work out that way," Marie recalls. Although the academy had a large collection of videos for their training courses, most of them were not appropriate or effective for the type of video clips required in an interactive program. Marie explains that standard training videos do not contain the scenarios or content that are needed to encourage interaction with the user. Videos for a CD-ROM require tighter shots, different camera angles and special "staging" to get a point across quickly and effectively. As an example, they wanted videos of scenarios that would illustrate some particular information the program was trying to convey, and these had to be specifically shot in order to accomplish this.

The program also contains numerous segments in which the users must indicate what hazard they are observing as a video pans across a scene. Many of these scenarios were not available in the academy's video collection. Marie points out, "Now when someone comes to us with a lot of video, we say 'That's nice, but we'll need a lot more'." Once the video clips were developed, voice-over narrations were provided by Jack Tyler, Battalion Chief at the Fire Academy who is in charge of their training. Marie showed him the clips and asked him to provide narrations that would reflect what the responders would say as they approached a situation and to indicate what they were looking for and where they would have to go.

Another interesting aspect involving the videos created for Multimedia Hazmat is the special effects that were added to enhance the testing process. For example, many of the videos that are displayed clearly in the teaching segments are shown with muted colors in the question/answer segments of the program in which the user is asked to respond to the hazardous incident shown in the video segment (see Figure 5.13 on page 106). The muted colors simulate smoke or fog, as might be encountered in a real situation, masking some of the more obvious information such as placard color. The user must then respond to other information such as the number or symbol on the plac-

Figure 5.13   *The Course Manager tracks the user's progress and assesses his or her skills. Courtesy of RJM Multimedia Inc.*

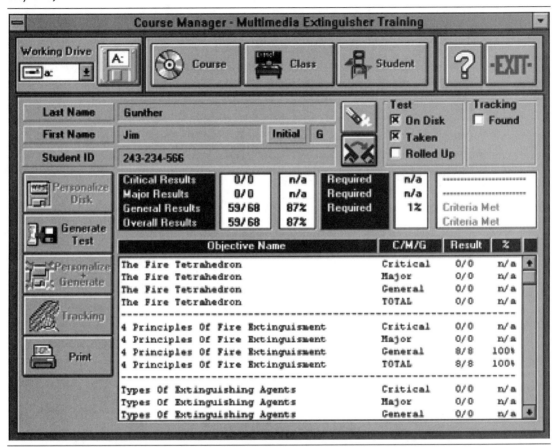

ard in order to identify the hazard depicted in the video. This provides a more realistic hands-on experience than would occur otherwise.

Acquiring copyrights to the content were quite time consuming. Marie estimates that it took a full six months to negotiate copyrights with the Fire Academy—"a very friendly collaborator" as Marie puts it. She points out that royalties can be even tougher to deal with because of the need to determine who made what contribution.

Marie believes that the key element in developing an effective title is the team itself and the way in which the various talents interact with each other. "We bring our instructional people and creative people and technical people together into a brainstorming session, and it gets really exciting." The instructional designer will outline what information needs to be conveyed, and the creative people will suggest a visual or interactive way of conveying that information, and this is where the "give-and-take" of the development process begins. Marie cites an example in which the creative designers suggest a game at the end of each learning unit. "The instructional designers will say, 'Okay, it has to be fun, but it has to convey what I need it to do. We have to make sure the user is going to open the book and look up the information and that they can't guess.' It's that interaction between the various talents that makes a more powerful product and makes the whole development process so exciting."

Multimedia Hazmat has been very successful in training emergency response personnel. As Paul Smith points out, "Anybody who completes this training and passes the tests in the program will be certified as having met the training requirements of 'first responder awareness' as set up by the National Fire Protection Association. I would say the people are better prepared after going through the disc because it is one-on-one learning as opposed to a single teacher trying to work with many students." He adds, "Our people are very positive about the program. They train according to their own schedule. And they can review their tests right away and get immediate feedback. The important part is that you don't have to understand a computer to use the technology. All you have to do is know how to turn on a computer and click a mouse." A new trainee can go through the program in about six hours. A refresher session takes only an hour or two. When compared to traditional training courses that nearly always involve travel and hotel costs as well as loss of work, the cost of the program ($1,199) is negligible.

Since their previous work had involved customized training systems, Marie found that developing a commercial product was very different. "With a custom product you are making it fit your client's exact needs. You have a well-defined client with pretty well-defined needs. You also have a far less diverse population that you're training, such as office workers or field personnel. So the scope of the learner capabilities is much tighter. In addition, if something goes wrong with installation or the program itself, it's pretty easy for you to get on the phone and walk them through it," Marie explains. "All these things are out the window when you're creating a product. First of all, you've got a far bigger and more divergent audience. So your user interface has to be really tight and bulletproof. And the content has to be more versatile to handle more levels of ability. You have to make greater provisions for that when you are creating a product." She also noted that a product has the additional aspects of packaging and marketing which are not encountered when creating custom programs.

Multimedia Hazmat is marketed to a number of emergency response organizations such as fire and police departments, emergency medical services, and the industrial market such as nuclear, petroleum, and chemical companies, and is also useful to the general public. It is marketed mainly within the United States, Canada, and Australia because of the similarities in the emergency response guidelines used by these countries. Their main distributor is Fire Protection Publications based in Stillwater, Oklahoma.

They have just released an interactive expert system that simulates scenarios of hazardous incidents. As the user watches a scenario unfold, he or she must make a decision, just as he or she would have to do in a real situation. Based on that decision, the scenario continues along the path and continues to "fork" as the user continues to try to resolve the problem until there is a final outcome—either resolution or disaster. The program then analyzes the user's decisions and advises him or her on how the situation could have been handled differently. This is linked to Multimedia Hazmat and provides an even greater means of hands-on training.

Marie offers the following advice for anyone thinking about developing an interactive training title: "There was a time in programming when you could do it all yourself. You had an idea, you sat down, and you started writing code. You can't do that with multimedia because no one person is good at instructional design, graphic design, writing, media production, and programming. It requires a team effort with lots of diverse talents." She adds, "We are NOT computer people, and we have to tell that to people all the time—we are trainers and educators and we're just using a different medium. It's a fascinating industry and an exciting industry, and I think most of the people who are involved are really happy they're doing what they are doing."

Further Reading

"Multimedia: IBM Multimedia Offerings for Training and Marketing Applications and Enhancements to Multimedia Product Line. 1991. *EDGE: Work-Group Computing Report* (June): 8.

Ganci, Michael, George Cicchetti, Thomas Goodkind, and David Monti. 1994. "SPT: A New Methodology for Instruction." *T.H.E. Journal* (August).

Jerram, Peter. 1994. "Who's Using Multimedia?" *NewMedia Magazine* (October): 48.

Raskin, Robin. 1990. "Multimedia: The Next Frontier for Business?" *PC Magazine* (July): 151.

Reveaux, Tony. 1993. "Learning Goes the Distance." *NewMedia Magazine* (June): 42.

Silver, Judith. 1992. "Show Provides Twelve Sessions for Fed Multimedia Advice." *Government Computer News* (August 3): 110.

Simone, Luisa. 1990. "TIE (Training Icon Environment)." *PC Magazine* (July): 184.

Starkey, Brigid. 1994. Negotiation Training Through Simulation: The Icons International Negotiation Seminars Initiative." *Educator's Tech Exchange* (Spring): 6.

Tynan, Daniel. 1993. "Just in Time: Multimedia Goes on the Job." *NewMedia Magazine* (July): 39.

THE MULTIMEDIA REFERENCE TOOL

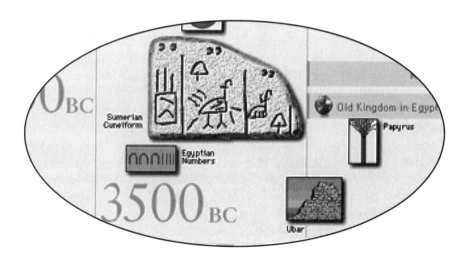

Introduction

The computer is one of the most powerful tools to access information quickly, whether a user is linking to one of the major online services such as the Internet and CompuServe or looking up information on a CD-ROM. (It is interesting that even though the Internet is a tremendous resource for information, of the 16 million people in the United States that have access to the Internet, more use it for communication such as e-mail than anything else.) Certainly, retrieving information stored in electronic format is a much faster and more thorough way to research material. Most libraries are moving texts and reference material to a digital format with the hopes of creating "virtual libraries." They are also trying to do so before their collections of printed material actually decay. Columbia University plans to scan and digitize 10,000 to 12,000 volumes each year and to store the information on a supercomputer, providing access to a wide network of users. Currently, most of these avenues of information retrieval do not involve multimedia elements.

Other ways of providing electronic information access to the general consumer include CD-ROMs and kiosks. CD-ROM technology is becoming increasingly popular because a CD-ROM can be used on a stand-alone computer or on a network. It is also becoming a standard feature of new computers. Not very long ago, CD-ROMs were used strictly for mass storage because of the amount of information that could be packed onto a single disc. The only people really using them were those who wanted to archive large amounts of data. As the cost of CD-ROM technology continued to drop and as multimedia development evolved, it became clear that this would be an ideal medium on which to deliver multimedia titles because of its storage capabilities. Unfortunately, many early CD-ROM–based "multimedia" titles were very disappointing. They tended to consist of large volumes of text that was simply in electronic format instead of printed format and had virtually no interactivity. Although one could access an abundance of reference material using a CD-ROM, it became clear that this was not the most effective use of CD-ROMs for information access.

Fortunately this has changed over the last few years. Just as interactivity enhances the learning process, it also provides a flexible and very powerful way to learn more about a particular subject. Its nonlinearity allows the user to quickly jump to other related topics to more thoroughly research a subject. When combined with other media such as sound and video, the user comes away with a richer understanding of the material. More recently released titles illustrate that information access is greatly enhanced by the addition of inter-activity and multimedia elements.

An interactive kiosk is another way to effectively deliver information to the general consumer. Most have a touchscreen that provides a very easy-to-use interface, and because the computer is hidden from view, even the most com-puter-phobic person will walk up and explore the content. Kiosks are used in museums, shopping malls, airports, trade shows, and restaurants, and although they are easy to use, it takes considerable planning and interface design to make them intuitive enough that the user needs only minimal instruc-tions to navigate and find the information he or she is seeking.

Overview of Profiles

The titles profiled in this chapter illustrate two very different ways in which multimedia may be used to enhance information access to the general con-sumer: one that is CD-ROM–based and one that is set in a kiosk.

Encarta is one of the top multimedia encyclopedias on the market, but it has many unique features that set it apart from the others. It illustrates how an encyclopedia designed specifically for the computer can greatly enhance the user's interactive experience.

Novato Electronic City Hall is an example of an interactive kiosk that pro-vides users with information on the city of Novato, California, including maps, public meeting agendas, and employment opportunities.

Encarta

An interactive encyclopedia is one of the applications in which multimedia can be used to its fullest potential. It is one thing to read text and view an accom panying photograph in printed format, but to be able to see a video and hear narration or music greatly enhances what one is able to learn from a reference book. Microsoft's Encarta has a rich visual and audio environment, and has won many awards including NewMedia's INVISION Silver Award for K–12 applications and book adaption, the World Class Award for reference from *PC World,* and the Readers Choice Award for reference software from *WordPerfect for Windows* magazine. The section on Dinosaurs (in Chapter 4) provides an overview of Microsoft's consumer division which develops all their multimedia titles.

Encarta '95 (see Figure 6.1) includes more than 26,000 articles (see Figure 6.2 on page 115) that are linked to each other with "hot words," making it

Figure 6.1   *Opening screen of Encarta. Courtesy of Microsoft Corp.*

Figure 6.2   *Screen display of an article and illustration. Courtesy of Microsoft Corp.*

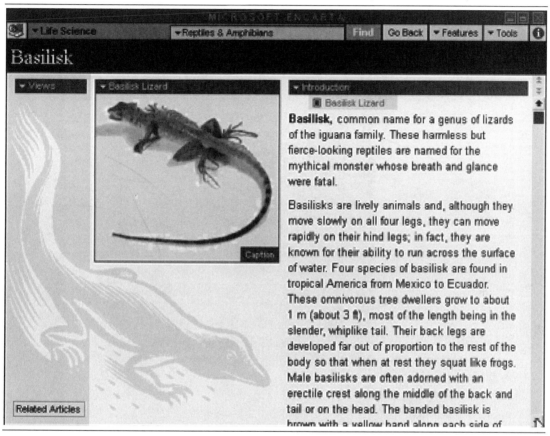

fast and easy to navigate from topic to topic. There are over 8,400 photographs and illustrations that may be displayed along with an associated article or accessed using the program's Media Gallery. Also included in the Media Gallery are sound and video clips. I was intrigued to be able to watch such videos as a chick hatching from its shell and the repair of the Hubble Space Telescope (see Figure 6.3 on page 116). Other features include an extensive Atlas (see Figure 6.4 on page 117)as well as a Timeline (see Figure 6.5 on page 118) that both allow the user to click on a portion of the illustration to access more detailed information. A challenging educational game called MindMaze (see Figure 6.6 on page 119) tests the user's knowledge in a variety of topics and adds an entertaining component to the program. Encarta even includes a full

Figure 6.3   *The Media Gallery has an enormous collection of graphics, sound, and video clips. Courtesy of Microsoft Corp.*

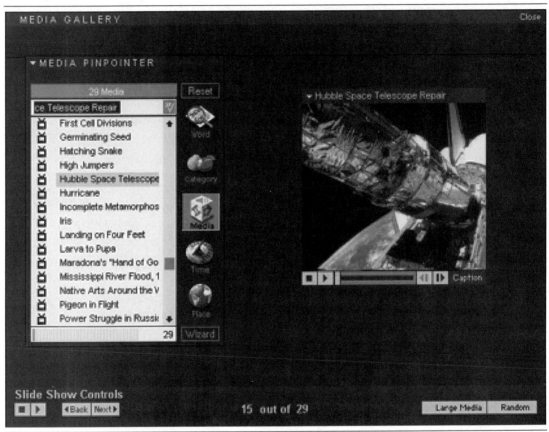

dictionary and thesaurus, and obviously has value and appeal to users of all levels. I was also impressed by how fast the program is in terms of navigation and display.

Of all the interactive encyclopedias currently on the market, Encarta is the only one that was created specifically for the multimedia environment instead of being tied to a printed version of an encyclopedia. Because of this, updates are not governed by printed updates, providing it with the most current information available on a CD-ROM encyclopedia and greater flexibility in terms of the timing of update releases. Kathy Fiander is the Product Manager for the Home Education Reference Unit at Microsoft and has been in marketing for over ten years. Before joining Microsoft five years ago, she was in bank mar-

Figure 6.4 *The Atlas allows the user to explore any area of the world in detail. Courtesy of Microsoft Corp.*

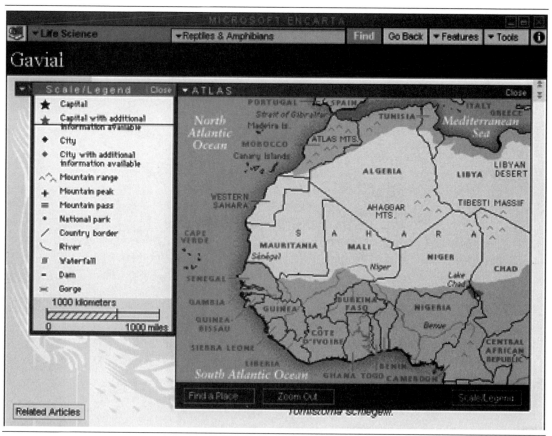

keting, which involved marketing directly to the consumer, giving her the experience she needed for her work at Microsoft. Kathy explains, "Because we can update independently of any printed version, we are able to provide the most up-to-date information. For example, about two weeks before we released our '94 version, the Middle East Peace Accord took place and we were able to get an audio clip and photograph of that into that version of Encarta." The '95 version is similarly very current and includes a video clip of the cleaning and repair of the Hubble space telescope and mentions the historic cease-fire agreement between the Sinn Fein and the British government. This last event occurred just two weeks before the release of the product.

Figure 6.5 *Using the Timeline, users can quickly jump to any historical period and explore important events that occurred at that time. Courtesy of Microsoft Corp.*

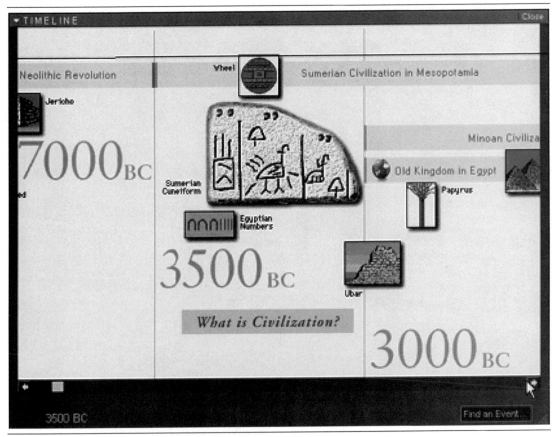

One of the restrictions of a print-based encyclopedia is the problem of adding last-minute content. For example, by adding a photograph to a page that has already been laid out generally means that an entire volume needs to be laid out again—something that is prohibitively costly and time consuming. A multimedia encyclopedia does not have such restrictions. Another difference is that when the team working on Encarta selects visual material, they do so with the computer screen in mind. This means that photos are selected that will look particularly good on a computer monitor which is backlit with light coming out at the "reader." Photos from a print-based encyclopedia are intended to be viewed on paper which reflects light. Similarly the Encarta team chooses

Figure 6.6 *An educational game, MindMaze, tests the user's knowledge of a variety of topics that may be explored in Encarta. Courtesy of Microsoft Corp.*

audio that is well-suited to the kind of speakers and the kind of audio equipment people have on their computers.

In order to stay as current as possible, Microsoft has an editorial staff of 25 for Encarta who review newspapers, press clippings, and wire service reports on a daily basis. Articles are constantly updated to reflect these rapidly changing events. As Kathy says, "In our attempt to stay current we have come out with three versions of Encarta between March of '93 and September of '94. Because we are not tied to a print-based encyclopedia, we have the flexibility to update Encarta this frequently." In addition, a large proportion of Encarta is updated with each version. "We have updated 10,000 of the 26,000 articles in our latest version of Encarta, which is unprecedented with both electronic and print-based encyclopedias. By the time we release our '96 version we will have a nearly 100% revision of our articles, which is absolutely unheard of in the publishing industry. This reflects our commitment to maintain very current content."

Jay Gibson is the Program Manager for Encarta. Of the many people I interviewed for this book, Jay is one of the very few whose roots are in computer programming. He has a degree in Computer Engineering from the University of Waterloo in Canada, and joined Microsoft as a program developer. He worked on the original Microsoft Bookshelf and Cinemania while devoting time to Encarta. Jay recalls, "I worked on Encarta when it was just a research project. We'd been working on an encyclopedia since 1988 from the standpoint of what the ultimate encyclopedia could be. We worked on it for years. We finally decided to switch from research mode to getting a product together." The result was the first version of Encarta which came out in March of 1993. Jay estimates that there were over 200 person years that went into the first version of Encarta, and that the latest version involved several hundred person years. While the majority of effort goes into the editorial process, a tremendous amount of time is devoted to code development, production, interface design, and testing.

The bulk of the original content for Encarta came from Funk & Wagnall's *New Encyclopedia*. Because of its good editorial structure it was well-suited to the type of encyclopedia Microsoft had in mind. They also used some material from Microsoft Press's *Computer Dictionary* as well as original material that was commissioned to outside writers. Now, all of the articles are rewritten by in-house personnel or by outside writers commissioned by Microsoft. They work with nearly 1,000 external consultants and contributors. Articles written by the contributors are credited in Encarta as are the consultants who include experts in various fields that read the articles to verify their accuracy. Most of the animations and illustrations are developed in-house.

By writing or commissioning the articles for Encarta, Microsoft is able to avoid some copyright issues, but not all. They have a large acquisitions department that seeks specific photographs, videos, or sound clips needed to accompany the textual information. Material may be acquired from dozens of large stock photo companies, major television networks, or even from individual people, so copyright negotiations are handled on an individual basis. The need to pay royalty fees is avoided whenever possible. Kathy says, "The general rule of thumb is to pay per piece and in some cases there are large photo houses that have literally millions of stock photos that we'll look through and purchase, sometimes in bulk." Great care is taken to select images that are not very common in the public domain. Kathy explains, "For example, for our article about JFK, we wanted to be sure not to include a photo of the assassination that you see in every single book. In such cases, we're careful to choose a different still shot that's just as meaningful but isn't as common. It's a way of adding a little extra value to the article." Jay adds, "Our acquisitions people are constantly learning new ways of getting material. For example, last year when the Peace Accord took place between Arafat and Rabin, we got a photo the day it happened from a very good photo house, and they sent it to us electronically. That meant we were able to get it into our product at the very last minute."

They also acquire quite a bit of video footage, but avoid what Jay refers to as "trendy" video. He explains, "Some products use video that really doesn't impart a message or teach something. They're simply filling up the disk with public domain video. We want to be sure that the video supports the article and has good editorial purpose. And hopefully people will have fun with it, too."

Of the material stored on the Encarta CD-ROM, less than 10% of it consists of text. The rest of the information is visual and audio, making it very rich in multimedia content. Jay points out, "We have such sophisticated compression technology that we can pack a lot more multimedia content onto a CD-ROM than other companies can." In fact, Jay joined the consumer division (which develops Microsoft's multimedia titles) because of the innovative techniques being developed for multimedia. "The code in this kind of environment is a little outside the traditional algorithm programming. There is a lot of interesting code having to do with handling different media and compressing images. It's really great software to write."

Encarta was developed using a proprietary engine modified from Microsoft's Viewer. A large multimedia database was also created for Encarta in order to keep track of the enormous number of multimedia files (such as text, illustrations, tables, videos, and sound). As Kathy explains, "This allows the team to keep track of which multimedia elements are associated with which articles so that at any given time, the editors and other people working on the database can go in and make changes much more quickly and easily."

Both Kathy and Jay were in agreement with John Porcaro, the Program Manager for Microsoft's Dinosaurs, regarding the value of usability testing. Encarta '95 went through more than 100 hours of usability testing involving children, adults, teachers, and librarians. Jay says, "One of the most important things we do to develop the computer interface is usability testing. When we design a new product, we make prototypes and bring in a variety of people to test some new feature. For instance, we may be trying to design a new search feature and we do a formal lab analysis. We have people sit in a room behind a one-way mirror and they know this. We then explain the test and how it will work, and then ask them questions to see how easily they can find certain information using this new search feature. On the other side of the mirror, there are often people from the design team who observe to see firsthand what the customer experiences. It's incredibly frustrating at times because we all know how to use the program—we designed it. We know that if the user presses a certain button, they'll find all the articles with photos. But the customers haven't seen this. It's not easy for them. So we're behind the one-way mirror watching them stumbling around trying to figure it out, and we're pulling our hair out thinking 'Click on that button!' And the reality is that it's not their fault. It's our design that's wrong and it can be tough at times because we think it should be easy. But that's the whole point of usability testing. We need to see the things that the customer finds frustrating or difficult to figure out. And so we go back to the drawing board to try to make our products easier and easier to use. But it IS very funny behind the mirror when people are so frustrated with what you have worked on so hard!"

Because of her involvement in marketing, Kathy stresses the importance of packaging and design. She points out some of Microsoft's strategies in terms of box design. "The packaging has to very quickly communicate what's in the box and has to stand out from anything else that's on the shelf because there are so many consumer packages out there right now. And the approach we've taken is to make sure that the graphic elements on the front will indicate what's going to be inside when you open the box. So we have an illustration that shows the main theme and other images such as filmstrips and musical notes that convey what the disc contains. Through the extensive packaging testing we've done, people have been able to look at that image with no words and say, 'Well, if I had to guess, I'd say these things come in that product'." I mentioned to Kathy Microsoft's tendency to use a lot of white space with their packaging. Kathy responds, "You have to be very careful when you use white space because space on a box is at such a premium. There is so much you want to communicate. It's a matter of balancing how much white space we need to get the package to jump out versus the minimum amount of space we need to present the images that will get someone to pick up the box and figure out what is in the product."

Kathy points out that Encarta is a product intended to be used by all members of the family. "We found an editorial style that works for the entire spectrum of audience—whether it's an eleven-year old or an adult. We also do a lot of work with the education and library market to ensure its value to a wide audience of users." They are also developing a children's version of the encyclopedia called Explorapedia intended for children ten years of age and younger. Although both products are very educational and would be ideal for schools, Kathy points out that by far the largest market for them is the consumer for the simple reason that funding in the school systems is so scarce that it doesn't allow schools to get heavily involved in technology. She recalls going out to schools in the Seattle area with Explorapedia to get the feedback of school children. "One of the criteria we had to use for our demonstrations was whether or not the school had a three-pronged outlet. Amazingly enough, we had to get to that level. That's the unfortunate state of a lot of schools that are really struggling with the kind of funding they need to bring technology into the classroom. And so we at Microsoft are doing what we can to help convey through a variety of efforts that funding for technology is to everyone's benefit."

And yet, as Kathy points out, a CD-ROM based encyclopedia will eventually be seen as more cost effective to schools and libraries. As I discussed earlier in this book, it is now possible to purchase a multimedia computer bundled with CD-ROM titles including an encyclopedia for about the same price as a full set of print-based encyclopedias. In addition, a CD-ROM encyclopedia takes up virtually no shelf space in libraries. But Kathy points to an added advantage. "I was part of a presentation that Bill Gates made earlier this year to a couple of thousand business people in South Africa who were trying to figure out how they can use technology to accelerate the learning and education process there. One of the benefits of CD-ROM technology for them, from a budgetary standpoint, is that they have neither the space nor the dollars to buy multiple sets of encyclopedias or reference materials to pass around. If *Volume A* is in use by someone else, you can't use *Volume A*, whereas if you have an encyclopedia on a network, it can be used by multiple kids. And that's a definite benefit from an education standpoint as well."

In keeping with all the other interviews I had in this book, Jay was quick to point out the diversity of people required to develop effective multimedia titles. He says, "Encarta involved a very large team effort and one of the biggest reasons for its success is that we have a team of incredibly talented, very diverse people. Multimedia brings together very different personalities. You have editors, designers, dancers, musicians, artists, and software people. That kind of diversity requires the recognition that each has a different way of thinking. There has to be the patience and willingness to cooperate with these different people. And I think that is where the biggest successes have come from—teaming up talented people with different perspectives and different approaches, and then figuring out how to get them to work together and cooperate." Jay remarks, "Trying to be a program manager at Microsoft is like try ing to herd kittens. I just try to get all the kittens to agree and it's one of th most fun parts of the job because it's not easy. But the results, when it doe work, are really great."

Novato Electronic City Hall

One of the most effective uses of multimedia for information access is a kios with a touchscreen that requires essentially no instructions for the user. This i because the user is usually part of the general public who may know little o nothing about a computer but is still able to walk up to a computer and easil access information in the form of text, photos, sound, and video without an assistance other than what is offered on the screen. And for the most par kiosks must be so easy to use that very few instructions are needed. It mus have a very intuitive design in order to be effective because it is intended to b used by people having a wide spectrum of computer literacy. Novato Elec tronic City Hall (see Figure 6.7 on page 125) is such a program and won New Media's INVISION Bronze Award as a public directory.

The program resides on a PC-compatible 386/33 computer with multimedi upgrade hardware, a Video 7 WIN.VGA graphics board, and Elographic Touchscreen and a 19" Mitsubishi monitor. It was developed to allow the citi zens and visitors of Novato, California, a means of looking up informatio regarding the community in general, public meeting agendas, maps (see Figur 6.8 on page 126), information on local schools and colleges (see Figure 6.9 o page 127), recreational activities (see Figure 6.10 on page 128), and city bud get information (see Figure 6.11 on page 129), employment opportunities other shopping areas, and a calendar of events. The program is very visual an interactive. For example, you may bring up a map of the city and all th schools. By selecting a particular school on the map you may bring up detaile information on the school. It also has a directory with all the phone number in the city. An introduction shows a video of the mayor of Novato welcomin the user to the program. In addition the program keeps track of what section were used most and is updated on a biweekly basis by the city to keep infor mation such as public meeting agendas and employment opportunities as cur rent as possible.

Figure 6.7   *Opening display of Novato Electronic City Hall. Courtesy of StudioGraphics.*

The kiosk is located in the Vintage Oaks Shopping Center in the city of Novato and was commissioned by the city in the hopes that it would help people become better aware of the facilities and services available to the residents of Novato. The kiosk supplements the normal methods of providing information using brochures or newsletters. Traditional methods of distributing this information are not only expensive but also time consuming. The kiosk provides a means of reaching a huge population who would not normally get this information through traditional channels, and is thus more effective. It is estimated that hundreds of people use the kiosk each day.

The Novato Electronic City Hall was developed by StudioGraphics, based in San Mateo, California. Richard Bennion is the President of StudioGraphics and founded the company in 1990. Prior to starting StudioGraphics, Richard

Figure 6.8   *The kiosk allows the user to access detailed maps of the city of Novato. Courtesy of StudioGraphics.*

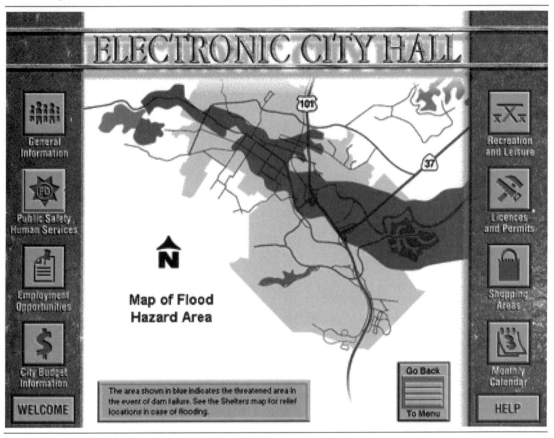

worked in technical sales for a distributor of high-end computer graphics equipment. He recalls, "While I was there, we started selling video capture cards, video output cards, all types of high-end equipment. But we were mainly providing 'solutions' to customers, which involved both hardware and software. In order to understand what we were doing, I began to test and experiment with all the new multimedia components and I began to see the power in being able to capture images in the computer as well as video, animation, and sound. Then I decided that for our next trade show, I should put together a little demonstration of how all this multimedia works. So I spent three weeks putting together a technical demonstration to show how all of the multimedia hardware and software could be put together and used."

Figure 6.9 *The user may look up detailed information on local schools and colleges. Courtesy of StudioGraphics.*

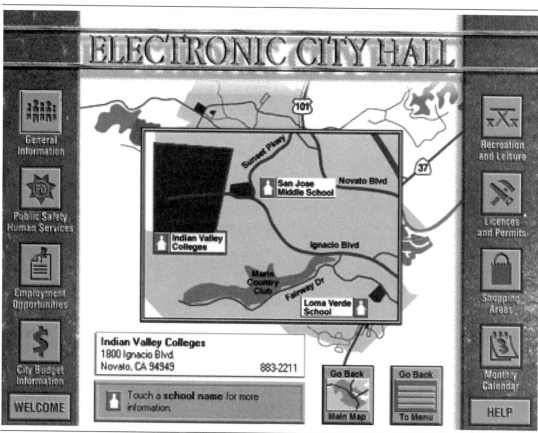

It was that trade show that was a turning point for Richard. He saw that he had been able to create an innovative marketing presentation that other high-tech dealers at the show raved about and hadn't been able to do themselves. As he was returning from the trade show, Richard decided to start his own company. As Richard says, it was a way to bring together his programming and design skills as well as his knowledge of sales and the high technology industry. StudioGraphics went from essentially no sales at the end of 1990 to over $750,000 at the end of 1994. Richard projects sales to be $1.5 million in 1995. Margins for their projects are an impressive 35–40%. StudioGraphics has been featured in *VAR Business Magazine* as one of the top 15 businesses to watch in the value-added reseller industry. There are currently eight full-time

Figure 6.10   *Information is provided regarding the city's recreation and leisure activities. Courtesy of StudioGraphics.*

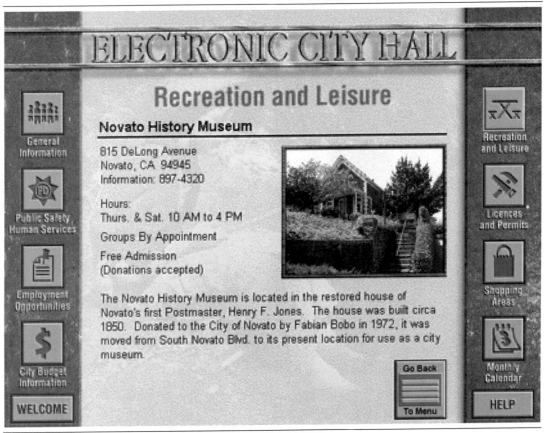

employees in the company, but they also use a number of outside contractors such as video productions companies, writers, photographers, musicians, designers, and illustrators.

StudioGraphics's clients include IBM, Hewlett-Packard, Chevron, Price Waterhouse, and medical companies, to name just a few. One of their recent programs is set up as kiosks at the exit of a chain of 47 restaurants in the San Francisco Bay area. As a person leaves the restaurant, he or she can use the kiosk to rate the service, cleanliness, quality of food, and other aspects of the dining experience. This information is downloaded to the restaurant's headquarters every night to provide them with an immediate evaluation of each of the restaurants in the chain.

Figure 6.11 *The program provides information on the city's budget as well as current job opportunities. Courtesy of StudioGraphics.*

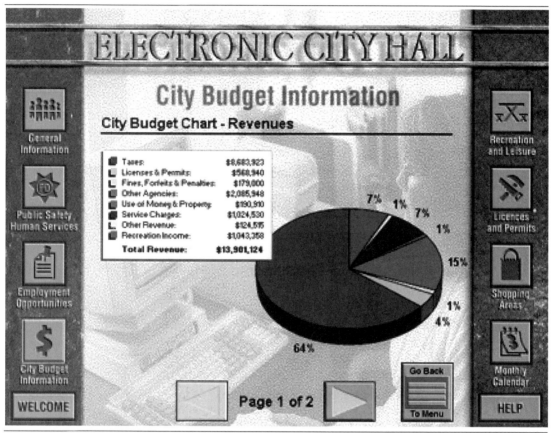

Although most of their applications are in the area of sales and marketing presentations, Novato Electronic City Hall was developed as an information access tool. As Richard says, "The city came to us and said they wanted to have an information kiosk. And I said 'We can do that.' So in order to get the job, we spent a day putting together a small demo. My ex-partner drove up to the city of Novato with his camera and took pictures. We had them quickly developed, scanned them and made a small program with a couple of fun menus to show what it could look like. I borrowed a touchscreen from Elographics and drove up to Novato with this little demo. When I set it up, the City Manager walked up to the touchscreen and started playing with it and was so impressed that basically we were hired right then."

Novato Electronic City Hall was developed for Windows using Authorware Professional along with other software such as Adobe Photoshop, Adobe Illustrator and Video for Windows. The project took approximately nine months to complete using a team of six people, who worked intermittently on that program, along with others. The greatest effort, Richard says, was getting all the information from the city that was to go into the kiosk. "The biggest problem we had was in putting together the content. That was an unbelievable effort. It took six months just to get all the information organized. We used all preexisting content. The city has a tremendous amount of resources. We took all their brochures, guides, books and newsletters—basically everything they had. We scanned in photos from brochures. We had three entire file boxes of information that the city sent to us. So it really took us four months to get all the information and another two months to figure out how we were ever going to put it all into a kiosk."

The program development and design took only about two to three months and went quite smoothly. As Richard points out, "Authorware is a very solid program, so it ran as expected." They had a woodshop design and build the kiosk and then installed it in the Vintage Oaks Shopping Center. The program tracks the number of times the various sections of the program are entered. They found that the two most popular areas of the application are the shopping center section that tells where all the shopping centers are in Novato and the job opportunities section. As Richard says, "The people who have money are interested in where to shop, and the people who don't have money are interested in finding a job." Because the city uploads information on a biweekly basis, the content remains very current. But Richard adds, "We've learned that you need to keep your touchscreens clean and you need to have someone whose job it is to clean the screen on a regular basis. Otherwise, they can get very dirty and not work properly. That's the one thing we've learned about touchscreens."

Richard feels strongly that developers should use tools that are proven and have been recommended by others. He says, "Here at StudioGraphics, we use Authorware Professional, Photoshop and Illustrator and we test our programs on Gateways, Dells, Compaqs and IBM computers. These are tools we can count on from companies that have put a lot of money into development. Even though Authorware costs $5,000, you need to spend the money on it. If you buy a tool for $500, you may get something that is not as reliable. So I tell people to choose your tools carefully."

Perhaps his greatest caution to developers pertains to the ability to communicate. Richard warns, "Don't ever underestimate the importance of communication when starting a company that will be developing multimedia applications just because you have good programming skills or just because you're good with graphics. Those are secondary things. The main concern is 'How do you communicate using this new technology?' So you need to make sure that either yourself or someone you're going to work with has those communications skills." Richard points out that interface design is really the same thing as communication. "One of the reasons that the City Hall project was so successful is that anybody can use it. You don't need instructions. You're able to go in to the program and intuitively get the information you need from it. The technology is transparent, and to do that you really have to focus on what it is the people are going to expect when they work with the interface design. That's where communication skills are so important."

Richard also stresses the importance of testing. "We have so many people come in and play with the product and give us feedback. We don't know everything and the only way to find out is to have good focus groups that will tell you what people are interested in. We are driven by peoples' demands— not what we think we should give them."

In spite of all the time StudioGraphics spends on testing, Richard admits to a scare he had right after Novato Electronic City Hall was installed in the shopping center. "We tested the kiosk in our office for two weeks. It worked perfectly. We tested the kiosk for three weeks in the City Hall before it was installed in the shopping center. So finally the kiosk got moved there and was there for a week. And I was very nervous. It was our 'baby,' and it was finally out in the world and was now on its own. And we were very nervous parents. A week later, I decided I'd better call up my contact at the city and find out how it was going. So I called him up and I said 'So, how's the kiosk doing?' And he said, 'Well, we're not really sure. What does "C:\" mean?'. The kiosk had been sitting there for a week with that DOS prompt. No one ever called us, no one ever said anything. Well we were immediately in our cars to make the hour and a half drive to Novato, but before leaving I said, 'Why don't you unplug the thing and plug it back in.' And so they did and sure enough it worked. But you can just imagine my reaction on the telephone." Richard laughs, "It's sort of like calling up your daughter who just went off to college for the first time and you get her roommate and ask if you can speak to your daughter, and she says 'No, she's in jail!' I almost dropped the phone and put the 'Out of Business' sign on the door and went home. That really stood out in my mind."

Richard still doesn't know what happened that week, but obviously the program has been running smoothly ever since and has been providing locals and tourists alike with a way to quickly and easily look up virtually anything having to do with the city of Novato.

Further Reading

Becker, Henry Jay. 1991. "Encyclopedias on CD-ROM: Two Orders of Magnitude More Than Any Other Educational Software Has Ever Delivered Before." *Educational Technology* (February): 7.

Berlin, Ed, Patricia Isaza, Mitt Jones, Don Trivette, et al. 1991. "From The Canterbury Tales to the Yellow Pages, CD-ROM Titles Are Ready to Deliver." *PC Magazine* (October): 286.

Bickford, Carolyn. 1994. "Reference Works." *MacUser* (October): 80.

Buchanan, Larry. 1994. "Connecting to the World: Getting Your School on the Internet." *Multimedia Schools* (May–June, 1994):14.

Caputo, Anne. 1994. "Seven Secrets of Searching: How and When to Choose Online." *Multimedia Schools* (May–June): 29.

Faulkner, John. 1992. "Kiosks: High Tech in Touch." *NewMedia Magazine* (December): 34.

McAllister, Celia. 1990. "Information Processing." *Business Week* (March 19): 122K.

McCracken, Harry. 1994. "Encyclopedias from A to Z." *Multimedia Worlds* (October): 75.

Rabinovitz, Rubin. 1993. "The Ideal CD-ROM Reference Library." *PC Magazine* (August): 554.

Stafford, Jan. 1994. Interacting with Multimedia Kiosks." *VARbusiness* (October): 71.

Stefanac, Suzanne. 1993. "Surfing the TeleNet in 2008." *NewMedia Magazine* (September): 40.

Stefanac, Suzanne. 1994. "Multimedia Online." *NewMedia Magazine* (November): 56.

Trivette, Don. 1990. "Electronic Encyclopedias Merge Text, High-Res Visuals, and Sound." *PC Magazine* (September): 537.

"Weather on CD-ROM." 1994. *Family PC* (September–October): 91.

MARKETING WITH MULTIMEDIA

Introduction

Multimedia presentations are very effective marketing tools, not only because of the different kinds of information that can be conveyed such as music and video, but also because they allow (and encourage) the user to interact with the program and thereby become more familiar with the product being marketed. Frequently the setting in which a sales presentation is available is one in which the users are "on their own." Examples are an unattended kiosk or a floppy disk that has been sent through the mail. Because of this the designer must be sure the program has a very easy-to-use interface since the user will have no manual and very likely will not have another person there to help with the program. On the other hand, the program should not be so passive that the user is bored or not paying attention to the material being presented. Balancing these two issues is one of the biggest challenges in creating a multimedia marketing presentation.

Most early desktop sales presentations simulated the traditional projector-based slide shows used in marketing, and although these are still commonly used, they frequently involve very little interaction from the user. In fact, simply giving the user the option to click to the Next or Previous page can result in a fairly boring presentation, even if it does involve animation and sound. I must admit that I have gone through several such programs and have found myself quickly clicking on the Next button while scarcely reading any of the text as the program continues. Fortunately, the advent of multimedia and the incorporation of more complex interaction has significantly changed the nature of software developed for advertising. The most effective sales and marketing titles encourage (and even require) a significant amount of user interaction to get to specific information, providing various "teasers" to do so. This keeps the user active and interested in the product.

Of course, the user may only interact effectively if the interface design is intuitive and easy to navigate. Most developers admit to spending literally hours deciding what label should go on a button. Next, More and → provide the most common conflicts, but there are countless others. Much of the decision is based on usability testing and a clear understanding of the demographics of the target audience. The developer must be constantly working toward creating a product that entices and encourages thinking and interaction, while providing an interface that is not frustrating to the user. Any instructions the computer provides should be minimal because the majority of users will not read very much text.

Another major consideration is the medium on which the product is to be displayed or delivered. Point-of-sale kiosks are a very common delivery medium and generally involve a touch screen. Storage space is generally not a big problem since the computer can be equipped with the hardware needed to run the presentation. However, other marketing software that is distributed to the masses presents challenges regarding the delivery medium. Although CD-ROM technology is becoming increasingly common, one may not yet assume that someone will have a CD-ROM drive. In these cases, it is necessary to provide the presentation software on a floppy disk. This is where some of the most interesting technical challenges come into play: fitting intriguing multimedia elements and an interactive program onto a single floppy disk. The titles presented in this chapter illustrate both examples quite well.

Overview of Profiles

Three very interesting titles are profiled in this chapter. Each was created to market very different kinds of "products" and uses distinctly different methods of delivery. Because of this, the development of each title involved unique challenges and solutions.

Electronic Business Card is exactly what it sounds like: a business "card" that is contained on a single floppy disk and is handed out to prospective clients in lieu of a paper card. It is full of multimedia elements and interactivity and is used to illustrate what the company is capable of producing.

Mary Chapin Carpenter, developed by the same company that developed the Electronic Business Card, promotes the work of a musical artist and provides the press with music samples and biographical information on two floppy disks.

Grow with Hawaii into the Pacific Century is a presentation that promotes the state of Hawaii as an excellent location to do business and to encourage businesses to move their operations to the state. It resides on an IBM Ultimedia computer and may be used in a kiosk environment.

Electronic Business Card and Mary Chapin Carpenter

A business card is one of the best ways to disseminate your company's name and let people know basically what the company does. But it can't actually give the person a firsthand look at what your company is capable of doing. Imagine instead being able to hand a person a floppy disk that they can load onto their computer and see a multimedia presentation that includes an overview of your company as well as a sampling of your work. The Electronic Business Card, developed by West End Post Interactive in Dallas, Texas, is an innovative replacement for a paper business card. It contains rich graphics, animation, and sound—and more importantly, it does so within the confines of a 1.4 MB floppy disk. Similarly, Mary Chapin Carpenter is an interactive portfolio that provides the news media with samples of an artist's music.

West End Post was founded in 1978 by Jay Rydman and specializes in film and video production and editing, mainly for commercials. It was one of the first companies in that area to install an Avid Media Composer for nonlinear video editing. Over the years, West End Post was able to put together a strong team of writers, producers, directors, and sound engineers. In an attempt to bring these talents to the multimedia arena, West End Post formed its interactive division in January of 1994. The Electronic Business Card was developed as a marketing tool to advertise the new interactive division of the company. The intent was to produce a very creative presentation that would reflect the imagination and vision of the company. It is certainly unlike any of the standard marketing presentations that are so often seen, and it won NewMedia's INVISION Gold Award for sales and marketing applications.

The program is actually an adventure in which the user must interact and use intellectual skills to go through three stages in time. As such, it is really an interactive puzzle that requires user input in order to get to the end of the puzzle. The first scene in time displays a screen rich in browns that make you feel as though you are in a prehistoric world (see Figure 7.1 on page 137). In this scene, called *Creation*, the user must select various objects that appear on the screen that could be used to create something. The next scene, called *Revolution* (see Figure 7.2 on page 138), shows rich colors of stained glass with a medieval theme and offers objects that, together, have led to revolutionary ways of doing things. The third time scene, called *Vision* (see Figure 7.3 on page 139), shows modern day objects that when used together lead to a vision of the future of such technologies as multimedia development. Finally, the user

Figure 7.1   *Creation scene from the Electronic Business Card. Courtesy of West End Post Interactive.*

is able to read about West End Post Interactive (see Figure 7.4 on page 140) and learn something about the development of the Electronic Business Card.

The graphics and 3-D animation are impressive, but the most unique feature of the program is its rich tapestry of sound. Unlike other presentations that loop the user through the same music or sounds, the audio in the Electronic Business Card is never the same no matter how many times you loop through the program. This is very effective in retaining the user's attention. The randomized sound is just one of the innovative features that gives the illusion that there is much more packed onto the disk than there really is.

It took about three months to develop the Electronic Business Card with a team of three people. The primary developer on the project was Tim Smith, a

Figure 7.2   *Revolution scene from the Electronic Business Card. Courtesy of West End Post Interactive.*

consultant who at that time had his own multimedia company called Tim Smith Interactive Media. (Tim currently works for Red Sky Interactive in California.) Tim provided the programming expertise and many of the design concepts that went into the product. Tim's codesigner on the project was James Marzano, who had been working in graphics design with West End Post. James says, "We worked on the project three months prior to the January kickoff of West End Post Interactive. We did most of our work at night on one of the Avid systems." James developed the majority of the graphics and sound. Through his work in film and video, he became involved with nonlinear editing, which led to his work in Director on the Mac. Another key person in the

Figure 7.3   *Vision scene from the Electronic Business Card. Courtesy of West End Post Interactive.*

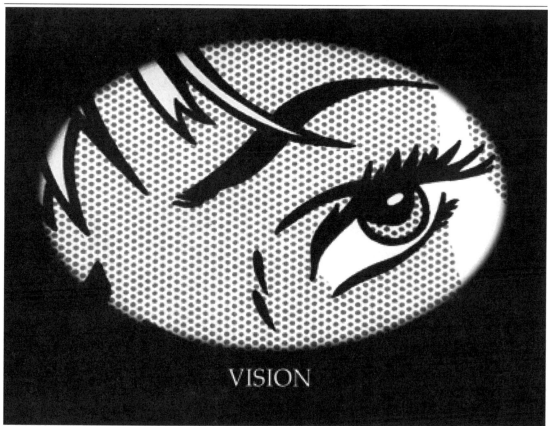

development was Mark Lennan, a graphics developer who also had been with West End Post for a number of years and who created the animations for the program. But as James points out, "When there are only a few developers, the lines cross and we all contributed to all aspects of development to some extent."

As the programmer for the project, Tim was confronted with a number of challenges to fit the various multimedia elements onto a floppy disk. Tim explains that they used two principle techniques to give the illusion of "magic" in terms of what is packed onto the floppy disk. He says, "In the three eras you go through during this story or trip—from prehistory to medieval to modern day—we wanted to develop an aural background or tapestry that would run

Figure 7.4   *Informational display from the Electronic Business Card. Courtesy of West End Post Interactive.*

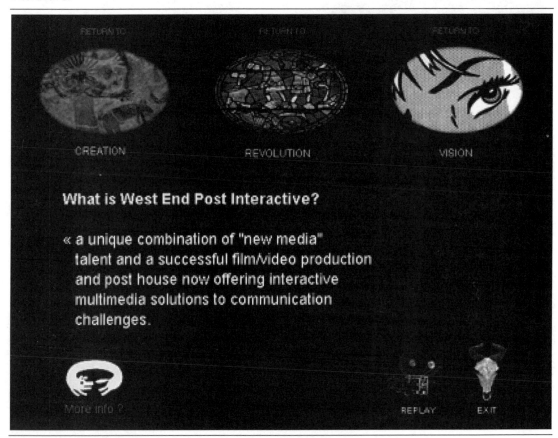

behind these scenes. That was difficult. We knew that the temporal length of the piece was completely determined by the user. Because of this, we first experimented with just long loops of sound to keep it interesting, but we found that even that got very boring after a while. So we came up with the idea of trying to randomize the sound."

The way in which they accomplished this was to create three main loops of sound for the three time periods depicted. The loops playing in the background are complex and therefore seamless because it is difficult to detect a beginning and end. For example, for the prehistory scene (in Figure 7.1), the background loop consists of the sound of crickets, and for the modern day scene (in Figure 7.3), they used the sound of traffic to create the loop. For the medieval scene (in Figure 7.2), they wanted to give the impression of monks mumbling in a cloister. James explains how they achieved this, "I got four of the guys in the company and we went down to the basement here. We set up a microphone and then we all just mumbled at low levels." After some modification of the recording they had achieved the sound they were looking for.

In addition to the seamless background loops that play randomly, they also created discreet "stinger" sounds such as drums or lions roaring that play randomly in the foreground. These short, discreet sounds are fired off by a random sampler algorithm that Tim coded into the program. As Tim says, "The net result is that as you sit there, you hear a background tapestry of sound, and you have these audible foreground sounds fired by the computer. Theoretically, you can sit there forever, and it will never be the same. If you have the luxury of a CD-ROM you can put long music or sound clips on there. We didn't have that luxury with a floppy disk, so we had to come up with some innovative ways to duplicate that."

Another strategy they used to cut back on storage requirements was to use only a portion of the screen display for the graphics. Rather than filling the screen, the Electronic Business Card shows up in an ellipse, thus cutting out nearly half of the graphics storage requirements. As James points out, "Disk space is THE biggest problem when you're creating these electronic business cards because you're trying to fit an entire interactive project onto one floppy disk. That is the modus operandi for every decision you make on every graphic and every sound that goes into it. It's a real art to get these elements to fit onto one floppy disk. Everything is trimmed down. We're constantly thinking of creative ways to do that, such as using only a portion of the screen and using sound loops."

Tim relays that there was another way in which they "fooled" people with the Electronic Business Card, namely in the use of color. Tim explains, "We completely take over the color palette in the piece and black out all the background elements such as the operating system and other applications that might be running at the same time. When you're developing a piece for the 8-bit world with 256 colors, there is a system palette which is a well-balanced palette of typical colors that are used by all applications. Director and other programs give you the control to change the color palette, but you can wreak havoc with the other applications running in the background because they're still numerically mapped to specific positions on the scale, regardless of what color is there. So we took over the color palettes in the Electronic Business Card to optimize them for whatever picture was on the screen."

He continues, "In the first scene, there is a palette of 256 colors which are mostly wonderful shades of brown that are close together. The cathedral scene with the stained glass window is the most gorgeous one in terms of colors. To save space we only wanted to take colors that were appropriate to that picture. But that can do very strange things to the background applications. Because of that, we blacked out the background. The whole piece is in 256 colors. So we used Debabelizer to analyze that photograph and pick out the 256 most appropriate colors from the millions of colors available that would make this particular photograph look the best. The palette was highly skewed toward the rich reds and blues and blacks that are in that picture and nothing else—no lime greens or hot pinks that you might find in the system's standard palette." As a result, they were able to achieve a graphic image that is virtually indistinguishable in normal hues from 24-bit color.

Carolyn Carmines is the Manager of Interactive Technologies at West End Post Interactive and was one of the people who participated in testing the Electronic Business Card in its early phases. She emphasizes the value of an interactive business card, especially because it is easily distributable over a network like America Online and Compuserve, allowing the user to download it and learn about the company. Carolyn says, "One of the important factors of an electronic business card on a network is the impact that it has in providing new leads for projects just because of the number of times it is downloaded. The development of that business card has more than paid for itself."

More recently, West End Post Interactive has been working with Sony Music/Nashville to produce electronic portfolios for musical artists. Because of their experience in packing so much multimedia onto a floppy disk, West End Post Interactive was a natural for such a project. Their recently released project for Mary Chapin Carpenter contains loops of her music to provide the media with a sample of her "new sound." Another disk contains extensive biographical information as well as a discography and lyrics to her songs. As Carolyn says, "The purpose of the disk was to entice the media because they are deluged with stacks of press kits every day. But when they get this brochure and open it up with its diskettes, they will load the program just to see what it's about. It's a way of bringing her to the top of the stack. Also I think it will improve the continuity and the accuracy of the information that is written about Mary Chapin Carpenter." The biographical disk contains about 30 pages of information in various word processor formats.

Many of the strategies to save space for the Electronic Business Card were also used for the Mary Chapin Carpenter project. For example, the images depict torn pages in the middle of the screen (see Figure 7.5 on page 143), saving storage space by not using the periphery of the display. In addition, they used musical loops to include as much music on the disk as possible. Although Sony guided them on what music to include, James had to decide

Figure 7.5   *Screen display from Mary Chapin Carpenter. Courtesy of West End Post Interactive.*

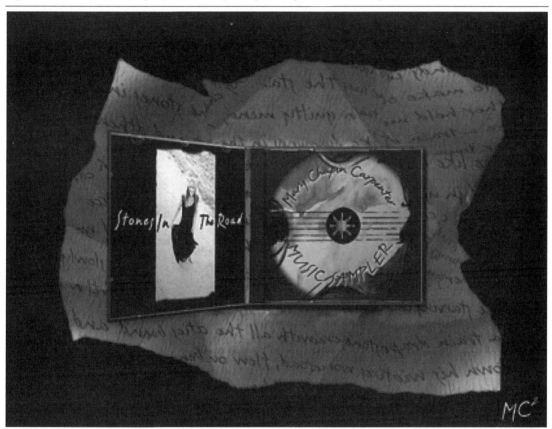

what clips would best fit onto the disk. Carolyn says, "In the opening, there is this beautiful instrumental that James edited in such a way that you can't tell it's not a continuous string." In fact, that continuous sounding melody is a loop, but it is cleverly deceptive.

Carolyn continues, "For this project it was important for people to hear the music and get a sense of the fabric and the style of this new release of Mary Chapin Carpenter." In order to do that, the development team had to have a good feeling for this themselves. They spent many hours sitting around a table listening to her music asking themselves "What does this make me feel like? What kind of images come to my mind? What is the story she is trying to tell here?" As James says, "We really had to get a feel for the music and the mood. That's what influenced the interface design—everything from the color to the layout."

West End Post Interactive has built a prototype for Sony to give them an idea of what an interactive sound sampler could look and sound like. Carolyn says, "We integrated a lot more elements in that prototype. But what intrigued Sony was the interface design itself. Anyone can have menu selections, but the trick is to find the right metaphor in which to present it." She refers to the guitar display (see Figure 7.6 on page 145) in the Mary Chapin Carpenter piece as an example. By double-clicking the mouse pointer on one of the guitar strings, the user is able to play one of the songs on the disk. In fact, the user may "strum" the guitar by moving the mouse pointer over the strings to play his or her own music. Not only is this a very creative design, it is intuitive to the user as well.

West End Post Interactive develops applications on both the PC and the Mac. They use as their determining factor which platform the client will be using. James points out, "It actually helps our development cycle if we develop on the machine that we're going to deliver it on. I don't think it's good business to force somebody into a specific platform, especially at this point when there are so many different platforms and different kinds of interactive applications you can deliver. The phrase we like to use here around the office is that we're 'platform agnostic.' We'll deliver on anything."

The company has also worked on some very large-scale projects. They recently created an interactive multimedia presentation program used at a worldwide corporate business presentation center that interfaces with remote cameras, video systems, and slide and film projectors. Carolyn explains that it was really a dual application. There is a touch-screen monitor in the podium. The presenter uses this to control the presentation as well as the room's "elements" such as curtains and lighting. The audience watches the presentation on an overhead screen. All of the control was programmed in Director.

I asked if they ran into any problems during the development of the Electronic Business Card. James admits that they went through three or four interface designs for the entire piece before it worked the way they wanted it to. He says, "We originally had no text at the bottom of the screens. Our original goal was to make people think and figure out what to do to go on to the next screen. But a lot of people thought it was 'broken' and didn't know how to use it." They then added text that gives hints to the user how to interact with the program. James voiced concern that too many people are passive when using a program. "Our impetus was to make people active and think in that piece. That's the whole point of this interactive media. It shouldn't be a passive experience. You control it—you do what you want to do and get the information out of it that you need." Carolyn adds, "A very important part of designing anything like this is understanding the behaviors and psychodynamics of the

Figure 7.6   *Guitar display from Mary Chapin Carpenter. The user may hear her songs by double-clicking on the strings, or strum the guitar by moving the mouse pointer over them. Courtesy of West End Post Interactive.*

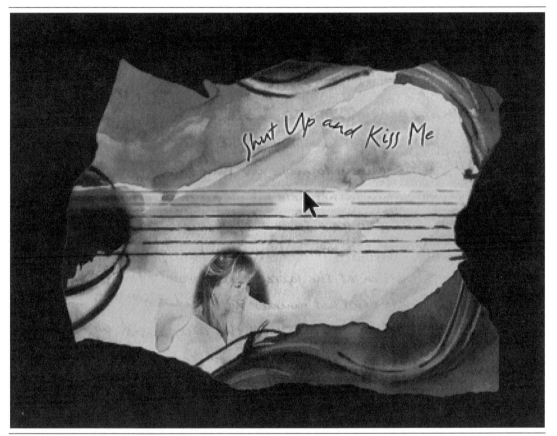

people who are going to be using it." She says that one of the considerations to be taken into account is the age group the program is targeted at because the younger generation is much more comfortable interacting with the computer.

The main problems they encountered on the Mary Chapin Carpenter program was the impact on the design that resulted from trying to include as much music as possible. Again, they had to try several different approaches before they came up with the final design for the product.

Both Carolyn and James advise others trying to develop similar products that they need to have someone on the team who is an experimenter and inventor in order to compress a grand scheme into a very small format. As

James says, "You really need a unique problem solver. It's not really that hard to put together a piece in Director. But once you have something that works, you need to figure out a way to do it in half the space and get it to play twice as fast. So it really involves looking at things uniquely and finding new solutions to problems." Carolyn adds that another crucial part is the team itself and how the various talents interact with each other. "You need to provide a space where ideas can flow and where everyone can take the risk of being way out there because all of the ideas have value."

Tim points to the value of rapidly prototyping the entire project before getting into the details of any one part. He says, "Too many developers tend to start at the beginning and refine as they go. That gets you into more trouble than anything else. You very quickly run out of space. You run out of ideas. It changes the way subsequent things run. Instead, we work at a very rough cut level before we start refining anything. One of the best resources you can possibly have is someone who can get things on the screen almost as fast as you can discuss them."

Tim also emphasizes the importance of testing. "My dad's a painter. I'll never forget growing up and my father painting watercolors. He would paint little squares on a piece of cardboard and hang it up in the sun inside his door. It would stay there for months. He was testing to see the rates of deterioration of different pigments by sunlight and ambient light. That's the same thing you have to do in the computer world. You need to quickly rough in a QuickTime movie with sample colors. Then you need to run it on a 4-bit machine, an 8-bit machine, then port it over to Windows and make sure it's doing what you want up front. The same is true of audio—you need to run it at 11 KHz, 22 KHz and 44 KHz. You really need to make a lot of 'test swatches' before you get into the details of the program."

Carolyn concurs and gives as an example the development of the application to be shown in the worldwide corporate center. This was the premier presentation for their client and was going to be shown to international analysts and consultants. But their client had only a limited budget and at that time could not afford 16-bit sound. The speakers to be used in the presentation, however, were very high end. Carolyn recalls, "We had to be sure the sound was as good as it could be. We had a very experienced sound engineer working in a recording studio for hours trying to get 8-bit sound to be as impressive as 16-bit sound." He worked to eliminate noise, retain the rich tonal quality of 16-bit sound, and compress it to 8-bit sound. And so again, West End Post Interactive was able to pull off some of the "magic" they've had to learn in order to deliver exciting multimedia presentations that are very "lean."

Grow with Hawaii into the Pacific Century

When we think of sales and marketing, most of us tend to think in terms of selling a product or marketing a company's capabilities to a potential customer. The Electronic Business Card profiled in this chapter is a very good example of that. However, when I saw Grow with Hawaii into the Pacific Century (see Figure 7.7) I was intrigued by the aspect of a program that marketed something very different—the state of Hawaii. Because of that different perspective), I thought it would be an interesting profile to include in this book. It

Figure 7.7 *Opening screen display from Grow with Hawaii into the Pacific Century. Courtesy of Tom Coffman Multimedia.*

won a Merit Award in NewMedia's INVISION competition and was given a Superior Award by the American Economic Development Council.

In some respects, Grow with Hawaii ... is similar to the Novato Electronic City Hall (profiled in Chapter 6) in that the user is able to access information about the state of Hawaii. However, the purpose of Grow with Hawaii ... is to promote Hawaii as a prime place to do business and to entice companies to choose Hawaii as either a location for a start-up enterprise or another office location for an existing business. Because Hawaii is situated between North America and Asia and because of its diverse cultural population, Hawaii has the advantage of offering an ideal environment for trans-Pacific business opportunities, many of which involve leading-edge technology. Grow with Hawaii ... was developed to inform businesses of these opportunities and to show them how the state of Hawaii can help them achieve their goals in terms of growth and success. Using Grow with Hawaii ... a person may access information about various aspects of doing business there (see Figure 7.8 on page 149), the culture of the islands (see Figure 7.9 on page 150), as well as the economy (see Figure 7.10 on page 151).

The program resides on an IBM Ultimedia computer that may be used in a kiosk environment at a conference or trade show. But it has its greatest usage by Hawaii's Department of Business, Economic Development and Tourism where it is shown to visiting business executives who may be considering Hawaii as a place to establish a business. Because so much of Hawaii's economy depends on tourism, the state is concerned about diversifying its economic base so that it is not so dependent on fluctuations in tourism. Grow with Hawaii ... was conceived as part of an ongoing marketing effort to bring other types of businesses to the state. The program was commissioned by the state of Hawaii, and Tom Coffman Multimedia successfully bid for the job against 11 other companies. Tom Coffman's company has been well-established in Hawaii for 17 years and has a solid reputation for creating multi-image slide shows, videos, and exhibits. With this project, which began in 1992, Tom Coffman Multimedia got involved in the world of interactive (or desktop) multimedia.

The lead person who was brought in to work on the project was David Teton-Landis, who like most of the people involved in multimedia has what he calls a "checkered" background. He has a Master's Degree in Psychology and a Master's Degree in Dance. He joined the University of Hawaii to teach as a Visiting Associate Professor in Dance after spending ten years in New York as a professional dancer. He was a computer hobbyist and had been using Hyper-Card on the Mac for years. Eventually his enthusiasm for teaching wore out.

Figure 7.8 *Screen display from Grow with Hawaii .... Courtesy of Tom Coffman Multimedia.*

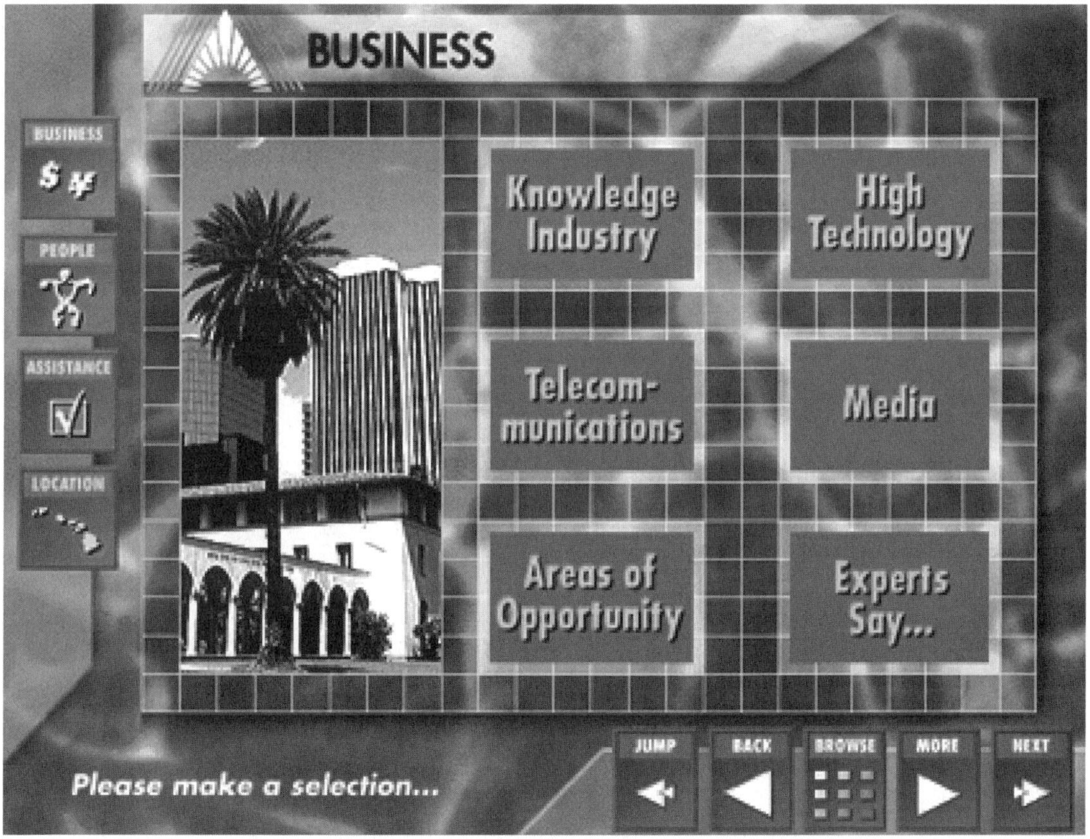

David recalls, "I was looking for another career because dancing doesn't go on forever unless you're an extreme fanatic. I'd drifted into desktop publishing and spent several years doing graphic design layout on the computer. I also spent a lot of time volunteering at the University of Hawaii's Hypermedia Lab where I learned basic skills of scanning, animation and sound, and I also was able to learn SuperCard and Director."

As a result of his participation with the Hypermedia Lab, David was part of a team bidding for the Grow with Hawaii ... project. When Tom Coffman Multimedia got the bid, David was asked to join the company to work on the project because of his experience in interactive design. Although there were only three people working full time on the project, Tom Coffman's extensive experience in other types of multimedia meant that he already had in place a

Figure 7.9　　*Screen display from Grow with Hawaii …. Courtesy of Tom Coffman Multimedia.*

network of outside people to help produce top-notch sound and video for the project. As David says, "We were able to produce everything from scratch. We went out and interviewed people for the videos in the program."

The program was developed under OS/2 for an IBM Ultimedia computer. David explains, "Tom Coffman Multimedia chose that platform partly because of the technological capabilities that were possible using this line of products as well as the fact that IBM was offering lucrative partnerships through what was called the *Ultimedia Developer's Program*. Through the program, developers were able to get the machines for four months without having to put any money down in order to develop products. Then they could purchase the equipment at a tremendous discount. What was great about the

Figure 7.10   *Screen display from Grow with Hawaii …. Courtesy of Tom Coffman Multimedia.*

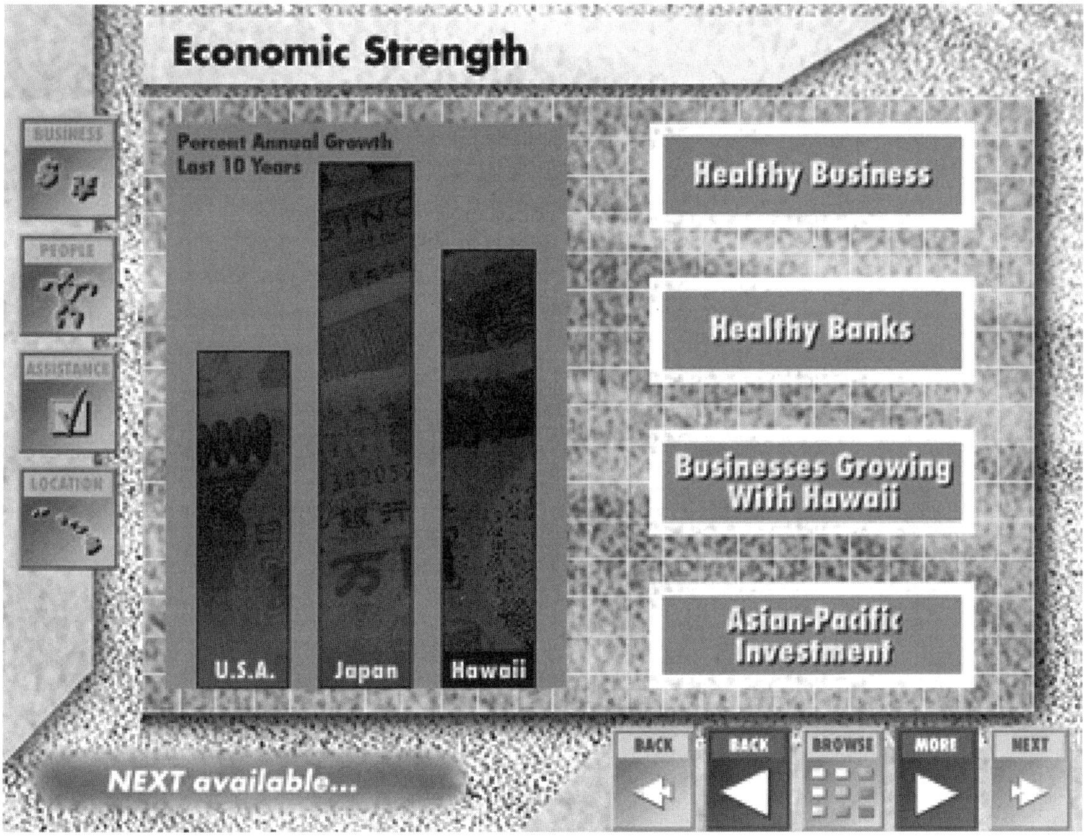

platform is that the Micro Channel Architecture had a faster and wider bus than was currently available with other PC clone architectures. It could carry a lot more information."

The system has an IBM-built touch-screen, a high-resolution XGA card, and an ActionMedia II board to handle the digitizing of video and audio as well as compression and decompression, which greatly enhances the program's performance. As David says, "The state was interested in having the best quality they could for this sales tool. This system provided better quality than QuickTime and a year or two before Video for Windows was available." The unfortunate result is that the program is not widely distributable because so few people have systems operating under OS/2 with an ActionMedia II board.

As David points out, "OS/2 is more of an enterprise solution than a desktop solution. The product ended up being a niche product because it's not Windows-based, but that's what it was intended to be in the first place. The platform enabled us to create a very good program with high-resolution graphics, full-motion video and great sound." The entire system is, as David puts it, "top to bottom an IBM package" and was developed using Audio Visual Connection as the authoring tool.

One of the intriguing parts of the program is that a person is able to control what is shown during the presentation. Essentially, the program was written as a shell so that the display may be controlled at various levels. And because much of the clientele the state is trying to attract is from Japan, there is a Japanese version of the program as well. The company subcontracted the translation of the project to a Japanese broadcaster who was teaching Japanese at the University of Hawaii. He did the textual translations as well as the male narrations, while a female drama student did the female narrations. He also provided the Japanese text that went into the program.

As David says, "It took three months of 11-hour days to get the basic program running to be shown at Comdex. Another four to five months were then devoted to the aspect of getting the program to allow customized one-on-one presentations that could be set up by the user." Tom Coffman was the producer and writer, while David did most of the graphic design and programming. Other people provided much of the video and audio content. David points out, "There are a lot of 'talking heads' in the program, such as testimonials from people about why they think Hawaii is a great place to do business, or talking about the different facets of the resources here—the university, the people and the different language groups. The video interviews take up about 375 MB of storage."

As other developers have pointed out, David recalls the time spent on what might appear to be trivial details, but are in fact very important issues from the standpoint of interface design. He says, "We had some seemingly endless discussions on what to call the button that ended up being labeled *More* to indicate that there was more information. We argued about *More* versus *Next* and what the user would be thinking as he or she was navigating through the program."

He also points to the diversity of people involved in a multimedia project and the need to be able to work with different talents to make a project work, especially if those people do not work with the company on a full-time basis. "Unless the company has the luxury to employ on a full-time basis all the people with the different talents needed to produce a multimedia title, then there is a major effort in team building. Once you find that team, you need to get everyone up to at least some level of understanding and cooperative thinking on what the project is all about. We were fortunate to have on our team someone who was great with sound, someone who was great with video, and a great composer. None of those people had worked with interactive multimedia before, including the producer and writer." But with these very diverse talents, they were able to put together a team that created an award-winning title that has done much to generate interest in Hawaii's resource base for new businesses.

David also points out that although this initial project was not particularly profitable, it did provide the capital (approximately $100,000) for Tom Coffman Multimedia to move into the area of interactive multimedia in terms of equipment and software purchases as well as the funding to develop the in-house expertise needed for future projects. Although the company was already well-equipped with extensive audio and video production facilities, the interactive multimedia project required them to purchase additional hardware and software and train the people working on the project. The state subsidized some of the costs involved in multimedia training, and helped to send five people working on the Grow with Hawaii … project to California for three to four day training sessions at the IBM Training Center. This training assistance in high-technology areas is part of the state's continuing efforts to ensure that it has the local talent needed to attract new businesses to the state.

David sees the company moving increasingly towards cross-platform applications to access a larger base of potential customers. As David says, "OS/2 is fabulous for a permanent installation, but we can't readily distribute the program. We're about to start working on a multimedia application for the Japanese Cultural Center of Hawaii, and it will be developed in Authorware and displayed on Windows machines. We're hoping to be able to sell the program on CD-ROMs at the center, so we'll have a product that is also marketable to the consumer." He sees such a product also being useful in the classroom to educate students about Hawaii's cross-cultural history. Most of their current projects are being developed using Authorware Professional for Macintosh and Windows, although they have developed some of their own proprietary presentation and navigation software.

When asked what guidelines he would give to other developers, David laughed and said, "Get all the sleep you need before you start the project." But in a more serious tone, he advises, "I think for me, multimedia is an extension of the interest and commitment to tell a story—to get people involved. You need to be expressive in this medium to tell stories, to educate, and to spark people's interest. I used to be told as a dancer, 'Don't do this unless you absolutely have to. Do anything else you can possibly do.' And in a sense that's true of multimedia because it takes an awful lot of commitment to be able to just keep from drowning in all the different facets of the information you need to know to do it. Not only do you have to be able to deal with all that information, you still need to have enough personality left over to have your work be worthwhile seeing. People involved in multimedia have a checkered background. They almost need to in order to understand and deal with so many different facets."

Further Reading

Burger, Jeff. 1994. "Presentations: Step by Step." *NewMedia Magazine* (April): 93.

Crowley, Aileen. 1992. "Buyers Add Verve to Presentations with Multimedia." *PC Week* (February 3): 67.

Greenberg, Jeff. 1993. "Adding Media to Your Message." *PC Magazine* (September 14): 259.

Jacobs, David, and Amy Shelton. 1992. "Make Your Move: Add Sound and Motion for Dynamic Presentations." *Publish* (June): 81.

Nelson, Ted. 1994. "The Big Scare." *NewMedia Magazine* (April): 41.

Stefanac, Suzanne. 1994. "Interactive Advertising." *NewMedia Magazine* (April): 43.

Tully, Tim. 1994. "High-Tech Show 'n' Tell." *CompuServe Magazine* (March): 30.

Weiss, Jiri. 1994. "Kiosks at the Point of Sale." *NewMedia Magazine* (April): 46.

THAT'S ENTERTAINMENT!

Introduction

There is no doubt the gaming industry is enormous. Computer games, cartridges and CD-ROMs brought in a staggering $4 billion in 1994 and are expected to bring in nearly double that by 1997. This is more than people have spent to see movies at the theater, something that has not gone unnoticed in Hollywood. Although cartridges have dominated the entertainment market, CD-ROM technology has evolved to such a state that it is expected to soon take the lead. For one thing, a CD-ROM can hold about 2,000 times as much data as a cartridge. It is also much cheaper (by a factor of about 10) and faster (by a factor of 4–6) to manufacture a CD-ROM than it is a cartridge. So why has CD-ROM not been the medium of choice for the gaming industry? One of the main reasons is that CD-ROM drives are slower and have not been able to provide the immediate performance response required by the "twitch 'n' flex" games that run on Nintendo and Sega systems.

Certainly, as CD-ROM drives become increasingly faster each year, slow response time will prove to be less problematic. But we are seeing another important trend in the computer market. The audience purchasing entertainment software is evolving to include a growing number of adults in their 20s and 30s. As a result, an increasing number of people are seeking entertainment that involves strategic thinking and problem solving. Lightning-speed responses are not crucial, whereas visually realistic graphics significantly enhance the "mood." Many such games are perhaps best described as interactive movies with complex plots, live actors and full-motion video. Such photo-realistic entertainment requires the large storage capacities of CD-ROM.

In fact, the line between a full-feature movie produced in Hollywood and interactive entertainment is rapidly blurring. Interactive games are being developed based on Hollywood movies and some, such as *Jurassic Park* and *Cliffhanger*, include video footage from them. And now we are beginning to see full-feature movies being produced in Hollywood based on interactive games such as Myst and Doom. Developers of entertainment software are faced with increasingly burdensome costs to hire actors, create expensive sets, and essentially produce a movie that will be played on a disc. Currently, a successful entertainment title typically costs between $1–3 million to produce, and it will only continue to increase as people's expectations of the quality of interactive entertainment increase. Developers of CD-ROM titles are quickly honing their skills in Hollywood production techniques while those in the entertainment industry are trying to learn all they can about computer technology.

In fact, the biggest players in the movie industry and the interactive entertainment business are scrambling to make deals to provide interactive entertainment on digital cable networks. This is resulting in complex partnerships involving movie studios, cable television companies, phone companies, software developers, and computer and electronics firms. For example, Time Warner Entertainment currently owns (among others) Time, Warner Brothers, HBO, Time Warner Cable, and its alliances include Sega, Toshiba, and SGI. Sony owns Columbia, Tristar, and CBS Records and is closely tied to Nintendo and Philips. Matsushita purchased MCA, Universal, and Panasonic and is heavily invested in 3DO. Paramount Communication's ownerships include Paramount Pictures, Simon and Schuster, Prentice Hall, USA Cable, and the SciFi Channel. The connections among companies is incredibly complex. And although nearly everyone is risking that interactive television (or ITV) is the wave of the future, there is still some question about how receptive of ITV the general public will be—whether people really want to interact with their television or if they would rather just sit back and watch a movie.

Even so, it appears that interactive entertainment, whether using a television or a computer, is an inevitability. The extent to which an individual chooses to interact will surely vary, but the technology will very soon be a part of all our lives.

Overview of Profiles

The games profiled here include some of the best-selling CD-ROM titles in the industry. All might be regarded as interactive fiction, and all are "thinking" games targeted at a more mature, intellectual audience.

The Journeyman Project developed by Presto Studios takes the user on an adventure into 3-D photorealistic worlds with aliens, space stations and time travel. Its sequel, *Buried in Time: The Journeyman Project 2,* is even more visually realistic and contains themes involving real historical events and people such as Leonardo DaVinci.

The 7th Guest was the first CD-ROM title that included full-motion video using professional actors and 3-D computer graphics. Its story centers on the haunted mansion of a mad toy maker and the guests he has invited to dinner. *The 11th Hour* is its sequel that picks up the story 70 years later. Both contain challenging puzzles that the user must solve to unravel the mystery.

The Journeyman Project and Buried in Time —The Journeyman Project 2

One of the most intriguing stories in this book surrounds the development of the well-known and best-selling game, The Journeyman Project, developed by Presto Studios in San Diego. The story is interesting partly because of the program's tremendous success, but more so because it was developed by a small group of young men fresh out of college who lived on the meager funding provided by families and friends while they worked hard to make their dream come true. Like many other titles profiled in this book, The Journeyman Project does not fit neatly into a single category. It is as much interactive fiction as it is a game, and is not at all comparable to the commonly seen CD-ROM games that have violent action as their focus.

The game begins in the year 2318 and the world is at peace. But the invention of time travel threatens to sabotage historical events that have led to this peace if the technology finds its way into the wrong hands. The user assumes the role of a special agent whose purpose is to prevent such sabotage and must travel through time to prevent corruption that may undermine world peace. The Journeyman Project involves a high technology/science fiction theme and uses 3-D photorealistic graphics to give the user a sense of virtual reality (see Figure 8.1 on page 159, Figure 8.2 on page 160, and Figure 8.3 on page 161 for some sample screen displays). It is the winner of a number of awards including NewMedia's INVISION Award of Excellence, Gold Award for best animation/graphics, Bronze Awards for adult games and for best production design. It was also voted the best entertainment title in *SVM Mac,* a leading French magazine. The Journeyman Project was available in Japanese in April of 1993, received the Apple Award at Apple Japan, and was the number-one selling Macintosh CD-ROM in Japan that year. The Turbo version of the product is available in French, German, Spanish, and will soon be translated

Figure 8.1   *A scene from The Journeyman Project. Courtesy of Presto Studios, Inc.*

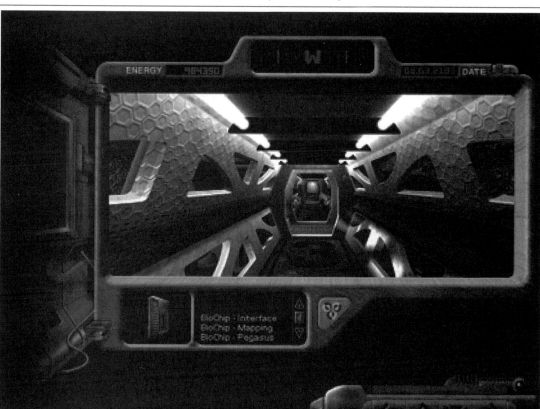

into Italian and Korean. A sequel is about to be released, Buried in Time: The Journeyman Project 2, and it picks up the story six months later.

The talent behind The Journeyman Project is a team of nine young people with very diverse backgrounds, including film and videography, writing, graphic design, and programming. Michel Kripalani cofounded Presto Studios in 1991 in order to realize a dream he had since he was very young— to create an interactive game. Michel admits that his early programming experience came from "hacking" on an Apple IIe when he was 15 years old, modifying games to enhance the characters. And he knew even then that someday he wanted to create a computer game of his own. Ironically, Michel didn't do well in computer classes but learned to program as a hobby, teaching himself how to use HyperCard and Director. He majored in Visual Arts with a specialty in film

Figure 8.2   *A scene from The Journeyman Project. Courtesy of Presto Studios, Inc.*

at the University of California in San Diego and got an internship during his senior year at a company called InterNetwork. There he worked with Macintosh computers, programming in HyperCard during the early days of multimedia and started working on his first CD-ROM project. After his internship and graduation in 1989, he left InterNetwork along with coworker Ed Coderre, and together they started their own company, MOOV Design.

For the next year and a half, they worked on a number of multimedia projects for kiosks and interactive training. Ed was the designer while Michel concentrated on the programming. They also developed some CD-ROMs, one of which was called *Verbum Interactive*. As Michel relays, "It was the world's first interactive multimedia magazine and was pretty exciting. We did this before QuickTime had come out. This was a two-CD set and it included

Figure 8.3   *A scene from The Journeyman Project. Courtesy of Presto Studios, Inc.*

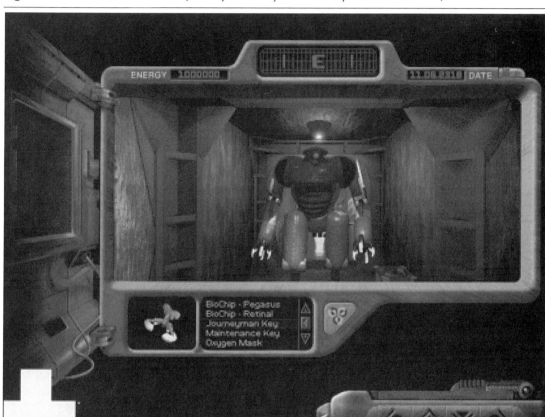

articles and interviews, with video movies, audio, and hypertext. It was way before its time." The project also involved a number of other contributors such as writers, content providers, and an art director named Jack Davis who was later the art director for The Journeyman Project.

Even though MOOV Design was involved in some exciting and break-through projects, it was mainly a client service business. Although his partner was happy with the type of work they were doing, Michel soon grew tired of working for other people. At about this time, he saw Spaceship Warlock—the first CD-ROM adventure game available for the Macintosh, which was released in 1991. Although Michel saw that the technology was there to distribute a great game, he felt that Spaceship Warlock hadn't pushed the limits in terms of graphics, story content, and adventure game concepts. Michel envisioned a game with photorealistic images and movielike content and was able to draw upon his background in film to create such a product. He left MOOV Design and founded Presto Studios to begin work on what was to become The Journeyman Project.

Michel had begun working on the concept for the program while he was living with Dave Flanagan who ended up being the lead writer on the project. Dave had graduated from the University of California in Irvine with a degree in English. Michel recalls, "We started writing the product in February of '91. At that point it just involved concepts and ideas, but we wanted to do something with science fiction. The thought of time travel intrigued us because it allowed us to go to different worlds, which is one of the things we thought CD-ROM would be great for in terms of visuals—to be able to jump instantly from location to location. And we were both influenced by science fiction and high tech movies, so it was just a natural direction for us to go."

Michel also felt strongly about avoiding the violence that dominates the game industry. He attributes much of this to his mother. "I first talked to my parents about writing a game when I was 15. Every time I told them I was going to do a game, my mother always said, 'Oh it's not going to one of those shoot 'em-up games, is it?' So when we started working on the project, I thought, 'Hey, why don't we make it nonviolent? There's no reason to have guns. Let's make it more of a thinking game.' And that really fit well not only with the story we were writing but also with the demographics we were appealing to. Journeyman is not for the 13- to 14-year-old twitch kids that want to sit in front of Genesis. It is for an older, mature adult audience, and I think they can appreciate the nonviolent theme."

In fact the target audience for The Journeyman Project was anyone who had a CD-ROM drive. Initially, this meant Caucasian males making over $50,000 a year who were in their upper 30s. As Michel points out, "It was a ridiculous bracket and it has significantly changed now. I'd say that the average Journeyman player is someone in their 20s or 30s. Unfortunately, it's still predominantly male, although we're trying to change that with Buried in Time. But the target market is still fairly well-educated and fairly well-to-do because you have to have a pretty expensive computer to run it on. But all of those things are changing rapidly."

When he started Presto, Michel knew he would require a top-notch team to develop the product. But his funding was too limited to be able to hire anyone. Fortunately, he had, over the years, made friends with people having the ideal mix of talents whom he was able to convince to work on the project at no cost. Michel recalls, "It took a little while to sell the vision to them, but once everyone saw what I was attempting and we were all in agreement about what we were going to do, it was easy to get everyone rallied together." The original team was made up of six people although three more joined shortly afterwards. All of them are tied into royalties, and they are all shareholders in the company. Although most members of the team initially tried to maintain their full-time jobs while working on The Journeyman Project at nights and on weekends, it soon became clear that they would need to devote their entire time to the project. They all agreed to give up their full-time jobs in early April of 1992 to work on the product.

Funding for the project came from family members and friends, and was used solely for their living expenses until they could complete the project. In fact, to save money, the team lived cramped together in a modest two-story house in San Diego. Michel says, "All of us already had our own computers and we had most of the software we needed to do the job. We did need to buy some hardware, but mostly what we needed was living expenses. We borrowed about $70,000 from friends and families and offered them 10% return on their money. And we all had some money we had saved up in the bank, but that lasted only so long. After that point, everyone had to draw off of whatever group funds we had—basically living money to take us all the way through the year until we started to see revenues coming in. It was a big risk. We thought we were going to ship in September of '92, but we didn't end up shipping until January of '93. In terms of most software, that was not really a big slip, but for us—four months of no additional money was scary."

One of their concerns was that they wanted to own the entire product, and so they wanted to avoid the pitfalls involved with getting money from venture capitalists. Michel recalls, "We knew that Journeyman was something we were going to take beyond even CD-ROM, and we wanted to own it in its entirety. It's why we set up the company the way that we did. We own the company and the company owns the entire product in full—every illustration, every design sketch, every piece of software that's related to it. Those were business decisions that we made to try and keep this company moving forward for many years to come. We realized if we were to go the route of investment banking or venture capital, we would lose control of what we wanted to do, and lose say in our own company. And that's one reason why we've struggled more than a lot of other companies, because a lot of people go the investment banking route. But in the end I think it's going to pay off for us."

Only a few members of the original team had previous experience working specifically on a CD-ROM project. Greg Uhler, whose background is in visual arts and computer media, had worked for Michel at MOOV Design and was the lead programmer on the project. Farshid Almassizadeh was a student at that time majoring in Cognitive Science at the University of California in San

Diego. He was also working part-time at GTE Interactive Media and was a good friend of Michel's. Farshid became the lead animator and also helped with the programming. But as Michel says, "Most of the other guys of the original six were fairly inexperienced. Everyone learned along the way. The best example is José Albanil, who is our lead 3-D modeler. We basically taught him how to model and at the same time we said 'Okay, now you're the lead modeler. Now do the entire game.' But he had an art background, and he had a very good eye for detail. So he just latched onto it and did it all very well."

Michel adds that they were careful to seek the advice of an attorney to write up a contract. He says, "We went to an attorney who was a family friend and she got us incorporated and set us up officially. We just moved forward from there. We didn't worry about it too much, though. There was a lot that was based on trust and friendship that went back for years. In early '94 we went in and properly restructured the entire company with local attorneys who really knew how to set us up, and we just reworked the paperwork. But in the beginning, we didn't have the money or the time to deal with it. So we did what we had to do to get moving and figured we'd deal with it later."

Although Michel put together a business plan, he looks back now and is amazed at how far off it was. The number of units that they were predicting they would need to sell in order to break even was 10,000. They have already sold more 150,000 units. Michel says, "It's been pretty phenomenal the way CD-ROM has taken off. I like to think sometimes that we've done so well because of foresight and planning but in all honesty, a lot of it is just being in the right place at the right time."

Michel explains one of the key events that led to the unexpected success of The Journeyman Project as well as other CD-ROM titles. "In 1992, Apple sold 50,000 CD-ROM drives, which was more than they had ever sold before. Most of the people in the industry were thinking that it was good but still not a very large installed base. We didn't really know enough about business. We thought 50,000 CD-ROM drives sounded like a lot and hoped we could sell the product to 20% of that market, in other words 10,000 units. So we just went ahead with those numbers in mind and did the product. But what happened in 1993 is that Apple made a commitment to sell 1 million CD-ROM drives. They ended up selling 1.2 million, and they didn't really tell anybody in advance. They just out of the blue decided to make Macintosh THE multimedia computer, and they sold all of their CD-ROM drives at cost just to get them everywhere. Based on that, all the PC manufacturers started doing similar things, and all of a sudden, all hardware manufacturers were putting CD-ROMs in their computers. And then people wanted to gobble up whatever software was good. And that's why you see not only Journeyman but also titles like Myst and The 7th Guest are having sales beyond their wildest dreams. Nobody really expected this."

Although it proved enormously successful, The Journeyman Project presented a number of challenges and difficulties in development. Michel says, "We are always fighting with the development software. That's the problem with working with off-the-shelf products. Director is good but you can only take it so far. I'm sure that Buried in Time [the sequel to Journeyman] will be the last Director-based product that we do, and it will only be Director-based on the Mac side. After that we're switching our whole programming staff over to C++. We're starting to use real tools and starting to build real software. We had some speed problems with Director on the Mac, and we worked with MacroMedia on them. They actually revved Director based on many of our suggestions, and we ended up getting a 300% increase in speed just from their help." The Windows version using Director presented even more problems. Michel expressed frustration with the speed of the first Windows version of Journeyman, but the recently released Turbo version was completely rewritten in C++, greatly increasing its performance.

Michel also explains that they had a lot of difficulty in getting The Journeyman Project published. "When we first went to publish Journeyman, everyone laughed at us because they didn't think there was a market for a CD-ROM game that required a color Mac and 8 MB of RAM. There was just not an installed base for it." They took the project to major publishers who showed no interest in the project. (Ironically, one of those publishers came out with a technologically similar title within nine months of the release of Journeyman.) Because of this, Presto Studios ended up publishing the product themselves, but found another publisher after nine months. Michel recalls, "Those first nine months when we self-published, it was just ridiculously distracting to everybody and we didn't get any production done. You've only got so much manpower." Michel explains that many developers are tempted to take on the publishing themselves by hiring more people. But he believes this is not a good choice, at least for Presto. "I'm looking at Sanctuary Woods [Presto Studios' current publisher] and how many people they have on the team prepared to launch Buried in Time, and it's something like a dozen people plus consultants. They're going to do it properly because of the budget they're spending, their experience, all kinds of things."

In fact, Michel is very excited about Buried in Time: The Journeyman Project 2, the sequel that picks up where the first story left off. "We have high expectations for the product. We really want to give The 11th Hour a run for its money. And we think that we're going to. I think that one of the big things Buried in Time has going for it is that we were able to keep the production costs low. Even though we're paying most of the people, we still pay some people on a royalty basis. We're getting Buried in Time done for less than a half million dollars whereas most titles these days are costing one to three million dollars to produce."

Michel also believes that Buried in Time will appeal to a much wider audience than The Journeyman Project, in part because its story will not be limited to high tech and sci-fi themes, which seem to appeal more to males. The sequel will also contain themes involving real historical events—something he believes will appeal more to females. In Buried in Time, the story picks up six months after the first one ends. Figure 8.4 on page 167 and Figure 8.5 on page 168 show scenes from the program. The user can visit a French medieval castle in 1204, or travel to Leonardo DaVinci's laboratory in Milan when he was building war machines and examine his works. Or the user can explore Mayan caverns in the Yucatan Peninsula.

Michel explains their shift in themes for Buried in Time. "There are an awful lot of sci-fi themes out there and while Journeyman is definitely still science fiction, we wanted to pull away from high-tech futuristic science fiction stories. So that's one of the reasons we wanted to go to real human history." Michel points to another reason as well. "We were looking at a title like Myst and we saw why it's so appealing. One of the reasons is it doesn't attack—it's not 'in your face' kind of stuff that a lot of CD-ROMs are. And we realized that it would be good to get some of that feel into the game. What we have now is a good marriage of both. We do have space stations and aliens and time travel, but we also have real history married with soft graphics."

Buried in Time is a three-CD set and is technologically much more advanced than Journeyman. Particularly impressive are the graphics. Michel elaborates, "It's amazing when you see the quality difference in the graphics. It's just unbelievable. Where before we were running step-by-step graphics with no in-between frames, now we're running full-motion video as you move through the environments. The production values and the technology have just gone through the roof in the two years since we did Journeyman. In this market, it's just incredible. The computers are faster and the tools are better." Michel is very enthusiastic about the release of Buried in Time. "I can't wait to show it to people. I've been seeing it for the last year. I knew what we were going to do and where we were going to go. We're still a few months from shipping, and I'm just pulling out my hair because I can't show this to somebody! It's going to be a tremendous surprise when we put it out and we're very excited about getting it out there." In fact, Buried in Time will be shipping in May of 1995.

There are other ways in which Buried in Time differs from the original title. Michel explains, "In the first game, in time travel you're tethered to the

Figure 8.4 *A scene from Buried in Time. Courtesy of Presto Studios, Inc.*

Pegasus Machine and have to use that as your home base. In the second game, you have a fully self-contained biosuit that you as the player are imagining wearing, and you also interact with other agents who are wearing their suits. So we went up to Hollywood and we got a company by the name of All Effects Company to build a custom biosuit for us. They are the same people that built the *Short Circuit* robot and *Teenage Mutant Ninja Turtles*. They built us an incredible costume with servo motors and bearings so you can spin the neck. We hired professional actors and actresses and we ended up doing a lot of blue-screen work—putting the suit into the environments, putting the medieval knights and actors in the environment. It was a lot of fun. And I finally got to draw on my film background."

Figure 8.5   *A scene from Buried in Time. Courtesy of Presto Studios, Inc.*

Some of the actors for Buried in Time were found through a local talent agency. Michel explains how the other actors were hired. "For the medieval actors, we went to a Renaissance Fair and hired some people for all of their armor and cool gear that they had. Then we dubbed in their voices later since they weren't great acting talents. But they came with armor and it saved us a lot of money." For the lead actress, they were able to get Michelle Scarabelli who has played in *Star Trek*, was the lead in *Alien Nation*, and is generally well known in science fiction circles. She also happens to be Michel's second cousin and was visiting for Christmas a year ago when Michel asked her if she would like to be in their next game.

The sequel involves many more live actors, requiring the team to shoot a lot of blue-screen video. Michel explains that they made a conscious decision to shoot with blue-screen. "The biosuit we had built looks like it's made out of metal. The problem is that metal is very reflective and when you put the green screen material up against the biosuit and other things, the green reflects in the object. The green has a lot higher reflectivity value so you tend to pick it up in the objects a lot more. We did a lot of tests and we realized it was best for us to shoot on blue. One of the other things we did is we used a very high-end professional compositing package to properly composite our blue-screen material into our world. Part of what the software does is it picks up that extra flash that's in the object and pulls it out of there. It's something that a lot of people overlook. You really need to use high-end tools to do this. And in all honesty, other than Buried in Time, the only other piece of software that I've ever seen that has properly done blue-screen is the new Wing Commander title."

Michel admits that much of his knowledge about shooting such video is his background in film. He points out that many of the people tackling these problems are programmers who are not up on the latest video production techniques. "They read the basic books that say 'Use the blue-screen and then pull the blue matte out' and they say 'Great, I can do that in programming.' But they don't realize that the blue-screen technique was invented back in the 70s and there have been a lot of improvements on it, and you need to track down the right software. To do it right, you need to buy a very expensive paint called *Ultimatte Blue* that is made specifically for keying."

Michel continues, "There's a difference when you look at a piece of video and can see that the guy is matted onto the background because he looks like a different channel." He compares this with good video in which the characters look as though they are truly part of the set. "That's the look we've been able to get with Buried in Time. It's more than just the blue wall. You also have to do interactive lighting and you have to do proper directing. There are a lot of things you have to pull off to make it work. You've got to convince people that you've built a real set." Such efforts to make Buried in Time so realistic have involved a team of 15 people with several additional consultants.

In keeping with their initial goal to take the Journeyman concept as far as they could, they are also pitching it as a movie and are talking to major companies in Hollywood, who want to make it into a $50 million production full feature film. As Michel says, "The material is there, the design is there, and the story is there. And if Buried in Time does well enough, there's a good chance that it will go." He pointed out that Cyan is pitching the movie rights to Myst and has already sold the book rights to produce three novels. The movie rights to Doom were just sold to Universal Studios, and Tom Berenger may play the lead. Ivan Reitman is to direct. "All of a sudden people are starting to rally around these computer games to turn them into movies. And I think that it could be that we're just going to find ourselves in the right place at the right time." Michel also feels that the Journeyman would work well as a television series because so much of it is based on individual scenarios. He says, "You could have one scenario per hour show, so it would fit really well."

Michel offers several guidelines for other developers based on their learning experiences. The first is to be as organized as possible. He says, "It's amazing how much stuff comes up later that you don't think about in advance, and you really need to think the whole project through. Know the overall picture, know what the goal is, know what you're trying to do, and have it all written down. The whole design document has to be as fleshed out as it possibly can be." He also cautions about underestimating development time, as has nearly every other developer I spoke with for this book. "Everyone in this industry underestimates on time. It happens to the best of us. No matter what you think it's going to take to get something done, you have to double it. I don't know of anyone who is successfully getting products out on time. It's just not happening. And it's weird because the more experienced you get, the more you begin to think you can nail it down. And the more you're always off by a factor of two."

Equally important to Michel is the need to be aware of designing for the direction the market is headed and where it will be when the product is going to be released. He says, "If you think a project is going to take a year to get done, then that means it's going to take two years to get done. Then you have to be designing a product that's going to be appropriate for the market in two years. And there's a big guessing game involved there. If you're putting out stuff with old technology, it's just not going to sell." And for the entrepreneur, Michel cautions to hire a good lawyer. Although it is costly to do so, he stresses the importance of protecting yourself and to be sure that you own your own content.

Michel expresses concern about the last minute panic that occurs in the software industry. But he sees this changing as people become more experienced, and he cites their interaction with Sanctuary Woods as a good example. "The Consumer Electronics Show is coming up soon and I've never felt more prepared for a show in my entire life. Sanctuary Woods was grilling us about CES in October, and they gave us ridiculous deadlines that were two months from what we thought they should have been. And all of a sudden now, we are at a point where we would normally be frantically adjusting our schedule to get ready for CES and I'm sitting here twiddling my thumbs about the show saying 'I think we're done.' I think that it's just a matter of getting experienced people involved in the business. The CEO of Sanctuary Woods and several other people there used to be at Macromedia. As companies get more and more experienced professionals involved, I think you're going to stop seeing products slip and you're going to stop seeing this mad rushing. Because it's not good. Personally, my stress level gets ridiculous. It's learning the proper way to get these things out."

Michel relays their own early experience with panic prior to the MacWorld at which they were introducing The Journeyman Project. They were just approaching the completion of the project and were, as Michel puts it, "all burning the candle at both ends." Michel did the final walk-through of the disc on Christmas Eve of 1992. He says, "The product was supposed to launch on January 6 in San Francisco, and we obviously had horrible problems trying to get the packaging and the discs pressed because of Christmas and New Years. And it got so close and so tight to the wire, it was incredibly stressful." They had set up a 20'×10' booth at MacWorld in San Francisco on the 4th and 5th and had spent in the neighborhood of $20,000 to launch the product. But still, they did not have the discs in hand. Michel says, "The discs arrived at 9:30 in the morning the day that the show opened at 10:00. So I don't think we could have cut it any tighter than that. I mean, the discs were airlifted in—Federal Express wasn't even going to make it early enough. They were custom airlifted to us from the night before. It was really wild and our hearts were just pounding." Michel laughs at the memory, "Then it was such a release that it was done, and we just wanted to let it all out and relax. But a half an hour later, there were swarms of people and it was just great having all these people lined up. We sold about a thousand discs at the show. It was a great kickoff!"

But even then, Michel was not to relax for sometime afterwards. "We had talked to a number of Japanese agents and we had finally cut a deal with an agent. So on the 6th of January, the discs arrived at the show. On the 8th, our agent told me at the show that he wanted to fly me to Japan on the 10th. So I drove from San Francisco to San Diego on the 9th and I unpacked and packed at the same time and then I was on a plane to Tokyo to go sign the Japanese rights to the product. It was a wild month. And definitely something that I'll remember my entire life. We've had such a great relationship with the Japanese." The company they signed on with was Bandai, the second largest toy manufacturer in the world. "Bandai is such a great company to work with. They realized that it really wasn't all about the money for us, and that it was really a bunch of young people who were really into it for the experience. When we signed with them, we became Bandai's first CD-ROM product of all time. As kickoff for them with the media, they decided to fly our entire company to Tokyo. So one month later, all of us at Presto were flying to Tokyo all expenses paid, and we were there for MacWorld Tokyo in February. It was just so great. This thing has just opened up so many doors."

The 7th Guest and The 11th Hour

When The 7th Guest was released in April of 1993, it was the first CD-ROM title to combine full-motion video using professional actors and 3-D computer graphics to create a haunted mansion so realistic that it became an immediate best seller. In fact, over a million copies of The 7th Guest have been sold throughout the world, and it has grossed more than $43 million in retail. It has received numerous awards including the 1994 NewMedia's INVISION Gold Award for Adventure Games and Gold Award for Technical and Creative Excellence, the Golden Triad Award from *PC Games* magazine, and the 1993 MVP Award from *PC Computing* magazine. Its sequel The 11th Hour, which is scheduled to be released in early 1995, will surpass The 7th Guest in terms of technology, visual and audio quality, and very likely, sales.

The 7th Guest (see Figure 8.6 on page 173) begins with video segments that portray the background of Henry Stauf, a crazed man with a shady past who rose to fame and fortune by creating mystical toys. But the story becomes increasingly bizarre as we see that the children owning the toys begin dying mysterious deaths. Stauf abruptly closes his toy business and becomes a recluse in the eerie mansion he has built. Years later he invites six guests to attend dinner for reasons none of them understands, but which become revealed during the game by solving a series of puzzles located in the different rooms in the house (see Figure 8.7 on page 174, Figure 8.8 on page 175, and Figure 8.9 on page 176). The player assumes the role of Ego, a spirit who moves through the house attempting to solve the mystery. Haunting music adds to the suspense, as do the animated icons such as a skull with a pulsating brain, clattering teeth, and a skeletal hand that beckons the user to explore the mansion.

Its sequel, called The 11th Hour, picks up the story 70 years later. In this game, the user plays the role of an investigative reporter, Carl Denning, who is searching for his producer who has disappeared during an investigation of a murder that has taken place in Henry Stauf's hometown. The deteriorating mansion appears to be connected in some way to the murders occurring in the small town. Live-action video is used in a feature-length movie that includes a cast of 18 characters. The game is much larger than The 7th Guest and involves much more sophisticated technologies. Figure 8.10 on page 177 and Figure 8.11 on page 177 illustrate some scenes from the sequel.

Both games were developed by Trilobyte, Inc., located in Medford, Oregon. Graeme Devine, cofounder and President of Trilobyte, was born in Scotland

Figure 8.6   *A scene from The 7th Guest. The ghostly appearance of the characters adds to the eeriness of the game. Courtesy of Trilobyte, Inc.*

and raised in England. His start in the computer industry began when he worked on British versions of Atari video games. He managed to get expelled from high school because he took a week off from school to finish one of those programming projects. He started two software companies in England before joining Virgin Games in 1987 to be their Vice President of R&D. The other cofounder of Trilobyte is Rob Landeros, who is also its Creative Director. His early interest in art led to his drawing underground comics in Berkeley. He later went to art school in Los Angeles and found the Amiga to be the perfect vehicle for expressing his artistic talents. Rob worked for Cinemaware, creating the

Figure 8.7   *A view of the mansion's spacious foyer. Courtesy of Trilobyte, Inc.*

graphics for Defender of the Crown and other PC games. Rob joined Virgin Games in 1988 to be their Art Director.

It was while Graeme and Rob were at Virgin Games that they began to formulate the concept for The 7th Guest. It all began in 1990 in an airport coffee shop where they decided they wanted to create a game about a haunted house. They purchased Word for Windows and began writing the script for the story. They knew that multimedia and CD-ROM were the directions they wanted to go, but unfortunately Virgin was moving increasingly in the direction of game cartridges. Still, they had hopes of convincing Virgin to go along with the project and spent hours writing up a proposal—"a work of art," as Graeme says—to present to the head of Virgin Games, Martin Alper. Shortly after he was presented with their proposal, Martin invited Graeme and Rob to have

Figure 8.8 *A view of the music room. Courtesy of Trilobyte, Inc.*

lunch. There, he announced to them that he didn't think their futures were with Virgin, and that they should set up their own company. Obviously, Graeme and Rob were stunned. But Virgin was very interested in the project and offered to publish it after Graeme and Rob wrote the program.

And so in 1991, the two of them set out to start their own company—Trilobyte. Although Virgin was hoping the pair would remain closeby in southern California, Graeme and Rob decided they wanted to move to Oregon instead. They found an office in Jacksonville, Oregon, where they began working on The 7th Guest. (They later moved the company to Medford.) They chose the PC platform over the Mac for their initial work, mainly because of their familiarity with PCs and also because they knew they weren't going to use Director (which was strictly a Mac product at that time). In fact, they didn't use Macs

Figure 8.9   *A view of the mansion's bathroom. Courtesy of Trilobyte, Inc.*

until quite late in the development of the program. Graeme says, "It's kind of funny because Jacksonville is the town that Apple adopted as its 'corporate town.' It gave all the businesses in Jacksonville a Macintosh to use. But we were using all PCs. I think that Apple was kind of frustrated that there was this multimedia company doing this multimedia project all on PCs." Graeme laughs, "So they didn't give us a Macintosh."

They have recently begun developing on Unix systems, which was an important decision for The 11th Hour. As Graeme relays, "The 11th Hour is about 12 times as big as The 7th Guest. So we made a shift over to using Unix systems to actually deal with most of the data preparation on The 11th Hour." They have been careful to develop proprietary software that is portable to

Figure 8.10 *A scene from The 11th Hour. Courtesy of Trilobyte, Inc.*

Figure 8.11 *A scene from The 11th Hour. Courtesy of Trilobyte, Inc.*

other platforms. Graeme explains, "We actually converted the player across to the Mac. The data is exactly the same and the scripts are exactly the same. So that's one of the powerful parts of our development environment. And actually we just pulled that player across to the 3DO as well. It took about three months to get it tuned and working on the 3DO, so it's very, very quick." Rob adds, "There's a term out there called *platform agnostics* and that's what we've tried to be. We were tied in there for a little while on the PC side, not that we wanted to be. But now we're running under Unix and our tools are in a state that they're so easily portable that we truly are platform independent."

One of the most important tools Graeme developed is GROOVIE (which stands for Graeme's object oriented viewer) that allows for the insertion of video and audio clips as well as the control of animation. GROOVIE3 is a more sophisticated version of the tool and provides even more photorealistic video sequences in The 11th Hour. The sequel contains about 65 minutes of full-motion video consisting of nearly 200,000 frames and is accompanied by true MIDI sound. The program takes up 134 GB uncompressed. Obviously, data compression was a major challenge. Early in the development of The 11th Hour, they found that a single video frame took a full hour to compress. At that rate, they knew it would take years to compress all the data. So they set out to develop a compression tool, called Encode, that provides them with compression ratios far greater than those possible with MPEG, and it does so without the need for the user to have special codec hardware. Using Encode, they were able to fit the final product onto two CD-ROM discs.

Other software used to develop The 7th Guest and The 11th Hour include 3-D Studio, Autodesk Animator Pro, Photoshop, PhotoStyler and Image Alchemy. Although the company currently employs about 35 people, Graeme and Rob were the only members of the team when they began working on The 7th Guest. During the early stages of development, Graeme was the only programmer working on the project while Rob concentrated on the graphics. They point out that the program for The 7th Guest is actually fairly small. But the amount of data involving graphics, sound, and music was enormous (though not nearly as large as they later created for its sequel). They soon hired another full-time employee, Robert Stein, to work on the graphics. Others were hired on a part-time basis, including a producer named Dave Luehmann who helped Matthew Costello write the script. In all, there were four 3-D Studio artists who worked on the project. Although they hired other programmers to help out, Graeme laughs, "They didn't last long. They went crazy and left."

They originally estimated that it would take 18 months to develop The 7th Guest. It ended up taking them closer to two and a half years to complete. As Graeme says, "Had we known how hard it was going to be we would have reconsidered a little bit ahead of time what we were doing." When they realized how much more time would be needed for development, they were faced with seeking additional funds. These were provided by a major gaming company, who didn't want them to create a version that would run on the platform of a leading competitor who had a CD-ROM player. Graeme says, "They were there with their checkbook because they didn't have a CD-ROM player."

Not only did the project take much more time than they estimated, it also presented other unforeseen problems. One was the color of the blue-screen they used to shoot the live video. Graeme explains, "The blue-screen we used wasn't quite blue. It had some red in it. That caused a lot of problems getting the red out of the image. So we wrote some specialized software that got rid of most of the red, but we had to touch up every single frame (about 27,000 frames in all). But we didn't want to have to touch up this halo around the characters, which would have taken forever. So we 'featured' it. We said, 'We have these halos. We've added in these great special effects'." And, indeed it did add to the ghostly appearance of the characters. But, they avoided this mistake in developing The 11th Hour.

The video in The 11th Hour is extremely impressive. Not only does it play at 30 frames per second (versus 15 fps in The 7th Guest), they used some different techniques while shooting the video. Traditionally, composite scenes shot against blue-screen use a camera in a fixed position, resulting in video shot from only one angle. For The 11th Hour, the scenes were shot from several angles. One of the scenes in a 3-D room was shot from 52 angles.

They also used some innovative approaches to animation that take into account how the human eye responds to images. They explain, "The Encode compression method in The 11th Hour allows for the efficient mapping of components of an animation that remain constant from one frame to the next. In essence, Encode hides from the human eye the fact that the program is making a screen when new pieces of the visual image are added to the frame. With Encode, the final animations of The 11th Hour look to players like 'real' rather than computer-generated movements." By exploiting these physiological aspects, they were able to skew the original compression algorithms toward the sensitivities of the human eye, thereby optimizing the visual signal-to-noise ratio and minimizing artifacts. The resulting images are bright and consistent with lifelike colors.

The 7th Guest used 22 KHz 8-bit mono sound that was digitally generated. The composer for the original score was George Alistair Sanger, nicknamed "The Fat Man." He has composed music for more than 80 popular computer games including Wing Commander and Loom. He creates the music using a Macintosh system connected to a synthesizer and includes additional musicians in the pieces. George also created the soundtrack for The 11th Hour, although the sound samples in the sequel are 16-bit stereo and the music player was upgraded to a waveform player, resulting in much richer sound quality.

The actors for the games have worked at the local Shakespearian theater in Medford, which holds an annual festival attended by a multitude of actors and screenwriters. Although they were experienced actors, they had not worked on a project involving blue-screen and video production for the computer. Graeme points out, "The whole interactive realm is very new to actors, and they're very inquisitive. When they come into the office and see themselves on the computer screen, they think that's the neatest thing in the world." In fact, it was such a new experience, one of the actors fell through the blue-screen immediately after being warned not to during the filming for "The 7th Guest." Rob recalls, "He was walking off the scene and he had to fall down, and we said 'Okay, now be careful not to fall through the blue paper.' And on the next take he went right through it."

Some of the actors who were in The 7th Guest made cameo reappearances in The 11th Hour, although the sequel is a contemporary story that takes place 70 years after the first story. And although it involves the same mansion, the rooms look very different. As Graeme says, "Seventy years has not been kind to the house." Rob adds, "In The 11th Hour, there are some new secret passages that weren't discovered the first time out, so the player can discover those. Also in The 7th Guest, the player was supposed to be a spirit so he could actually travel down the pool table pocket and end up in this oven in the kitchen. Well our character this time is a mortal, so he can't do that kind of stuff. He has to find an actual passageway."

The script for the two games was written by Matthew Costello, an award-winning author of science fiction and mystery novels. For The 11th Hour, Matthew worked closely with director and writer David Wheeler. Their goal for the sequel was to create an interactive thriller with multiple endings. The puzzles in The 11th Hour add to its interactivity. When the player enters a room, he or she must find a "hot spot," which is a puzzle. When the puzzle is solved, other objects in the room are brought to life. By selecting the right object, the player is given a hint about the story.

Because both games involve a complex story and challenging problem solving, they are targeted to a mature audience. Graeme points out, "I think that we tried to aim the product squarely at normal human beings who go to the theater, watch television, and read books rather than the normal game playing market which is the 14–17 year old male. The problem we have is that most people who go to the software store to pick up a product are 14–17 year olds and they want to buy games that they like. It's hard for us to find our exact target audience right now. Cartridges for Nintendo systems are shoot and twitch games for kids. They do really well. They sell millions of units and there are certainly no complaints about that portion of the business."

Rob adds, "On our side of the interactive entertainment business, which is the PC side, it involves a different type of approach. The game designers are a little more cerebral. It's a little more sedate entertainment involving a little more strategy and thinking. These designers have always looked around and said 'Gee, computer games are so much fun. Why aren't we a bigger market?' And there's a lot of complaint about not having tapped into the mainstream and doing as well as other forms of entertainment. The reason I think is in large part because it's a niche market and a niche audience, and not everybody is a computer nerd or a fantasy role-playing geek. Strong language, but there is a smaller market for that kind of entertainment. Not everybody can handle it. If your product is a little too complex to get through a game, it's not much fun. It appeals to a smaller group. What we're trying to do is just appeal to, as Graeme says, the normal, average guy out there watching TV whose idea of interactivity is not that high."

Both feel strongly that good multimedia entertainment involves quality and care in the design. Graeme says, "All too often you see a badly designed product that has shoddy thought applied to a shoddy interface, shoddy design, and bad characters. The quality of the product is not representative of where it should be. I think a lot of the current CD software is very shoddy." Rob points out that many people think that all they need is the right hardware and software to develop a quality product. He says, "It's very possible to put together a piece of software using those tools but you have to have good content and put a lot of thought into it. People expect a lot of information in these things. And there are those products out there that are fine and work well. But a lot of it is shovelware and people see through that right away."

Rob continues, "Adding sound isn't going to improve a floppy disk game and make it what they're expecting out of CD-ROM. I think what people expect is high-quality production. It takes a lot of data to make it possible to present things that are more televisual—in other words the quality of video presentations you might expect to see on your television. The 7th Guest was one of the first projects to realize that. But we had to take the time and the money to present it that way to fulfill those expectations. I think a lot of people are mad at us for raising the ante. Our little $100,000 budgets aren't going to cut it anymore. Wing Commander is coming out—a $3-million production. It's a little scary even for us. There has to be a balance with the return on investment. It's kind of a juggling act right now."

Although Virgin provided the startup funds for The 7th Guest, there were times when Graeme and Rob were concerned that they might not be able to complete the project. Graeme says, "There were times when we didn't know if we were going to be able to pay our mortgages or credit cards because basically halfway through The 7th Guest, Virgin gave up and said that's it. They just gave up and it was up to Rob and me to carry the rest of the project." They admit that the major mistake they made was in their estimation of the time it would take to produce the amount of data in the program. Graeme says, "We see that happening with almost every other CD title out there—even with the larger companies. People really underestimate how hard it is to move all that data around and how many manhours it really takes to make a good product."

Rob recalls, "We almost died making this product. Especially Graeme who had to pull the whole thing together at the end. Being on the art production side, you can walk away from the project a little earlier than the technical side. Graeme was in there, and he looked pretty bad somedays." The two laugh while Graeme adds, "I always remember right before the end of The 7th Guest, I'd been at the office for most of the week straight, and I remember Rob saying 'Go home! You need some sleep.' It was about four in the morning, and I could see behind my head watching myself type. Then, I'm going home and I only live five minutes down the road, and I'm driving home in my car. Several times I was totally convinced there was someone in the backseat of my car. I would stop my car and get out and look. And then I was driving again and I thought 'Wow, there's something in the road,' and I'd stop my car and look. I was just so tired I could barely make it home, and I was quite lucky I didn't end up in the ditch that night."

Rob says, "After The 7th Guest came out, a lot of publishers and developers looked at it and said, 'Okay, that's cool. We'll go do one of our own,' and at the time I was thinking, 'Boy, you know, you should be calling us for help.' We thought that they'd want to work with us. We spent three hard years working out these problems. But that's the arrogance of a lot of companies, and of course if they have an idea, they're going to have their own crack at it. My advice at the time was, 'Hey, if you're going to do it, you'd better realize what you're getting into. It's not that easy. If you want to talk to me, talk to me. I'll tell you about some of the problems we faced—mass storage, moving around data, and handling all that.' It's a different level."

They also point to the importance of producers. Graeme says, "Good producers make a real big difference as well. Dave Luehmann was a good producer on the project. He really brought everything together and was in there toughing it out with the rest of us. He made sure that we kept on track. When we couldn't see our own problems anymore because we were so close to them, he was able to drag us out and show us what the big picture looked like. I can't say enough about having a good producer."

The small company that started out with only two employees has quickly grown into one of the leaders in the development of interactive CD-ROM entertainment and now employs about 35 people. They currently have five additional titles in progress. One is a third game in The 7th Guest trilogy. They are also coming out with a product using similar game design philosophies. Rob says, "It still has to do with ghosts but it's a very lighthearted approach—very fun and comedic." And they are also producing a title with a different theme—office politics. It involves character interaction between people with different types of personalities, and the object is to rise to higher levels in a corporation. Rob points out, "It's a very satirical look at the business world."

The enormous impact The 7th Guest was to have on the industry was apparent at its first public showing. When The 7th Guest debuted at the Computer Electronics Show, the crowd of people wanting to see the program was so big that the booth was actually leaning over. Some of those who looked at the program were Steven Spielberg's agent and someone from Microsoft. After the show, Microsoft called Trilobyte and told them that Bill Gates wanted to demo it at the Microsoft Multimedia Conference the next month. They asked Trilobyte if they could make a Windows version, and they [Trilobyte] replied "Sure." Graeme recalls, "It seemed like a pretty simple thing to us. It had to run in Windows. It couldn't run in DOS, and The 7th Guest is a DOS game." Microsoft provided the programmer who worked with the code to ensure that it ran in Windows. Because the programmer was in Washington, all the data for the demo had to be transferred via modem. The deadline became so tight that in the end, in order to make it in time for the conference, they had to get the final data to Microsoft on the same day, which FedEx couldn't do. So they purchased the only high-speed modem in Medford to transfer the program— something that took nine hours. As Graeme happily points out, Microsoft paid for the phone call.

Further Reading

Bank, David. 1994. "Coming Attraction: 'Hollywood Meets High Technology.'" *San Jose Mercury News* (February 14): 1D.

Dvorak, John C. 1993. "Game Machines: Trend or Fiasco?" *PC Magazine* (November 9): 93.

Evans, David. 1994. "Gore Wars: Is the Dark Side Winning the War for the Home PC?" *Marketing Computers* (December): 22.

Graves, Gaye. 1994. "Tinseltown in Cyberspace." *NewMedia Magazine* (August): 32.

"Interactive games." 1994. *Computer Conference Analysis Newsletter* (April 1): 9.

Lambert, Sandra. 1994. "Developer Beware: Interactive TV's Raw Deal." *NewMedia Magazine* (August): 17.

Langberg, Mike. 1994. "Nintendo Rejects CDs for Cartridges." *San Jose Mercury News* (February 11): 1E.

Levander, Michelle. 1994. "Want to Perform in a Video Game? Get a Union Card." *San Jose Mercury News* (January 26): 826.

McCarthy, Shawn P. 1993. "Virtual Reality Isn't All Just Fun and Games; Sandia Lab Uses Real-world Situations for its Simulations in Computer-Human Interaction." *Government Computer News* (September 13): 70.

Mitchell, Gabrielle, and Kevin Ferguson. 1994. "Movie, Music Moguls Ink Interactive Deals: Fox, MCA, Sony and BMG Ready Multimedia SKUs from New Units." *Computer Retail Week* (May 23): 5.

Mohan, Suruchi. 1994. "Users Eye Game Technology to Spice up Service." *Computerworld* (October 10): 24.

Rahlmann, Reed Kirk. 1994. "Characters in Search of a CD-ROM." *NewMedia Magazine* (July): 16.

Reveaux, Tony. 1994. "Let the Games Begin." *NewMedia Magazine* (January): 48.

Sandler, Corey. 1993. "The Game of Life." *PC World* (August): M89.

Silverthorne, Sean. 1994. "Merger Mania: The EA/Brøderbund Deal Shows the Dynamics of Entertainment Software are Changing. Better Partner Up." *PC Week* (February 28): A1.

Stefanac, Suzanne. 1993. "Interactive Hollywood." *NewMedia Magazine* (August): 40.

Wolfe, Alexander. 1994. "That's Intellitainment." *Electronic Engineering Times* (June 20): 51.

Worthington, Paul. 1993. "Software Developer or Hollywood Studio? The Line Blurs Further." *PC World* (August): M7.

ADAPTING BOOKS TO INTERACT

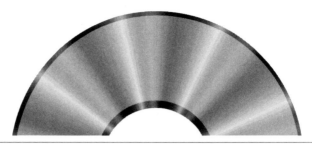

Introduction

There are those who argue that, although it makes sense to provide reference material in electronic format, books that are intended to be read are not well-suited to the computer. Indeed, some of their reasoning is valid. It is still more difficult to read text on a computer screen than it is on a page. Most people do not want to sit at a computer to read an electronic novel, opting instead for a comfortable chair. And many users were turned off by early attempts in which text was simply placed onto a CD-ROM, offering the reader no advantages over a printed version. After all, why sit at a computer and be forced to scroll through pages and pages of text?

But there are many advantages of an electronic book that incorporates inter-activity and multimedia elements. Like electronic reference books (discussed in Chapter 6), the user can quickly locate keywords and topics and can easily jump to related topics using hyperlinks. But the real advantages lie in the richer environment provided by graphics, video, and sound. Imagine reading a novel set in a country unfamiliar to you. By clicking on the country's name, you may bring up background information on the location and its culture, and view photographs or video footage taken in that region. You are given an instant geography lesson that enriches your understanding of the story being told.

Electronic books generally fall into two categories: those that have been adapted from a printed version and those that have been created specifically for the computer. Many printed books are good candidates for electronic adaptation. An example is a children's book because it tends to be very visually oriented and usually contains more graphics than text. The various graphic elements can be brought to life through animation, while sound effects and music add to the experience. Young children can learn to read by clicking on text and hearing how the word is pronounced. None of these features is possible with a printed version.

Literary classics may also be greatly enhanced by the addition of multimedia elements. The user may want to read about the author's background and societal environment to better understand the message being conveyed in the story. By providing the user with illustrations, photographs, and video clips explaining various aspects of the book, the user comes away with a much deeper appreciation of it. And the use of music can help create a "mood" appropriate to the story. I personally would have appreciated more of the literary classics I had to read in school if they had included elements that helped me better understand the era (and hence the characters) in which the book had been written.

Increasingly, we are seeing books created for the interactive environment, particularly fiction. Such interactive fiction (also called hyperfiction) usually has several different endings to the story. One reader may come away from the book with a completely different perspective than another because of selecting alternative outcomes to situations, or choosing to follow the story from a different character's point of view. Hyperfiction is nonlinear, and in some cases there is no real beginning or ending to the story. A well-known example is *Victory Garden,* which is a fictionalized story about the Persian Gulf War. The "book" is stored in HyperCard stacks that contain a maze of events and characters. Writing the interactive novel requires a different approach from that used in linear storytelling, and authors are having to learn a new way of writing a novel.

All of these examples illustrate how interactivity and multimedia provide the electronic book with many advantages over printed versions. Even though the user may not yet be enamored with the idea of reading a book on a computer screen, even that is likely to change as screen resolution continues to improve. The traveler will find it much more convenient to bring along a single CD-ROM disk containing a hundred books rather than pack a half-dozen printed copies. And now with the availability of portable flat-screen players, a person actually can curl up in a chair and read a good electronic book.

Overview of Profiles

The titles I chose to profile here involve very different types of book adaptations aimed at different age groups. Both illustrate how an electronic version of a book can offer much more to the reader than the original one.

Living Books is a series of interactive children's books based on best-selling stories written by Mercer Mayer, Marc Brown, and others. All of the books are very visually oriented with brightly colored graphics and delightful animations.

The Essential Frankenstein is an electronic adaptation of classic literature that effectively combines all the various multimedia elements to enrich the reader's understanding of the original story. Its development is compared with that of another title, called *Mark Twain,* which contains all the literary works of the great author. Also included is a look into their recently released *Slaughterhouse Five.*

Living Books

I can't look at any of the Living Books interactive stories without laughing at the unexpected antics of the characters and "props" in the stories—squirrels that pop out of trees, tap dancing starfish, a picket fence that can be played like a xylophone, and a garden with singing tomatoes. Every page in a Living Book is pure enchantment. Although intended for children, the software is equally entertaining for adults. Many of my friends have asked to see one of the Living Books, and although they initially plan to spend just a few minutes with it they inevitably get hooked and stay for an hour or more. It's almost impossible to leave a page in the book before you've clicked on every "object" to see what happens. Obviously many other people share my enthusiasm. The Living Books are some of the hottest selling childrens' software on the market. And they have received over 45 awards for categories including technical and design excellence, education, innovation, and entertainment.

Living Books is a company jointly owned by Random House and Brøderbund Software. Random House was founded in 1925 and is one of the largest general trade book publishers in the world. It currently has ten divisions, one of which is the Juvenile and Merchandise Group, a leader in children's book publishing. This division includes Random House Children's Media, which encompasses children's projects involving audio, video, and CD-ROM. Brøderbund Software, founded in 1980, has been a leader in the development of consumer software—particularly children's multimedia titles. Their award-winning software includes the Carmen Sandiego series and Myst. In 1993, the two companies formed a joint venture—Living Books—to develop and market multimedia storybooks for children.

Most of the Living Books are based on published works. Examples include *Just Grandma and Me,* a multimedia adaptation of Mercer Mayer's popular children's book, and *Arthur's Teacher Trouble,* and *Arthur's Birthday,* based on Marc Brown's best sellers. Others are original stories written specifically for the Living Books series. For example, *Harry and the Haunted House* is a tradi-

Figure 9.1 *This is Harry D. Rabbit from the Living Book,* Harry and the Haunted House. *Courtesy of Living Books.*

tional book that was written and illustrated with the interactivity of the software in mind (Figure 9.1 shows one of the characters from the book). *The Tortoise and the Hare,* based on Aesop's fable, was rewritten for the series.

In a typical Living Book, an opening screen (accompanied by some lighthearted music) shows a character from the book who introduces him- or herself and the "book." The reader may either listen to the story being read or "play" inside the story (see Figure 9.2 on page 190). Although having the story read may be preferable for very young children, the latter option is eminently more fun. Each screen depicts a page from the book (see Figure 9.3 on page 191, Figure 9.4 on page 192, and Figure 9.5 on page 193 for some examples), and nearly every object on the screen may be clicked on, resulting in that object coming to animated life. You may also choose to have the narratives read in English or Spanish. *Just Grandma and Me* even offers a Japanese narrative.

The creative mind that led to the Living Books series is Mark Schlichting, Product Designer and Creative Director at Living Books. Mark admits that he loved to watch cartoons as a child, an activity that led his parents to ask "What good will watching all these cartoons do for you?" As Mark points out

Figure 9.2   *In the Living Books series, the user is given the option to listen to the book read or to play and interact with the program. Courtesy of Living Books.*

now, "Little did they know." Mark studied painting and graphic design at California State University at Hayward and animation at San Francisco State University. As a natural extension of his creative work, he also wrote stories and drew cartoon characters for his children. He later formed his own production company to create video and special effects, and eventually decided that he wanted to use his skills to tell stories on the computer.

Mark initially freelanced as a computer artist for Brøderbund Software as well as other companies over nine years ago. He had the idea for Living Books before CD-ROM technology had hit its stride. He knew he wanted to take the concept to a software company that would understand the need to balance entertainment and education. "You can have an educational product that kids

Figure 9.3   *A screen display from* Just Grandma and Me. *Courtesy of Living Books.*

won't play with. If it isn't entertaining enough, then it doesn't empower them to explore," says Mark. "The Carmen series was just starting to take off, and I really felt that Brøderbund was the place to bring the idea. I got hired here as an animator and then talked them into letting me do a prototype—and away we went." Mark started working full time for Brøderbund in 1989.

What drew Mark into the Living Books concept was not only his interest in graphic design and animation, but also the fact that he is the father of three boys. One summer day, his middle son and a couple of his friends rented a Nintendo game with no manual. As Mark describes, "They launched off into this game that they'd never seen before. In three hours they had gotten to the 52nd level and I was thinking, 'What an incredible ability these games have to draw their attention!' Just try and get your kids to focus this much on their

Figure 9.4   *A screen display from* The Tortoise and the Hare. *Courtesy of Living Books.*

homework. On the other hand, I was amazed at the level of critical thinking skills being used in an environment where there was absolutely no content. So I was thinking that you need to use this in an environment that *has* content. Here was something that kept three ten-year olds' attention for three hours solid. I thought that was impressive."

"Our first story, *Just Grandma and Me,* was designed for four- and five-year olds because that's the age when they're making the cognitive link between the graphic of a word and its sound. It turns out that children as young as two use Living Books regularly. They also like the ability to explore at their own speed where there's no pressure. The environment offers a lot of instantaneous, positive feedback that empowers them to continue to explore."

Figure 9.5   *A screen display from* Arthur's Birthday. *Courtesy of Living Books.*

Teachers find the Living Books to be motivational as well as educational and entertaining. Mark says, "I had a teacher tell me that they had shown *Arthur's Teacher Trouble* in the classroom before school let out for the summer. And when school started again in the fall, several of the students said to the teacher, 'Did you know there are more Arthur books?' They had bought and read all of the Arthur books during the summer based on the motivation they got from the CD-ROM. The reason I got into this whole thing is that I really want to make a difference in the future of education. For me that's really the payoff."

The Living Books have proven to be equally effective with children having very different learning skills. As Mark points out, "I've gotten some wonderful

Figure 9.6   *A screen display from* Harry and the Haunted House. *Courtesy of Living Books.*

letters from parents of children who are autistic or learning disabled. One couple told us about their daughter who has Down's Syndrome who learned to read with *Just Grandma and Me.* Another mother related that her child was very withdrawn but learned to speak mimicking the program and now deals with the whole world as though it's a 'clickable' item. Kids see computers as people. It's very interesting."

Mark explains that teachers told him they wanted a program that kids can run themselves, that requires little supervision so that the teacher can spend time with children in the classroom who need more personal attention. He says, "The Living Books were designed to be as easy to use as CD audio. All you have to do is put your disk in, double-click on an icon and it launches.

When you click on anything on the page, you get an instantaneous reaction. That's really important because kids won't wait. After a second they begin clicking again. They expect the computer to act like the real world. That really influenced our design. We wanted to make it simple and straightforward and easy to use so that even kids who can't read can use it."

Mark recalls the "evolution" of the CD-ROM industry and its impact on multimedia. "When I looked at the market in 1988, I saw that CD-ROM had this incredible potential, and everyone expected it to happen. But it wasn't happening and there was a reason for that. The manufacturers all saw CD-ROM as a storage device. What we wanted was the ability to use all the space on a CD-ROM and have it perform just like a regular floppy disk–based game. With floppies, we were really limited in the amount of graphics, animation, and sound we could put into a program. Then suddenly with CD-ROM, we could expand to 600 MB. At first, everyone felt they had to fill the whole disc with things like the works of Shakespeare, the encyclopedia, the *Whole Earth Catalog*."

Mark's idea was use early CD-ROM technology for something beyond storage. He saw it as the perfect player for multimedia. He says, "We had an excellent programming team here, and over the course of about a year we were able to create a platform-independent engine so we could develop software for the Mac and Windows at the same time. It also allowed us to stream the audio simultaneous to the animation, and nobody that we knew of had done that before. When people see the Living Books play, they look at it and say, 'Oh I could do that' because it looks very simple. That's the whole idea—it looks simple and straightforward." But as Mark explains, when others tried to duplicate the Living Books, they realized that it wasn't at all easy to do. "I think that stalled a lot of our major competition for the first couple of years because they hadn't thought far enough ahead to see the real challenges involved." *Just Grandma and Me* was bundled with many CD-ROM drives and was even used by several CD-ROM manufacturers for testing. Mark recalls, "We were trying to set a standard for multimedia, and in many ways we became an early ad hoc standard."

Most development is done on a Mac and ported to Windows, although some titles have been ported to CD-I and Tandy's VIS. A Living Book disc typically contains both the Mac and Windows versions. This is important because of the limited shelf space in retail stores, especially since the explosion of multimedia titles. And although bookstores have begun to carry some interactive books such as the Living Books, they are not yet providing very much space for multimedia.

The production team at Living Books consists of about 20 people. Part of their strategy in creating the Living Books series was to develop a "program-merless" product—one that could be readily changed for a new book and not require any major reprogramming. Because of this, most of the project team consists of artists and animators. Several are taught animation on the computer after joining the company. As Mark explains, "The industry is still very new. Those of us who have been in the industry longer are almost all generalists who have done a wide variety of things. This works really well because it all comes together with multimedia. I'm part actor, part painter, part dancer, and I think that's true of most of the team. It keeps our work interesting. We have a love of the power of technology. It really amplifies our ability to create."

Mark describes his own attraction to computerized animation. "I learned to do traditional animation. You'd start with pencil sketches and then you test them on film. You'd get them back after a couple of weeks and try to fix what was wrong. Then you'd do another version, and maybe you got far enough along that you'd ink your characters on animation cells and then shoot the animation again on film. Months and months would go by before you actually saw your original idea working as animation." Mark explains how the computer facilitates the animation process. "On the computer, I can sit down, sketch out an idea, draw it, animate it, record a sound and attach it to the animation. The same day I can see the whole thing and know if it worked or not. You have this nearly instant gratification."

Because the members of the team contribute so much of their own creativity, they have a sense of ownership in the project. Although they hire outside talent, Mark points out that they try to keep the production in-house as much as possible. Because most of the sound designers are also musicians, they play the music, sing many of the songs, and create the special sound effects. Marks says, "Our musicians are wonderful and add a lot of emotional content." Almost everyone on the production team has been a voice in a Living Book. Mark was the voice of Grandma in *Just Grandma and Me,* and much to my delight he began talking in Grandma's voice during our interview. But Mark points out that they also use children's voices. "We always use real children for the main characters because kids have a real spontaneous feeling that adults never can imitate."

Mark wrote the script for *The Tortoise and the Hare* and admits that he dreamed several of the pages in the book (such as the one shown in Figure 9.4) while he was asleep. Other aspects of the creative process involved "work" that would appear to be humorous to many. "Imagine a job where what you have to do all day is figure out funny walks for tortoises, songs for singing doorknobs, and dances for starfish." Mark laughs, "It's a tough job, but somebody has to do it."

Most of the development problems encountered have involved the limitations of the changing marketplace. Mark says, "We've designed our products to work with the widest range of computers. Currently, all the Living Books only need 2.5 MB of RAM to run and take up no space on your hard drive. As systems get more complicated, operating systems take up more of the RAM and we're always having to figure out ways to make the program more efficient just because operating systems are filling up the available RAM."

Todd Power was the Product Manager for many of the Living Books titles. As Todd points out, testing is an important part of production. They begin testing after a few pages in a book have been completed. Living Books has an extensive Quality Assurance lab made up of numerous computers with many different configurations, although the Windows versions provide the most challenge. Todd says, "Computers with every imaginable configuration are set up to run the Living Books, and the PC end of the testing is especially tricky due to all the different device drivers. Currently, QA takes about a month, although early on it took perhaps twice that amount of time when we were first learning and before the PC environment became more standardardized. The Mac testing has never been as problematic."

Living Books continues to bring to life children's classics. Currently, Mark's team is working on a series of Dr. Seuss books that will captivate child and adult alike—just as the other Living Books have done. But as Mark says, "Many adults still have computer phobia, although as computers become easier to use, this is beginning to go away. When I bought my first computer (a Mac), I opened up the manual and started reading it. My kids came up and immediately jumped onto the computer and started playing. I kept saying, 'Wait a minute, wait a minute! I'm reading the manual!' and they were saying 'Let me drive!' Kids aren't afraid the computer is going to blow up. They've grown up with the technology and they're not afraid of it." There's no doubt that the Living Books are contributing significantly to the computer literacy of an even younger generation.

The Essential Frankenstein

When classic literature is put into electronic format, it can provide the reader with a much richer experience, but only if the various multimedia elements are effectively incorporated. Nearly everyone agrees that curling up and reading a book is more pleasant than reading the same text from a computer screen. But when photographs, illustrations, video, and sound are added, the reader is able to experience more and hence have a greater sense of appreciation for the work. A good example of this is The Essential Frankenstein, published by Byron Preiss Multimedia in New York City.

Throughout The Essential Frankenstein (see Figure 9.7 on page 199), the user is thrust into another world in which haunting music and visual effects set moods that bring to life Mary Shelley's classic tale. The user may access chapters in the book that are accompanied by supplemental graphics of Mary Shelley's original manuscript and watch an interview with Leonard Wolf (see Figure 9.8 on page 200), the film consultant to the recent Kenneth Branagh film. The title also includes classic movie trailers, images from various *Frankenstein* movies (see Figure 9.9 on page 201), a game, a cartoon (see Figure 9.10 on page 202), and two video screen savers.

The sister company of Byron Preiss Multimedia is Byron Preiss Visual Publications which has been successfully publishing a variety of books since 1984 and is perhaps best known for what Byron Preiss (the President and founder of the companies) refers to as "bringing elements together"—books that involve a collaborative effort. Examples include *Robot Dreams,* which brought together Isaac Asimov and a production designer of *Star Wars,* and *The Secret Life of Pandas,* which involved Jane Goodall and Chinese naturalists. In 1992, Byron Preiss started Byron Preiss Multimedia to publish books in electronic format.

The multimedia company has 35 employees and five different imprints, each of which publishes different kinds of titles. Digital Bauhaus is an imprint that focuses on nonfiction edutainment and includes titles such as *The Ultimate Frank Lloyd Wright* and *The American Heritage History of the Civil War.* The Arts and Commerce imprint is devoted to desktop tools such as Seinfeld's ScreenSaver & Planner. Brooklyn Multimedia is a game imprint, and Crayon Multimedia is a children's imprint. Finally, the 21st Century Classics division covers classic literature such as *Frankenstein* and the works of Steinbeck. The Director of this division is Rachel Forrest. When I spoke with Rachel, she was very pleased because The Essential Frankenstein had just received an excellent review in *Computer Life* magazine and had been featured on *Entertainment Tonight* along with the popular Seinfeld disc.

Rachel has a long and varied background in literature. She has a Master's Degree in English Literature and was working on her Ph.D. when she took a job as Product Manager at the Bureau of Electronic Publishing, a company that publishes a variety of CD-ROM titles. It was here that she began developing electronic titles such as *U.S. History, Great Literature* and *Twain's World,*

Figure 9.7 The Essential Frankenstein. *Courtesy of Byron Preiss Multimedia.*

Figure 9.8   *Along with text from the book, the user may also view the original notes of the author as well as a video interview with Leonard Wolf. Courtesy of Byron Preiss Multimedia.*

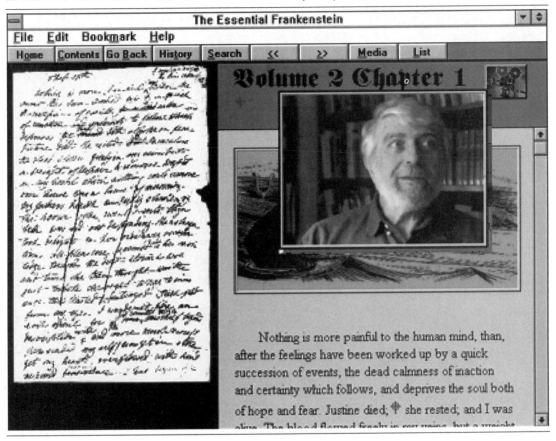

a compilation of all the works of Mark Twain. One of Rachel's responsibilities was to design the discs to determine where the hypermedia links would go. She eventually got more involved in programming and came to understand all aspects of digitizing information. As Rachel puts it, "In order to manage a disc you have to understand everything."

After working at the bureau for several years, Rachel was hired by Byron Preiss Multimedia to direct the development of classic literature. There she has worked on a number of projects including The Essential Frankenstein, Slaughterhouse Five, and Of Mice and Men. Through part of our interview, Rachel compared the development of titles such as Frankenstein, which is more consumer oriented, with that of Twain's World, a title used more for reference.

Figure 9.9 *The user may view video clips and photographs from the various movie versions of* Frankenstein. *Courtesy of Byron Preiss Multimedia.*

The birth of the Creature in Mel Brook's "Young Frankenstein".

Rachel explains, "Twain's World contains over 300 of his works on the disc. Because of this, we had to identify this as a product that would be used to compare and mostly do research. It would provide the user with an entire library on a disc. So we really had to concentrate on text manipulation. The multimedia aspects were really used to augment the text rather than to immerse the user into an experience. With Frankenstein, we were able to concentrate on a single work, and the multimedia elements were used to create moods for each chapter. The multimedia allows the user to experience all aspects of what Frankenstein means to different people such as filmgoers and

Figure 9.10   *A scene from a cartoon in* The Essential Frankenstein. *Courtesy of Byron Preiss Multimedia.*

modern writers. The user can really be immersed in the whole history of Frankenstein throughout the last couple of hundred years."

To create moods, they used video and commentaries from various people. As Rachel points out, this would be very difficult to do for a disc that contains over 300 works. The many multimedia diversions in Frankenstein enhance the experience of what the user is reading. Rachel says, "There is one question that people ask all the time with a title like this and that is, 'Are people really reading the literature from the disc on the computer?' And I think that with a disc like Frankenstein, they will be because there are so many things to learn along the way."

With Twain's World, they were more concerned about textual content because it would be used for reference. This meant that they needed to set up a lot of tag words for searches. They also needed to make it as complete as possible. A question they had to ask themselves was whether they could fit all of Twain's work onto the disc. The only work they left off of the disc was a book that was published posthumously called *Letters from the Earth* because it would have involved copyright issues that they didn't have time to work out. Rachel says, "It's virtually complete. But people still call us up and say 'Hey! You didn't include *Letters from the Earth*.' It's just amazing how much people know about Mark Twain!"

The project team for Frankenstein consisted of ten people, including programmers, a video digitizer, a sound engineer, graphic artists, and animators. They hired an outside composer to write the music. The program was developed using Microsoft Viewer with some programming modifications, although Rachel believes that in the future they will migrate to Director and Visual Basic because they are more graphically oriented. Frankenstein took six months to develop, but as Rachel points out much of the work was already done because it was based on the book version published by Byron Preiss Visual Publications. The book is heavily annotated and illustrated and includes an extensive filmography. The editor of the book was Leonard Wolf who specializes in horror fiction and horror films and was the consultant for Kenneth Branagh's recent film *Frankenstein*.

The multimedia version of The Essential Frankenstein was a natural extension of the book and focuses heavily on the historical context and theme. The disc includes all the book's annotations and illustrations, as well as narratives such as Mary Shelley's journal in what might be her own voice. Along with the original music, these elements help to set moods in the various chapters. Besides video clips from the various Frankenstein trailers, the disc also includes an interview with Leonard Wolf, although Rachel admits that he was initially skeptical about multimedia. She says, "I think sometimes academics are very skeptical because they think multimedia is going to diminish their work in some way. But when Leonard saw the disc he was very pleased. That's one of the reasons we like to get academics involved in the discs. It helps serve as a learning experience, and they are generally very excited to participate."

Slaughterhouse Five has an especially appropriate theme for multimedia. As Rachel says, "I took the theme of the hero, Billy Pilgrim, being randomly thrust through worlds and different time periods. The user has the option to travel in that way with the program." Figure 9.11 on page 204 and Figure 9.12 on page 205 illustrate scenes from that title. Rachel points to multimedia as a

Figure 9.11   Slaughterhouse Five *contains a video of an interview with its author, Kurt Vonnegut. Courtesy of Byron Preiss Multimedia.*

whole new genre of literature, and has noticed an interesting trend in recent years. "Instead of people coming to you with a pitch for a book, they're coming to you with a pitch for a multimedia disc that tells a story. They're leaping over the middle step of giving you a linear book and are instead saying, 'I have an idea for a novel, but I think I can adapt this idea for multimedia.' You have to make a little paradigm shift in your own head and see things in a different way." Rachel sees the electronic book industry including increasingly more interactive fiction.

Figure 9.12 *A screen display from* Slaughterhouse Five. *Courtesy of Byron Preiss Multimedia.*

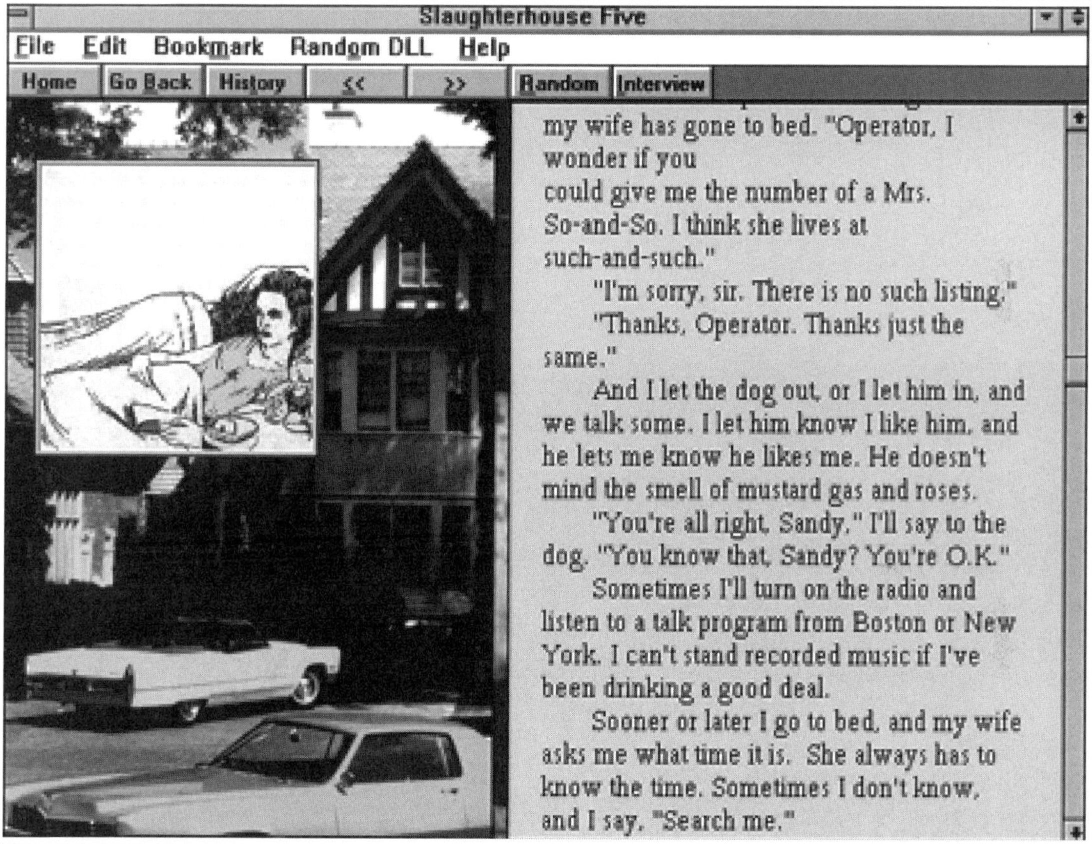

my wife has gone to bed. "Operator, I wonder if you could give me the number of a Mrs. So-and-So. I think she lives at such-and-such."

"I'm sorry, sir. There is no such listing."

"Thanks, Operator. Thanks just the same."

And I let the dog out, or I let him in, and we talk some. I let him know I like him, and he lets me know he likes me. He doesn't mind the smell of mustard gas and roses.

"You're all right, Sandy," I'll say to the dog. "You know that, Sandy? You're O.K."

Sometimes I'll turn on the radio and listen to a talk program from Boston or New York. I can't stand recorded music if I've been drinking a good deal.

Sooner or later I go to bed, and my wife asks me what time it is. She always has to know the time. Sometimes I don't know, and I say, "Search me."

Since working with multimedia, Rachel doesn't look at a book in the same way she used to. "Now when I look at a book, I automatically see it in terms of what I would do and how I would arrange it to make it into a multimedia product. For example, I ask myself where I would put video and what video I would use to make this scene come alive, or what would I do with the characters. The characters have different perceptions of an action, and the user would have the option of selecting different characters with their perspectives of the activity. It would provide an understanding of what plot and characterization really mean in a novel. To be able to offer the complexity of what the author meant would be a very interesting thing to do. It's almost performance art on a disc."

The main problem they encounter with any title is in acquiring content. Although the text for many of the titles is in the public domain (because it was published over 75 years ago and is no longer protected by a copyright), other content such as film presents complications. As Rachel says, "Getting Hollywood film is very difficult because most of the owners of film rights have their own multimedia divisions. They are making their own deals and they don't want you to have it." Rachel explains that getting textual content from books with copyrights is just as difficult. "All of the big book publishers have their own electronic divisions now. So they are deciding whether to take that property in-house or let somebody else do it. Consequently large book companies are rapidly developing relationships with companies like Byron Preiss."

Rachel also points to the problems involved with the immaturity of the industry. "The industry is so new that the rules are still being made about what's in copyright and what's out of copyright. What you are able to get in acquisition will often change your original plan and will often mold how the product will be developed." And as Rachel says, "There is a lot of competition among the multimedia companies to get hot modern twentieth century authors, and that's another issue. We're publishing Steinbeck right now, and everybody wanted to publish Steinbeck."

The company tries to avoid copyright issues by commissioning for creative content. For example, Rachel recently worked on a disc about Raymond Chandler. Although she could have tried to obtain the rights to use photographs from books about Hollywood, Rachel instead commissioned someone who lived in Los Angeles to take similar pictures. By doing so, she was able to avoid copyright issues. Rachel says, "It was much cheaper in the long run, and the photographs were much better." For any project, they must decide whether to license material such as a documentary or to hire an expert and have it filmed themselves.

Rachel advises that book adaptations should have a real purpose. She says, "You need to make sure there's a reason you're putting a book into multimedia. Too often people just take a book and add some pictures and call it multimedia. But I think you need to have a real idea, a real concept, a real purpose in making it a multimedia disc. For *Of Mice and Men*, we wanted to graphically represent the themes, and to allow the user to really understand the historical context of the migrant worker. And hopefully that would relate to things that are going on today such as poverty and homelessness. So I think people need to be sure that they aren't just doing multimedia for the sake of doing multimedia. They need to have a well-thought-out concept in mind."

Rachel continues, "Everybody wants to be involved with multimedia. I was thinking the other day that they should do a remake of *The Graduate* where they're at the party and the guy comes up and says 'Multimedia' instead of 'Plastics.' Everyone has an idea for a disc. Every graphic designer thinks he should start his own company, and really there are so many development packages out there that are fairly inexpensive that you can do it. But marketing it is the big thing. We have distribution through Microsoft and Time Warner and that takes care of it for people who come to Byron Preiss with good ideas. As a matter of fact, a multimedia agent called me up the other day representing someone with an idea for a multimedia title. You know it's an established industry when you have 'multimedia' agents."

Further Reading

Butterbaugh, Sean. 1994. "CD-ROMs Seek Toehold in Bookstores." *InterActive Week* (November 7): 67.

Delaney, Paul, and George P. Landow (eds.). 1991. *Hypermedia and Literary Studies.* Cambridge, MA: MIT Press.

Gossage, Lew, and Bill Bayer. 1994. "Moving College Textbooks to CD-ROM." *CD-ROM Professional* (March): 90.

Green, Jeff. 1993. "CD-ROM Publishing Arrives." *MacWeek* (December 6): 32.

Jonas, Gerald. 1993. "The Disappearing $2,000 Book." *New York Times Book Review* (August 29): 12.

Mike, Dennis G. 1994. "Interactive Literacy: CD-ROM Reading Programs that put Education First." *Electronic Learning* (May/June): 50.

Mitchell, Gabrielle. 1994. "Electronic Titles May Become Latest Chapter for Many Booksellers: From the ABA Convention." *Computer Retail Week* (June 6): 6.

Newman, Keith. 1994. "Tribune Taps New Media." *Computer Retail Week* (July 11): 8.

Norton, Priscilla. 1992. "When Technology Meets the Subject-Matter Disciplines in Education. Part Two: Understanding the Computer as Discourse." *Educational Technology* (July): 36.

Osborn, Barbara Bliss. 1994. "Write on the Money." *Film and Video Monthly* (January/February): 14.

Pack, Thomas. 1994. "Electronic Books: A New Spin on the Great American Novel." *CD-ROM Professional* (March): 54.

Poor, Alfred. 1995. "Searching for the Right Words." *Computer Shopper* (January): 808.

Reynold, Louis R., and Steven J. Derose. 1992. "Electronic Books." *Byte* (June):264.

Schwartz, Evan I. 1992. "Scrolled Any Good Books Lately?" *Business Week* (September 7): 61.

Smith, Dawn. 1994. "A First Look at Interactive Books." *Marketing Computers* (November): 42.

Stansberry, Domenic. 1993. "Hyperfiction: Beyond the Garden of the Forking Paths." *NewMedia Magazine* (May): 52.

CONSULTING IN THE MULTIMEDIA WORLD

Introduction

Consulting is tough to do, no matter what area one is working in. Any mistakes you make along the way come out of your own pocket. You are faced with buying your own hardware and software, and the time you spend learning to use that software is not covered by a salary. When starting out, you are constantly trying to balance the need to get a contract by bidding a job lower than you should with the need to get the work and grow financially. And many times you feel you cannot take any time off because that next contract has just come in and it means more business.

Consulting in multimedia involves additional challenges. The very nature of multimedia requires diverse talents and involves legal issues regarding ownership of content. And it is still an area that many people just do not yet understand. But like all areas of consulting there are some basic things one needs to constantly keep in mind.

Perhaps the toughest part of consulting is in finding those first clients. Most agree that it is best to target a specific type of client and focus on the types of applications you, as the consultant, are most familiar with. For example, someone who has come from a corporate sales background might want to specialize in sales presentation applications, while someone with training experience might focus on developing training software. As has been apparent from the profiles in this book, probably no other area of technology has attracted people from such diverse backgrounds. This can be an advantage because the consultant can tap into the industry with which he or she is most familiar and likely to already have contacts.

In addition, it is much easier to sell clients on an idea if you understand their needs and can communicate with them using their own "language." This can be crucial in terms of understanding the program to be developed and setting up a realistic schedule for the project. One of the greatest reasons consultants inadvertently underbid a job is miscommunication. Either the client has unrealistic expectations or the consultant does not fully understand what the client wants.

Because of this, it is crucial to work closely with the client and have frequent reviews to ensure that both sides are aware of the direction in which the project is going. In doing so, one should set up milestones that involve a set of goals to be completed at specified times. At the end of each of those time periods, the consultant should have the client sign off that portion of the work.

Even so, nearly every consultant has encountered clients who really do not know what they want or, worse yet, clients who keep changing their minds along the way. They may have initially wanted the interface to work one way, only to decide that they now want it to work in a very different way. The most important rule is to keep a very good paper trail to record these deviations from the initial plan. Never have a discussion on the phone and agree to make changes without immediately writing a formal document clearly stating the changes requested by the client and having the client sign the document. This is crucial in case you need to renegotiate the contract and request more money to cover those changes.

Most projects involve unforeseen problems or additions, and if the client is unwilling to work with you on a time and materials basis, it is important to build in cost overruns when bidding a job. Nearly every project takes more time and effort than was initially expected. In part, this is because a client who sees what is possible with multimedia often wants to add other elements that escalate the cost to complete the project. In such cases, the client must understand that any additions will change the scope of work and involve an additional fee. If money is tight, the client may decide that the program does not really need those additions or, if it is possible, have some of the additional work done in-house to keep costs down. And frequently it is possible, if the necessary expertise is available within the company. Many times, the costs may be renegotiated.

Starting a multimedia consulting firm, like any other business, is not for everyone. It involves a lot of financial risk and tenacity to make it work. You suffer the early frustrations of submitting proposal after proposal only to strike out many more times than you can land a contract. You must work very long hours and weekends to get a foothold in the industry. But it can also be one of the most rewarding and interesting jobs you can have.

Overview of Profiles

Two consulting companies are profiled here and demonstrate how people with very different backgrounds have successfully developed multimedia applications targeted at the markets with which they are most familiar.

Imagix Productions is headed by Gary Chapman, whose background is in corporate marketing. Gary has created a number of applications involving sales presentations and has also begun developing portions of multimedia titles for very large companies on a subcontractual basis.

Sapphire Pacific is a company that specializes in developing customized interactive programs for research scientists and environmental consultants. Most of the applications also involve expert system capabilities that help inexperienced people make decisions closely matching those of an expert in that field.

Imagix Productions

Many people getting started in multimedia do so on a consultancy basis, bidding on projects that eventually lead to the growth of the company. Gary Chapman started out this way when he founded Imagix Productions in 1992, a small firm based in San Diego. Imagix has developed a variety of multimedia software, including corporate presentations, trade show kiosks, and interactive training programs for several large companies. One of these is a psychological self-help title which deals with attention training that can be applied to business and sports. For example, it teaches the user how to remain calm in stressful situations and includes games that reinforce the messages conveyed in the program. The content for the program was provided by a publishing company who will also market the title, while Imagix provided the artistic treatment and programming. Imagix has also produced an interactive guided tour to accompany a best-selling CD-ROM title for a leading multimedia company. Figures 10.1–10.5 illustrate some of the programs Gary has developed.

Prior to starting his own company, Gary was Vice President of Product Marketing for Fujitsu Systems of America. He first got interested in multimedia in 1989 when he attended a CD-ROM conference in Boston. He realized then that the technology was going to be a major force in the industry. Gary recalls, "That conference was a real watershed for me. I really wanted to get involved." Because Gary was responsible for new product development, he had a budget that allowed him to purchase multimedia development software such as Director and various graphics packages. Because Gary's field was marketing, he didn't have programming experience at that time and wanted an

Figure 10.1 *This screen is a somple of an animated sales demonstration used by Applied Retail Solutions in a trade show exhibit booth. The demo features eye-catching graphics and animation and a variety of different soundtracks, which can be modified by booth personnel while the demo is running. Courtesy of Imagix Productions.*

authoring tool that would allow him to develop creative presentations without requiring extensive programming skills. "I looked at Authorware, but that had some limitations in terms of the amount of animation you could create directly in it, and it had a really expensive price tag. Director was the right tool for me."

Gary began working with Fujitsu's marketing/communications department to develop interactive presentations. But in 1992, Gary decided to start his own company to develop multimedia software. Gary says, "Fortunately, I had the resources to carry myself financially while I got more proficient with the

Figure 10.2   *Imagix Productions created a summary of the MacWorld Conference for the San Diego Macintosh Multimedia user group. The summary featured QuickTime video of key exhibits. This screen shows the video that was used to identify the setting of the conference as San Francisco. Courtesy of Imagix Productions.*

tools. Although I thought I knew what I was doing in the beginning, I really didn't. There's a big difference between creating some interactive presentations for internal use and being able to make a living at it. So I honed my own skills for a year. But I was able to start out with a couple of contracts and that helped."

One of those contracts was a multimedia presentation for his former firm that illustrated how to install a slot scanner. The company initially was going to have a training video produced, but Gary convinced them that they should instead have a multimedia presentation developed that would include animation, still photography, video, and voiceovers to accomplish the same thing.

Figure 10.3 *This is the interactive menu of the Imagix Productions marketing demonstration, which outlines the benefits of using multimedia and describes the firm's capabilities. Courtesy of Imagix Productions.*

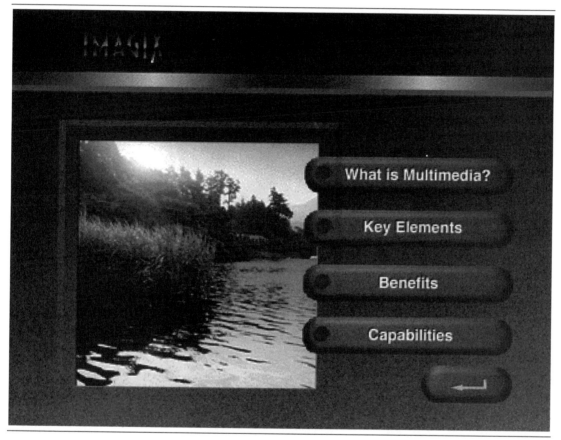

Gary explains, "It was very difficult to describe in words how to install their slot scanner. But once you saw it being done, you could do it. We included about five minutes of live video with the program and then spun the whole thing out to videotape. We were able to bring it in for considerably less than what a full training video would have cost to produce."

Gary used several strategies to get contracts when he started out. He gave talks at local computer conferences and set up a booth at trade shows, although he admits that the latter did not bring him sufficient business to justify the time and cost involved. He joined local multimedia user groups such as the Digital Multimedia Association through which he has made several valuable contacts. In addition, Gary has taught multimedia courses at the

Figure 10.4   *A slide from a presentation made by Gary Chapman to the San Diego Chapter of the IICS. The topic was development processes for creating CD-ROM titles. Courtesy of Imagix Productions.*

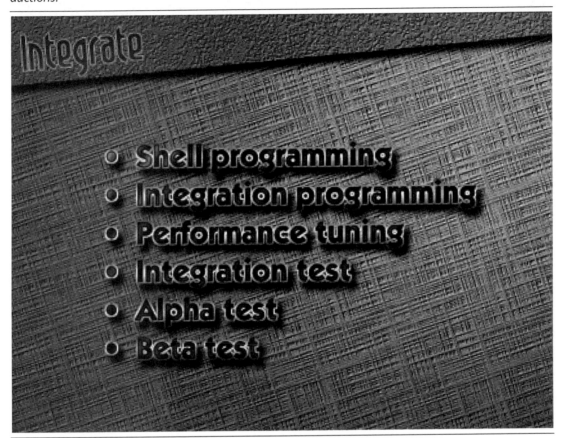

University of California's Extension College in San Diego. He also helped develop the multimedia program for the Foundation for Educational Achievement, a nonprofit organization funded in part by the state of California to train qualifying people for free who needed to upgrade their job skills or who were in danger of being laid off. And he has written articles for newspapers and has just completed a book on multimedia.

Gary also went back to his previous business associates and developed sales presentations for many of them. As his skills grew, he was able to continue to bring in more and more contracts, and eventually began subcontracting to other large multimedia companies. Because most of his consulting work has

Figure 10.5 *Another slide from the presentation described in Figure 10.4. Courtesy of Imagix Productions.*

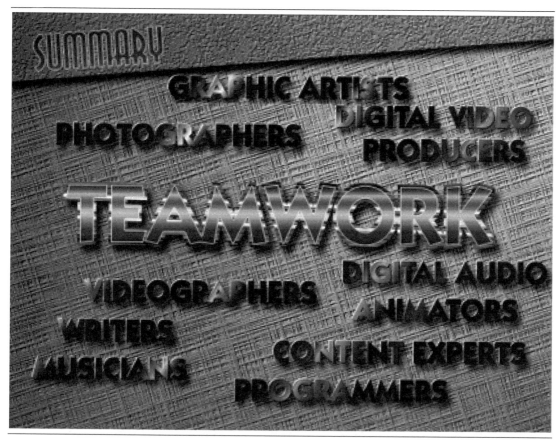

involved local companies, networking and referrals have been very important. As is true with any type of networking, it helps to live in or near a large city. San Diego provides an ideal locality for entrepreneurial companies, particularly those involved in high technology, and proved to be a fruitful city to network in multimedia. Gary says, "There is a strong and thriving multimedia community here. It is easier to get started if you are near a city like San Diego, although it can still be done if you live in a small town because of modems, networks, and on-line bulletin boards. But it's really nice to be able to get together with other people and help each other figure out how to develop various aspects of multimedia."

Gary concedes that his first year in business was lean, but he is now well established in his third year. He currently has two full-time employees and subcontracts out work according to the size and requirements of various projects. On large contracts, he has subcontracted work to as many as six people. Gary points out that it is very costly to start a multimedia development company. "In the course of three years, I've probably put $100,000 into this company for hardware, software, and upgrades. I literally spend close to $200 a month just in software upgrades to stay current with all the tools. There are what I call the *big four*. You have to have Director, Photoshop, SoundEdit 16, and Premiere. But in addition to that, you need a host of other ancillary tools such as Strata StudioPro, FreeHand, Illustrator, Painter, Morph, and clip media. And you need to continually upgrade your equipment. It saves you money in the long run because it saves you time."

Gary avoids copyright issues as much as possible and has been successful in doing so, in part because Imagix Productions creates much of the needed material, including sound and video. Other material is provided by the company for which they develop software. As Gary points out, "When you're a small company, the best way to avoid copyright issues is to create everything yourself. When we develop something for a large company, they assume the responsibility for any material they provide to us."

As with most multimedia development teams, Gary's projects involve some division of labor. Gary does most of the programming and animation, while his associate, Gary Holley, does most of the backgrounds and graphics. As Gary (Chapman) points out, "We can work in parallel that way, which is important when you're looking to meet schedules. Many times, I'll program a shell of the presentation, such as a sales demo. I'll prototype it with all the buttons and text placeholders to indicate where the graphics and animations will go. Then as the artwork gets done, we integrate it into the program." Another associate, Mark Sylvester, also handles much of the graphics production and manipulation. Mark also works on incorporating many of the standard Lingo handlers needed on a given project. For larger projects, Gary hires additional people to help with the graphics and programming effort. His teaching and networking have also helped him find the right people to hire. Gary Holley was, in fact, a student in one of Gary's multimedia classes.

Although formerly a math major, Gary Holley became interested in art, which eventually led to computer graphics and an interest in multimedia. Gary (Chapman) has found him to be a valuable asset to the company. He says, "He's a phenomenal artist and he can also program. But we tend to gravitate toward a division of labor."

Although most of their programs are developed for the Windows environment, they use the Mac for development. Perhaps the greatest problem Gary has encountered has been in porting applications from the Mac to Windows. Gary says, "Before Director was seamless between Mac and Windows, it was a very difficult and tedious process to port an application. Once you finished your Director presentation on the Mac, you had to compile it into a PC-playable runtime package, which you moved to the PC using a LAN or some transfer tool. Then you would test it on the PC. The problem was that the PC runtime package always lagged behind the current Director release for the Mac, and there were always some commands you couldn't use. If you had an illegal command, you'd have to go back to the Mac and rewrite the code, then recompile and go through the same process. It was very time consuming. With the new 4.0 version of Director, it's much easier." However, Gary points to problems with the PC environment because it is not yet standardized. He finds that the differences between various video cards have caused them the most problems.

One of the most difficult tasks faced by every consultant is bidding a job, especially when he or she is first getting established. There is always the dilemma of bidding low in order to get the contract while ensuring that the work is contributing to the financial growth of the company. Gary admits that bidding a contract can be tough. "Companies have different expectations, and they all want to operate on a fixed-cost basis. I don't understand why companies don't want to do things on a time and materials basis. That really offers them the greatest flexibility and protection because they can just cut off the project if it's not giving them the results they want. Instead, they want to be absolutely certain what the project is going to cost. If I were to go back to corporate life, I would view how we did things very differently now."

Gary believes this is especially problematic with creative media such as interactive programs. "When you see multimedia, you immediately think of a dozen more things you'd like to do. So as a consultant, you need to build a certain cushion into your estimates to cover changes the client is going to want. The problem is that many clients won't want to pay for the additions because they think it ought to be part of the original contract." As Gary points out, it's very difficult to get a multimedia program's concept down the first time. It involves a more iterative process than other types of software development. Most clients believe that they can get the concept right during the first meeting, but as Gary says, they really can't—and this needs to be taken into account when bidding any job.

I asked Gary if he had ever underbid a job and what can be done to rectify such situations. Gary says that in many cases it is possible to renegotiate the scope and/or cost of the project if the client understands the situations and is amenable to renegotiation. In other cases, the client may be willing to take on part of the work in-house, but he points out the client often will take the easy aspects of the program, leaving him to handle the more difficult ones. And he admits there are times when you simply lose. Gary says, "When you're starting out, you tend to low-bid jobs to get the work, and you just don't make as much money from a project as you should. But you're getting your name established, and that makes it easier to get the next job—especially if you're doing work for major companies."

Like many developers that start out in consulting, Gary sees himself moving away from consulting and putting more effort into developing products. Gary says, "I think that consulting is a way of generating revenue while you're gearing up and acquiring skills and people to work with you on a regular basis so that you can produce titles. There is a lot more money in producing titles, but you really need to get to a critical mass of about a half dozen people, and they each have to have areas of specialization. I'm sure there are people who can be successful just being consultants, but my personal interest lies in the development and creativity of producing a title that looks great and does well."

Gary offers some advice to others starting out as consultants in the field. "Don't grab at any new tool that comes along unless you have a lot of resources or unless the tool is going to have a significant impact in the title you're developing. Don't pay the penalty of being the beta tester as a small shop. Let the big companies with the staff and R&D money be the beta testers. I have seen titles that were actually delayed because the company jumped on the new tool bandwagon, and the new tool was faulty and had to be reworked. And so the company couldn't release its title because it depended on that tool. So the small developer has to be especially careful how he invests his money. Newest isn't always best." Gary admits that he has gotten involved in beta versions at the direction of larger companies that were paying for a title he was working on. But he says, "In every case it turned out to be a bad experience. I think title productions should not be based on beta tools."

Marketing is another area in which Gary has learned some lessons. "It's important to be careful how you spend your marketing dollars as a small company. Networking and word of mouth is still the best way to promote yourself. I've gone to large trade shows and set up booths, and that hasn't always been successful. You get a lot of interested people who just want to look, and it is a way of getting your name into the community. But the dividends that come from that are usually minimal. I still go to trade shows, but I go as a seminar speaker. I find you can get some fairly decent leads from that kind of activity."

Gary's plans for the future involve the development of three titles in the next year. Although he has developed titles for other major companies, he wants his company name to be on these. One is a title for children that has a circus theme. He says, "My ideal business is to have about ten people working on two titles concurrently—one that is almost done, and one that is just starting up. We're not quite there yet, but we're getting closer." He also hopes to be working on titles for other companies on a work-for-hire basis and to have four full-time employees by the end of 1995. Gary also has another goal—to have more free time for his personal life. "When you're in a startup mode, you tend to work six to seven days a week, and you can get pretty burned out. So one of my goals is to continue to do what I'm doing, but to take a little bit more time for myself."

Sapphire Pacific

Finally, I come to the profile of my own small company in La Jolla, California, called Sapphire Pacific, which develops interactive applications, many of which involve expert system capabilities. Although most of our clients have been research organizations and environmental consultants, we have also developed applications in other areas such as social services and manufacturing. All of the programs rely heavily on high-resolution photographs and most involve decision support concerning complex information using rules based on the knowledge of an "expert" in that field. A brief overview of a few of them will make it clearer why we use certain software, and how we have targeted clients.

COREXPERT is a program developed for Scripps Institution of Oceanography (part of the University of California in San Diego) to help their geological curating staff record descriptions of sediment cores taken from the sea floor. Because accurate descriptions must be made by people who do not all have the expertise needed to identify microscopic-sized mineral grains and fossils, the program contains photographs and narrations to help them recognize what they are seeing in the microscope (see Figure 10.6 on page 222). An important aspect in recognizing certain constituents is to rotate them on a microscope stage in polarized light, and such "animations" may be seen in the program. Rules check the user's input and warn about inconsistent entries, such as sediment components that don't generally occur in the entered abundance, or fossils recorded by the user that don't commonly occur together.

Fossil Notes is a series of electronic catalogs of various microfossil groups that contain high-resolution photographs, textual descriptions, and other data

Figure 10.6   *A screen display from COREXPERT. Throughout the program, the user may access textual descriptions, graphic illustrations, and animation that help in the recognition of sediment components. Courtesy of Sapphire Pacific.*

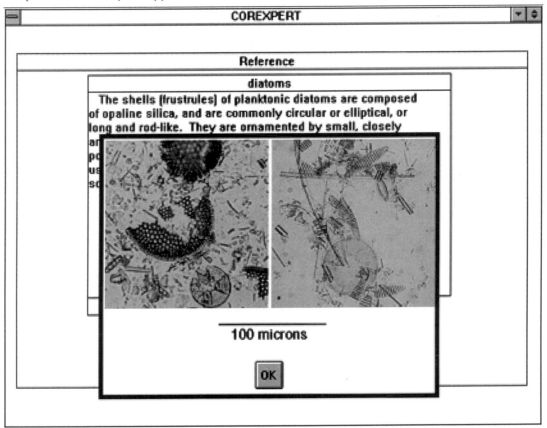

used by paleontologists (see Figures 10.7 on page 223 and 10.8 on page 224). The user may view animations of evolutionary changes while a narration describes what is being displayed. We have also developed a number of programs for environmental firms that help them assess impacts resulting from development. For example, one program allows the user to scroll through and zoom in on large aerial photographs (see Figure 10.9 on page 225) and maps of a region and to compare photographs taken before and after an area has been disturbed. A recent project, funded by the National Institutes of Health, is being developed for use by social service organizations to recommend the most appropriate housing for the elderly based on their needs and preferences.

Figure 10.7 *A screen display from one of the Fossil Notes series of electronic catalogs for a particular group of microfossils. By clicking on one of the illustrations of major categories of these microfossils, the user may then view the various species contained in the catalog. Courtesy of Sapphire Pacific.*

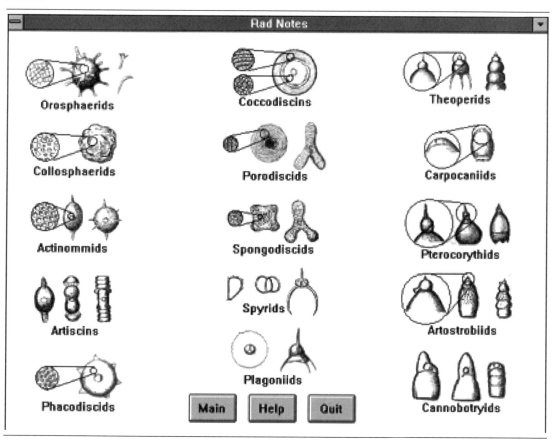

Using MATCH the client may view photographs of the facility as well as floor plans, menus, and activities while a narrative describes the residence and its amenities (see Figure 10.10 on page 226 and Figure 10.11 on page 227).

Like most of the other people I interviewed for this book, my background is not in computers or multimedia. I became involved in the technology to assist with various projects I was working on. I used to be a research scientist in Paleontology and I have a Ph.D. in Biology and Geology. After receiving my degree in 1982, I began doing research at Scripps Institution of Oceanography. As part of our work there, we relied heavily on computers to analyze large

Figure 10.8 *While viewing photographs of individual species, the user may display photographs of similar species to assist with an accurate identification. Courtesy of Sapphire Pacific.*

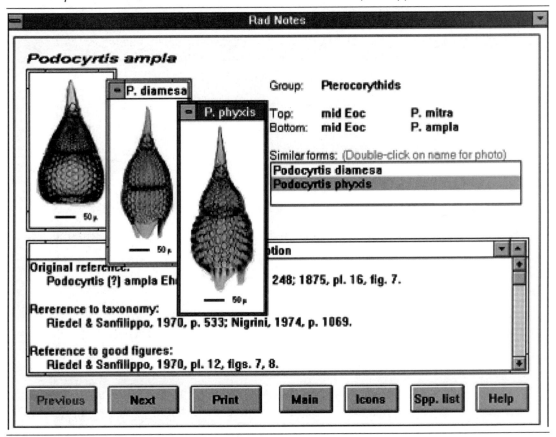

amounts of data. I eventually became involved in projects that used computers to help identify microfossils recovered from sediment cores taken from the sea floor. Microfossils are used to determine the ages of the various layers in the cores. This information is then used to interpret the history of the earth in terms of events that took place tens of millions of years ago such as climatic changes and the movement of the earth's crust.

During this time I worked closely with Bill Riedel, a well-known paleontologist who also has been a pioneer in the area of applied artificial intelligence. (Bill continues to work with my company on a number of projects.) When I began working at Scripps, he had been attempting for a number of years to have computers help identify microfossils in the hope that a computer would

Figure 10.9 *Several environmental programs Saphhire Pacific has been involved in include aerial photographs that the user can zoom in on to view specific regions in greater detail. Courtesy of Sapphire Pacific.*

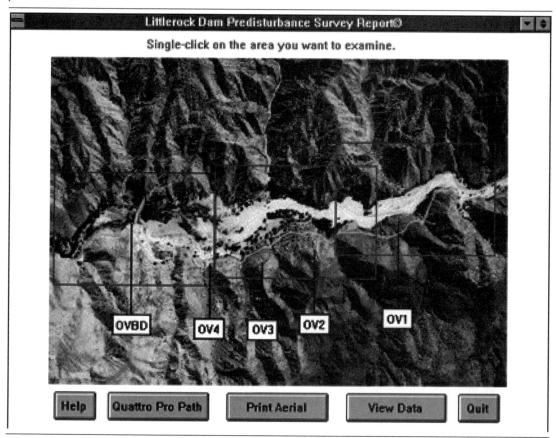

be more accurate and consistent in recognizing the various species. For this work, we had a video card in a computer connected to a camera attached to a microscope. We tried to write programs that would allow the computer to recognize the various shapes and features of the microfossils that would distinguish one species from another.

We eventually came to the conclusion that the human observer is better able to quickly recognize certain features using his or her eyes and mind, and that with expert assistance someone with little experience in paleontology could make accurate identifications. This led to our work in expert systems and neural networks, and we found multimedia elements to be an important way of

Figure 10.10   *A screen display from MATCH. Courtesy of Sapphire Pacific.*

helping the user answer essential questions such as "What is the shape of the outline?" or "What does this look like when rotated in polarized light?" We began by implementing high-resolution photographs and eventually added other elements such as animation and sound. Morphing proved to be an effective way to illustrate the evolutionary development of fossils.

I eventually decided to leave the research environment and started Sapphire Pacific in 1989. Although I wanted to work on similar projects, I also wanted to apply the technologies we had been using to other areas. My first clients were research organizations who were familiar with my work at Scripps and who wanted similar programs written to assist in their work. Many of these projects started out as a small program that was expanded each year as the client came up with additional funding. Because my background in the sciences is

Figure 10.11 *A screen display from MATCH. Courtesy of Sapphire Pacific.*

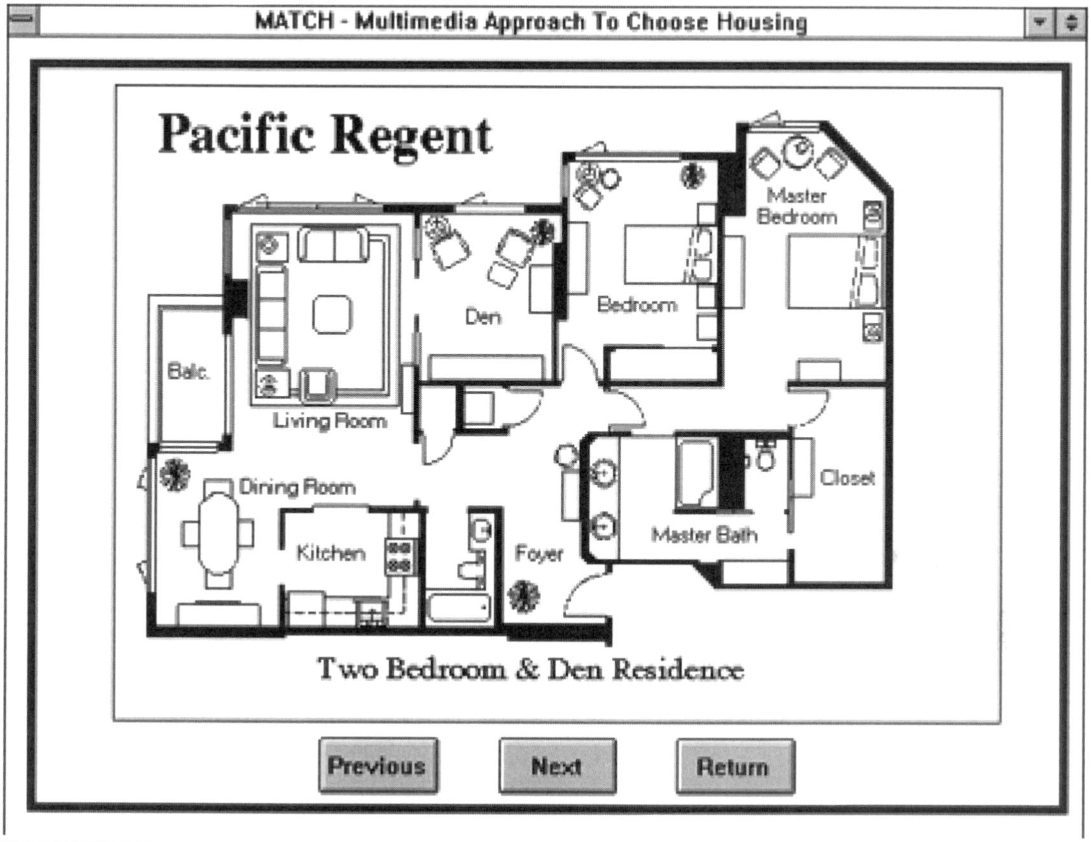

fairly broad, I had a number of contacts in both the geological and biological fields, and soon began working with environmental firms. Our work initially focused on expert system development but has since moved increasingly toward interactive multimedia applications, many of which do not involve decision support. This evolution has dictated many of the choices we have made over the years—from the software we use to the funding we seek.

Because so many of our programs are written for scientists, we have found that we need to keep the screen design very simple—almost austere. Any glitz wouldn't be accepted well by most of our clients, and in some sense this makes our development a bit easier from the standpoint of design. All of our work is done on a PC. Like others developing interactive multimedia programs, we use a number of software packages such as PhotoMorph, Autodesk Animator Pro,

MediaDB, PhotoFinish, OmniPage, and many more. Because much of our work has involved expert system development, we have done most of our programming using a Windows application development language called Knowledge Pro. We find it has a powerful programming language and a very flexible expert system engine, and the final code may be translated into C++. We incorporate multimedia using Microsoft's Multimedia Development Kit. For multimedia projects that don't require expert system capabilities, we frequently use a more "traditional" authoring tool such as Authorware or Multimedia Tool-Book.

Like Gary Chapman of Imagix, I have found networking to be the most useful way to build a client base. Because most of our clients are not local, I need to attend major conferences (usually in other states or even countries) in order to make contacts—something that is very costly. When I first started my company, I set up a booth at these meetings, and although many people expressed interest in our work, we never landed a contract large enough to pay for the expense and time we had invested. A booth is really more valuable if one is marketing a product rather than a service—particularly if the service involves a very specialized clientele. However, I still find it valuable to attend the meetings to keep in contact with our various (and potential) clients. Although I have not taken advantage of them, there are programs such as the Small Disadvantaged Business Program that can help woman- and minority-owned businesses get started. Such programs ensure that large companies that subcontract out work have a certain percentage of the work go to a disadvantaged business.

Like many people who begin a consulting business, we are moving increasingly in the direction of product development rather than custom application development. And like many companies struggling in a high technology field, we spend much of our time doing research and development. Because of this, one of the most important sources of money we have discovered is the Small Business Innovation Research (SBIR) program sponsored by the federal government. Because I have found that very few companies are aware of the program, I feel it is worth explaining the program in some detail here. I hope that many reading this book will benefit from the information.

Various agencies of the government such as the National Institutes of Health, the Environmental Protection Agency, the Department of Defense, and the National Science Foundation provide funds to small businesses that are developing products on the leading edge of technology. In order to compete for this funding, the company must be "small" (that is, less than 500 employees) and for-profit. You must also submit a lengthy proposal detailing the project to be undertaken. Key factors in getting funded are innovation and risk. The project must involve technology that does not currently exist or technology that will be used in a very innovative way. The project is thus risky enough that the company would likely have difficulty in getting funds from other sources.

The SBIR program typically involves three phases, and a proposal must be submitted for each one. During the Phase I period, a company tests the feasibility of its project to determine if the proposed technological innovation is, in fact, possible. A Phase I project is intended to take about six months to complete and typically involves funding from $50,000–75,000. The proportion of submitted proposals that are awarded range from one in five to one in eight. Once a company has been awarded a Phase I grant and successfully shown the technology to be feasible, it may write a proposal for Phase II funds to continue development of the product. A Phase II project generally lasts two years and may be awarded funds of $500,000 or more. Phase III involves commercialization of the product, and the company must find its own funding to bring the product to market. The SBIR program is meant to help defray the costs involved in the initial R&D stages of product development.

We have received SBIR funding and found it has allowed us to be involved with innovative development while helping us stay afloat to do so. Although in the past, the technologies we focused on involved artificial intelligence, we are now working to develop programs also involving innovative techniques in multimedia. Because we are in the initial phases on these projects, I'm not able to provide details. However, I believe that the SBIR program is something that those involved in leading edge technology should look into.

Although we have been fortunate to obtain funding from the SBIR program, I might offer a few cautionary notes. First of all, one needs to be able to write academic-like proposals and must have the patience (and finances) to wait for six months (or longer) before hearing if the proposal will be funded. Many companies feel they can't wait that long, particularly if they have other means of acquiring money. In addition, it is important to realize that if you team with another company on an SBIR project, only one of the companies can submit the proposal as the "Principal Investigator" and that company must assume the lead from that point on. If after the first phase of the project the lead company decides that it does not want to pursue a Phase II grant for that project (perhaps because the focus of the company has shifted to another area), the other company of the team cannot assume the lead and submit a Phase II proposal under its own name. Obviously, this can result in tension between the two companies, but this is an aspect of any type of partnership. It's vital to think through who should be the lead company submitting the grant proposal.

In developing applications, one of our main concerns has involved content and ownership of a program, particularly as we are beginning to develop products that can be sold to multiple users. A good case in point is Fossil Notes, which I mentioned earlier. This is the first program we developed with the intention of selling to multiple users. Because of this, we were careful to write the program as a shell so that it could be used for other microfossil groups. In fact, the program could be adapted for flowers, trees, and almost anything one wants to catalog. The problem, of course, is content. Once one collaborates with the owner of content, there is inevitably some conflict about who owns the software. In most cases so far, we have been approached by others who want us to modify our program to work with their content; that is, the particular microfossil group that they work with. Our strategy has been to make it clear that Sapphire Pacific owns the program and they own the database. Each of these components of the software is sold separately, although Sapphire Pacific handles the production, marketing, and handling of the product.

Throughout this book, I have asked the people I interviewed what mistakes they made that they would be willing to share. I know that we made several, especially when I first started the company. I underbid many jobs in order to get the work, and although this wasn't necessarily a mistake, I believe that I did this more than I had to. It finally came to the point where I decided I'd rather not get the contract than work as hard as I did for what I was being paid. It was then that I began to double the amount I was initially bidding, and to my delight we still got the contracts.

Another mistake I made with a couple of clients was in not documenting changes they requested via phone, in part because I know them fairly well. I recall one project in which the client requested a specific interface design. After we set this up in the program and sent it to him, he decided he wanted a different interface, which we discussed at length on the phone. I made the fatal error of not documenting our conversation and having him sign the document. After we reprogrammed the interface design, he had no recollection of requesting the change and wanted it set up the way we had first designed it. Although we had saved some of the initial program, we hadn't saved all of it (another mistake). Unfortunately I had to swallow the cost because we knew that the client had a set amount he could spend on the project. But we learn from our mistakes, and I have never made that one again. I document even the most minor changes requested by a client.

On the other hand, I think we have done a good job in predicting the emerging technologies and moving in those directions before others have. And we have been fortunate in our SBIR endeavors. Many companies submit a dozen or so proposals before getting one of them funded. We were lucky to get our first proposal funded, and we foresee continuing in that direction. So much of our work is developed for such a small market, and yet I find it fulfilling to work with people with whom I share a common interest and understanding of the content involved. And I enjoy the excitement of working with emerging technologies. I am fond of a saying I heard not too long ago that I think applies to all of us working in multimedia (and AI): "If you're going to work on the cutting edge, be sure to keep yourself away from the blade." I try to, but I don't always succeed.

Further Reading

Berger, Jeff. 1993. "Decisions, Decisions." *NewMedia Magazine* (February): 56.

Bozman, Jean S. 1993. "Looking Forward to Office 2001; Multimedia, Collaborative Technologies Will Find Their Niche in the Office of the Future." *Computerworld* (January 11): 28.

Chepetsky, Susan M. 1994. "Despite Obstacles, Multimedia Is Gathering Adherents." *Digital News and Review* (January 3): 38.

Clark, Carla M. 1994. "Applications-Development Experts to Offer Tips." *Computer Reseller News* (August 29): 30.

Coupland, Ken. 1993. "Declarations of Independents." *NewMedia Magazine* (October): 48.

Dunlap, Charlotte. 1994. "Convergence VARs Consult, for Now." *Computer Reseller News* (September 26): 243.

Jerram, Peter. 1994. "Careers in Multimedia." *NewMedia Magazine* (February): 34.

Menn, Don. 1994. "Profitable Partnerships: The Life of a Media Consultant." *Multimedia World* (April): 89.

"Multimedia Markets." 1994. *Computer Conference Analysis Newsletter* (April 1): 7.

Ricciuti, Mike. 1993. "Making Multimedia Work." *Datamation* (September 1): 30.

Sager, Ira. 1993. "Turning Upside Down? Dataquest Chief Judy Hamilton Confidently Looks Ahead." *Information Week* (January 18): 27.

Schneier, Bruce. 1993. "So, You Want to Be a Multimedia Star." *New Media Magazine* (February): 53.

Shillingford, Joia. 1994. "1994—The Year of Multimedia." *IBM System User* (May): 13.

Resource Directory

Magazines and Newsletters

CD-ROM Professional
462 Danbury Road
Wilton, CT 06897
(800) 248-8466

Communications Industries Report
International Communications Industries
Association
3150 Spring St.
Fairfax, VA 22031-2399
(703) 723-7200

Interactive Age
P.O. Box 194
Skokie, IL 60076
(708) 647-6834

Multimedia and Videodisc Monitor
Monitor Information Services
Future Systems Inc.
P.O. Box 26
Falls Church, VA 22040
(800) 323-3472 or (703) 241-1799

*Multimedia Computing and Presenta-
tions, and New Media in Education and
Entertainment*
Simba Information Inc.
213 Danbury Rd.
Box 7430
Wilton, CT 06897
(203) 834-0033

Multimedia World
501 Second St.
San Francisco, CA 94107
(415) 281-8650

New Media
Hypermedia Communications Inc.
901 Mariner's Island Blvd., Suite 365
San Mateo, CA 94404
(415) 573-5170

Organizations

Interactive Multimedia Association
3 Church Circle, Suite 800
Annapolis, MD 21401
(410) 626-1380

*International Communications Industries
Association*
3150 Spring St.
Fairfax, VA 22031-2399
(703) 273-7200

*International Interactive Communications
Society*
P.O. Box 1862
Lake Oswego, OR 97035
(503) 649-2065

Multimedia Business Communications
1580 Oakland Rd., Suite C206
San Jose, CA 95131
(408) 453-3950

Multimedia Computing Corp.
3501 Ryder St.
Santa Clara, CA 95051
(408) 737-7575

Simba Information Inc.
213 Danbury Rd.
Box 7430
Wilton, CT 06897
(203) 834-0033

CD-ROM Sources

CD-ROM, Inc.
1667 Cole Blvd., Suite 400
Golden, CO 80401
(303) 231-9373

Nautilus
7001 Discovery Blvd.
Dublin, OH 43017-3299
(800) 637-3472

NewMedia Source
3830 Valley Center Dr., Suite 2153
San Diego, CA 92130
(800) 344-2621

UniDisc
4401 Capitola Rd., Suite 4
Capitola, CA 95010
(408) 464-0707

Software

Animation clip software

Animation Clip Art Collections
Visual Magic
620 C. Street, #201
San Diego, CA 92101
(800) 367-6240

Clip Animation Vol I & 2
Illusion Art
P.O. Box 21398
Oakland, CA 94611

Autodesk Animation Library
Autodesk Inc.
2320 Marinship Way
Sausalito, CA 94965
(800) 525-2763

Animation/morphing software

ADDmotion
Motion Works Inc.
1020 Mainland St., Suite 130
Vancouver, British Columbia, Canada
V6B2T4
(604) 685-9975

Animation Stand
Linker Systems
13612 Onkayha Circle
Irvine, CA 92720
(714) 552-1904

Animation Works
Gold Disk, Inc.
385 Van Ness, Suite 110
Torrance, CA 90501
(310) 320-5080

Animation Studio
Walt Disney Computer Software Co. Inc.
500 S. Buena Vista St.
Burbank, CA 91521
(818) 567-5340

Autodesk Animator Pro
Autodesk Inc.
2320 Marinship Way
Sausalito, CA 94965
(800) 525-2763

Cinemation
Vividus Corp.
651 Kendall Avenue
Palo Alto, CA 94306
(415) 494-2111

Deluxe Animation
Electronic Arts
1820 Gateway Drive
San Mateo, CA 94404
(415) 571-7171

Director
Macromedia, Inc.
600 Townsend
San Francisco, CA 94103
(415) 442-0200

Grasp
Paul Mace Software
400 Williamson Way
Ashland, OR 97520
(800) 523-0258

Magic
Macromedia, Inc.
600 Townsend
San Francisco, CA 94103
(415) 442-0200

PC Animate Plus
Brown Wagh Publishing
130-D Knowles Drive
Los Gatos, CA 95030
(408) 378-3838

PROmotion
Motion Works Inc.
1020 Mainland St., Suite 130
Vancouver, British Columbia, Canada
V6B2T4
(604) 685-9975

Visual Magic
620 C. Street, #201
San Diego, CA 92101
(800) 367-6240

Authoring/presentation software

Action
Macromedia, Inc.
600 Townsend St.
San Francisco, CA 94103
(415) 442-0200

Applause II
Borland International, Inc.
1800 Green Hills Road
Scotts Valley, CA 95067
(800) 437-4329

Ask-Me 2000
Innovative Communications Systems
(ICS)
7100 Northland Circle, Suite 401
Minneapolis, MN 55428
(612) 531-0603

Astound
Gold Disk, Inc.
20675 S. Western Avenue, Suite 120
Torrance, CA 90501
(310) 320-5080

Audio Visual Connection
IBM Corp.
Multimedia Information Center
P.O. Box 2150
Atlanta, GA 30301
(800) 426-9402

Authorware
Macromedia, Inc.
600 Townsend St.
San Francisco, CA 94103
(415) 252-2000

CanDo
INOVAtronics
8499 Greenville Ave., Suite 209B
Dallas, TX 74231
(214) 340-4992

Compel
Asymetrix Corp.
110 110th Ave. N.E., Suite 700
Bellevue, WA 98004
(800) 448-6543

Director
Macromedia, Inc.
600 Townsend
San Francisco, CA 94103
(415) 442-0200

GraphShow
Chartersoft Corp.
80 Fennel Street
Winnipeg, Manitoba, Canada R3T3M4
(204) 453-4444

Grasp
Paul Mace Software
400 Williamson Way
Ashland, OR 97520
(800) 523-0258

Guide
OWL International
2800 156th Avenue, S.E.
Bellevue, WA 98007
(206) 747-3203

Hollywood
Claris Corporation
5201 Patrick Henry Drive
Santa Clara, CA 95054
(408) 987-7000

HSC InterActive
Harvard Systems Corp.
1661 Lincoln Blvd., Suite 101

Santa Monica, CA 90404
(310) 392-8441

HyperCard
Claris Corporation
5201 Patrick Henry Drive
Santa Clara, CA 95052
(408) 987-7000

IconAuthor
AimTech Corporation
20 Trafalgar Square
Nashua, NH 03063
(603) 883-0220

Linkway Live!
IBM Corp.
Multimedia Information Center
P.O. Box 2150
Atlanta, GA 30301
(800) 426-9402

MacPresents
Educational Multimedia Concepts, Inc.
1313 Fifth SE, Suite 202E
Minneapolis, MN 44414
(612) 379-3842

Magic
Macromedia, Inc.
600 Townsend
San Francisco, CA 94103
(415) 442-0200

MediaBlitz
Asymetrix Corp.
110 110th Ave. N.E., Suite 717
Bellevue, WA 98004
(206) 462-0501

MediaDeveloper
Lenel Systems International Inc.
19 Tobey Village Office Park
Pittsford, NY 14534-1763
(716) 248-9720

MediaMaker
Macromedia, Inc.
600 Townsend
San Francisco, CA 94103
(415) 442-0200

Multimedia Make Your Point
Asymetrix Corp.
110 110th Ave. N.E., Suite 717
Bellevue, WA 98004
(206) 462-0501

Multimedia ToolBook
Asymetrix Corp.
110 110th Ave. N.E., Suite 717
Bellevue, WA 98004
(206) 462-0501

Persuasion
Aldus Corporation
411 First Avenue, S.
Seattle, WA 98104
(800) 333-2538

PowerPoint
Microsoft Corp.
1 Microsoft Way
Redmond, WA 98052
(800) 227-4679

Presenting Now...
ISM, Inc.
2103 Harmony Woods Road
Owings Mills, MD 21117

(410) 560-0973

Quest Multimedia Authoring System
Allen Communication Inc.
5225 Wiley Post Way, Suite 140
Salt Lake City, UT 84116
(801) 537-7800

Storyboard Live!
IBM Corp.
Multimedia Information Center
P.O. Box 2150
Atlanta, GA 30301
(800) 426-9402

SuperCard
Aldus Corporation
411 First Avenue, S.
Seattle, WA 98104
(800) 333-2538

Tempra Show
Mathematica Inc.
402 S. Kentucky Ave.
Lakeland, FL 33801
(813) 682-1128

Clip art software

Adobe Collector's Edition
Adobe Systems, Inc.
1585 Charleston Road
Mountain View, CA 94039
(415) 961-4400

ArtRoom CD
Image Club Graphics
Suite 5, 1902 11th Street

SE Calgary, Alberta, Canada, T2G3G2
(800) 661-9410

Chinese Clip Art
Pacific Rim Connections
3030 Atwater Drive
Burlingame, CA 94010
(415) 697-9439

Design Clips
LetterSpace
338 E. 53rd Street, #2C
New York, NY 10022
(212) 935-8130

Designer's Club Collection
Dynamic Graphics, Inc.
6000 N. Forest Park Drive
Peoria, IL 61614
(800) 255-8800

EduClip Images
Teach Yourself By Computer Software,
Inc.
3400 Monroe Avenue
Rochester, NY 14618
(716) 381-5450

EPS Clip Art collections
T/Maker Company
1390 Villa Street
Mountain View, CA 94041
(415) 962-0195

Japanese Clip Art
Qualitas Trading Co.
6907 Norfolk Road
Berkeley, CA 94705
(415) 848-8080

MacKids Kolor Klips
Nordic Software, Inc.
917 Carlos Drive
Lincoln, NE 68505
(402) 488-5086

Media Line
Free Spirit Software, Inc.
58 Noble Street
Kutztown, PA 19530
(215) 683-5609

Medical Clip Art
TechPool Studios
1463 Warrenville Center
Cleveland, OH 44121
(800) 777-8930

MultiWare CD ROM
BeachWare
5234 Via Valarta
San Diego, CA 92124
(619) 492-9529

ProArt
Multi-Ad Services, Inc.
1720 W. Detweiller Drive
Peoria, IL 61615
(800) 447-1950

SoftClips
SoftWood Inc.
P.O. Box 50178
Phoenix, AZ 85076
(800) 247-8330

Visual Delights CD-ROM
SunShine
P.O. Box 4351

Austin, TX 78765
(512) 453-2334

Vivid Impressions
Cassady & Green, Inc.
P.O. Box 223779
Carmel, CA 93922
(800) 359-4920

Graphics software

Adobe Illustrator
Adobe Systems, Inc.
1585 Charleston Road
Mountain View, CA 94039
(415) 961-4400

Adobe Photoshop
Adobe Systems, Inc.
1585 Charleston Road
Mountain View, CA 94039
(415) 961-4400

Aldus PhotoStyler
Aldus Corporation
411 First Avenue, S.
Seattle, WA 98104
(800) 333-2538

Arts & Letters Graphics Editor
Computer Support Corporation
15925 Midway Road
Dallas, TX 75244
(214) 661-8960

Canvas
Deneba Software
3305 N.W. 74th Avenue

Miami, FL 33122
(800) 622-6827

CorelDraw!
Corel Bldg.
1600 Carling Avenue
Ottawa, Ontario, Canada K1Z8R7
(613) 728-8200

Designer
Micrografx, Inc.
1303 Arapaho
Richardson, TX 75081
(800) 272-3728

Designworks
New Horizons Software
206 Wold Basin Road, Suite 109
Austin, TX 78746
(512) 328-6650

Freehand
Aldus Corporation
411 First Avenue, S.
Seattle, WA 98104
(800) 333-2538

IntelliDraw
Aldus Corporation
411 First Avenue, S.
Seattle, WA 98104
(800) 333-2538

MacDraw Pro
Claris Corporation
5201 Patrick Henry Drive
Box 58168
Santa Clara, CA 95052
(408) 987-7000

PhotoFinish
Softkey
450 Franklin Road, Suite 100
Marietta, GA 30067
(404) 428-0008

Picture Publisher
Micrografx, Inc.
1303 Arapaho
Richardson, TX 75081
(800) 272-3728

Professional Draw
Gold Disk, Inc.
20675 S. Western Avenue, Suite 120
Torrance, CA 90501
(310) 320-5080

Publisher's Paintbrush
Softkey
450 Franklin Road, Suite 100
Marietta, GA 30067
(404) 428-0008

SuperPaint
Aldus Corporation
411 First Avenue, S.
Seattle, WA 98104
(800) 333-2538

Windows Draw
Micrografx, Inc.
1303 Arapaho
Richardson, TX 75081
(800) 272-3728

Morphing software

Elastic-Reality
ASDG Inc.
925 Steward St.
Madison, WI 53713
(608) 273-6585

Digital Morph
HSC Software
1661 Lincoln Blvd., Suite 101
Santa Monica, CA 90404
(310) 392-8441

Flo', MetaFlo'
The Valis Group
P..O. Box 422
Point Richmond, CA 94807
(510) 236-4124

Morph
Gryphon Software Corp.
7220 Trade St., Suite 120
San Diego, CA 92121
(619) 536-8815

PhotoMorph
North Coast Software Inc.
P.O. Box 459
265 Scruton Pond. Rd.
Barrington, NH 03825
(603) 664-6000

VideoFusion
VideoFusion Ltd.
1722 Indian Wood Circle, Suite H
Maumee, OH 43537
(419) 891-1090

WinImages:Morph
Black Belt Systems
398 Johnson Rd.
Glasgow, MT 59230

Multimedia database software

Mariah
Symmetry
8603 E. Royal Road, Suite 110
Scottsdale, AZ 85285
(602) 998-9106

MediaTree
Tulip Software
P.O. Box 3046
Andover, MA 01810
(508) 475-8711

MPC Organizer
Lenel Systems International Inc.
19 Tobey Village Office Park
Pittsford, NY 14534-1763
(716) 248-9720

MediaDB
MediaWay, Inc.
3080 Ocott St., Suite 220C
Santa Clara, CA 95054
(800) 632-7401

Portfolio
SoftShell International
715 Horizon Drive, Suite 390
Grand Junction, CO 81506
(303) 242-7502

Music clip software

*250 of the World's Greatest
Music Clips*
Future Vision
60 Cutter Mill Road
Great Neck, NY 11021
(516) 482-0088

MultiWare CD-ROM
BeachWare
5234 Via Valarta
San Diego, CA 92124
(619) 492-9529

MusicBytes
Prosonus
11126 Weddington
North Hollywood, CA 91601
(818) 766-5221

QuickTunes
Passport Designs Inc.
100 Stone Pine Road
Half Moon Bay, CA 94019
(415) 726-0280

SoundSavers
Animotion Development Corp.
3720 Fourth Ave. South, Suite 205
Birmingham, AL 35222
(800) 536-4175

Sound software

Alchemy
Passport Designs Inc.
100 Stone Pine Road

Half Moon Bay, CA 94019
(415) 726-0280

AudioShop
Opcode Systems Inc.
3950 Fabian Way, Suite 100
Palo Alto, CA 94303
(415) 856-3333

Audio Trax
Passport Designs Inc.
100 Stone Pine Road
Half Moon Bay, CA 94019
(415) 726-0280

AudioView
Voyetra Technologies
333 Fifth Ave.
Pelham, NY 10803
(800) 233-9377

Digital Performer
Mark of the Unicorn
222 Third St.
Cambridge, MA 02142
(617) 576-2760

Master Tracks Pro-5
Passport Designs Inc.
100 Stone Pine Road
Half Moon Bay, CA 94019
(415) 726-0280

MCS Stereo
Animotion Development Corp.
3720 Fourth Ave. South, Suite 205
Birmingham, AL 35222
(800) 536-4175

Monologue
First Byte
19840 Pioneer Avenue
Torrance, CA 90503

SoundEdit Pro
Macromedia, Inc.
600 Townsend St.
San Francisco, CA 94103
(415) 442-0200

SoundTrak
Animotion Development Corp.
3720 Fourth Ave. South, Suite 205
Birmingham, AL 35222
(800) 536-4175

Studio 3.04
Midisoft Corp.
263 N.E. 90th St.
Redmond, WA 98502
(206) 8817176   [sic!]

Trax
Passport Designs Inc.
100 Stone Pine Road
Half Moon Bay, CA 94019
(415) 726-0280

Wave for Windows
Turtle Beach Systems Inc.
Cyber Center, Unit 33
1600 Pennsylvania Ave.
York, PA 17404
(717) 767-0200

Video software

Deluxe Video III
Electronic Arts
1820 Gateway Drive
San Mateo, CA 94404
(415) 571-7171

D/Vision-Pro
TouchVision Systems Inc.
1800 W. Winnemac
Chicago, IL 60640
(312) 989-2160

Sundance 2.0
Sundance Technology Group
6309 N. O'Connor Road, Suite 111
Irving, TX 75039
(214) 869-1002

Video Director
Gold Disk, Inc.
20675 S. Western Avenue, Suite 120
Torrance, CA 90501
(408) 982-0200
(analog vs. digital, so may not work)

VideoToolkit
Abbate Video
83 Main Street
Norfolk, MA 02056
(508) 520-0197

VideoWare
HSC Software
1661 Lincoln Blvd., Suite 101
Santa Monica, CA 90404
(310) 392-8441

Virtual/Video Producer
V_Graph Inc.
1275 Westtown Thornton Road
Westtown, PA 19396
(215) 399-1521

Hardware Peripherals

CD-ROM drives

Chinon America Inc.
660 Maple Ave.
Torrance, CA 90503
(800) 441-0222 or (213) 533-0274

Hitachi Home Electronics (America) Inc.
401 West Artesia Blvd.
Compton, CA 90220
(800) 369-0422 or (213) 537-8383

NEC Technologies Inc.
1414 Massachusetts Ave.
Boxborough, MA 01719
(800) 632-4636 or (508) 254-8000

Panasonic
2 Panasonic Way
Secaucus, NJ 07094
(800) 742-8086

Peripheral Land Inc.
47421 Bayside Pkwy.
Fremont, CA 94538
(800) 288-8754

Sony Corp.
3 Paragon Drive
Montvale, NJ 07645-1735
(800) 352-7669

Texel America Inc.
1080-C East Duane Ave.
Sunnyvale, CA 94086
(800) 886-3935

Toshiba America Consumer Products
1010 Johnson Drive
Buffalo Grove, IL 600089
(800) 253-5429

Sound boards

Artisoft Inc.
691 East River Road
Tucson, AZ 85704
(800) 846-9726 or (602) 293-4000

Convox Inc.
675 Conger St.
Eugene, OR 97402
(503) 342-1271

Creative Labs Inc.
1901 McCarthy Blvd.
Milpitas, CA 95035
(800) 544-6146 or (408) 428-6600

Macromedia Inc.
600 Townsend St.
San Francisco, CA 94103
(415) 442-0200

Media Vision Inc.
47221 Fremont Blvd.
Fremont, CA 94538
(800) 348-7116 or (510) 770-8600

Turtle Beach Systems
Cyber Center, Unit 33
1600 Pennsylvania Ave.

York, PA 17404
(717) 843-6916

Video boards

Creative Labs Inc.
1901 McCarthy Blvd.
Milpitas, CA 95035
(408) 428-6600

Digital F/X Inc.
755 Ravendale Drive
Mountain View, CA 94042
(415) 961-2800

Digital Vision Inc.
ComputerEyes/RT
270 Bridge St.
Dedham, MA 02026
(617) 329-5400

New Media Graphics
780 Boston Rd.
Billerica, MA 01821-5925
(508) 663-0666

TrueVision
7340 Shadeland Station
Indianapolis, IN 46256
(800) 344-8783

Turtle Beach Systems
Cyber Center, Unit 33
1600 Pennsylvania Ave.
York, PA 17404
(717) 843-6916

VIP video capture subsystem
Ventek Corp.
31336 Via Colinas, Suite 102
Westlake Village, CA 91362-9897
(818) 991-3868

Scanners

Flatbed scanners

Advanced Vision Research Inc.
562 S. Milpitas Blvd.
Milpitas, CA 95035
(408) 956-0350

Epson America Inc.
20770 Madrona Ave.
Torrance, CA 90509
(800) 922-8911 or (310) 782-0770

Hewlett-Packard Co.
19310 Pruneridge Ave.
Cupertino, CA 95014
(800) 752-0900

Howtek Inc.
21 Park Avenue
Hudson, NH 03051
(603) 882-5200

Microtek Lab Inc.
680 Knox St.
Torrance, CA 90502
(800) 654-4160 or (213) 321-2121

Mustek Inc.
15225 Alton Parkway

Irvine, CA 92718
(800) 366-4620 or (714) 833-7740

Sayett Technology Inc.
17 Tobey Village
Pittsford, NY 14534
(716) 264-9250

Sharp Electronics Corp.
Sharp Plaza MS 1
P.O. Box 650
Mahwah, NJ 07430
(800) 237-4277 or (201) 529-9593

UMAX Technologies Inc.
3170 Coronado Drive
Santa Clara, CA 95054
(800) 562-0311 or (408) 982-0771

Hand-held scanners

Computer Friends Inc.
14250 Northwest Science Park Dr.
Portland, OR 97229
(800) 547-3303 or (503) 626-2291

Intel Corp.
5200 Northeast Elam Young Pkwy.
Hillsboro, OR 97124
(800) 525-3019 or (503) 629-7354

KYE International Corp.
2605 E. Cedar St.
Ontario, CA 91761
(800) 456-7593 or (714) 923-3510

Logitech Inc.
6505 Kaiser Drive

Fremont, CA 94555
(800) 231-7717 or (510) 795-8500

Touch-screen and Pen input

Arthur Dent Associates
500 Clark Rd.
Tewksbury, MA 01876-1639
(508) 858-3742

Elographics Inc.
105 Randolph Rd.
Oak Ridge, TN 38730
(615) 482-4100

IBM Corp.
1133 Westchester Ave.
White Plains, NY 10604
(800) 426-9402 or (914) 642-4662

Ink Development Corp.
1300 South El Camino Real, Suite 201
San Mateo, CA 94402
(415) 573-6565

MicroTouch Systems Inc.
55 Jonspin Rd.
Wilmington, MA 01887
(508) 694-9900

NCR Corp.
1700 S. Patterson Blvd.
Dayton, OH 45479
(800) 225-5627 or (513) 445-5000

Visage Inc.
1881 Worcester Rd.

Framingham, MA 01701
(508) 620-7100

Removable storage/portable hard drives

Iomega Corp.
1821 West 4000 South
Roy, Utah 84067
(800) 456-5522

Kingston Technology Corp.
17600 Newhope Street
Fountain Valley, CA 92708
(714) 435-2600

Mega Drive Systems
489 South Robertson Blvd.
Beverly Hills, CA 90211
(310) 247-0006

SyQuest Technologies Inc.
47071 Bayside Parkway
Fremont, CA 94538
(510) 226-4000

Vision Logic
283 E. Brokaw Rd.
San Jose, CA 95112
(408) 437-1000

Glossary

2-D animation
> Animation involving the creation of a series of 2-dimensional images that appear to move on the screen.

3-D animation
> Animation used for virtual reality in which an object may be viewed from different perspectives, giving the impression of a third dimension.

adaptive differential pulse code modulation (ADCPM)
> Translator that compresses high-quality audio files.

ADC
> *see analog-to-digital converter*

ADCPM
> *see adaptive differential pulse code modulation*

analog-to-digital converter (ADC)
> Used to convert analog sound to digital sound.

animation
> Technique in which several images are displayed in rapid succession, giving the appearance of movement.

artificial intelligence
> Technology in which the computer is programmed to perform various tasks in the same way that humans do; areas include robotics, expert systems and neural networks.

authoring software
> Software that allows the developer to incorporate all the elements of multimedia (such as sound, graphics and video) into a cohesive, interactive application.

CAV
> *see constant angular velocity*

CD-DA
> *see compact disc-digital audio*

CD-I
> *see compact disc-interactive*

CD-R
> *see compact disc-recordable*

CD-ROM
> *see compact disc-read only memory*

CD-ROM XA
> *see compact disc-read only memory extended architecture*

codec
> Compression/decompression techniques used for digital video recordings; may be either software- or hardware-based.

CLV
> *see constant linear velocity*

compact disc
> Optical storage medium in which a laser beam is used to encode the data.

compact disc-digital audio (CD-DA)
> Compact disc which is the standard for playing audio; uses the Red Book specification.

compact disc-interactive (CD-I)
> Compact disc which relies on a Motorola 68000 microprocessor, a real-time operating system (RTOS) and specific audio and video hardware; uses the Green Book specification.

compact disc-read only memory (CD-ROM)
> Compact disc used to deliver most multimedia titles and software; this uses the Yellow Book Standard

compact disc-read only memory extended architecture (CD-ROM XA)
> CD-ROM technology that allows for synchronous playback of video and sound; uses an extension of the Yellow Book specification.

compact disc-recordable (CD-R)
> Compact discs such as Photo-CDs on which the user may record their own data using either single-session or multi-session technologies; this uses the Orange Book standard.

constant angular velocity (CAV)
> Videodisc technology in which the disc rotates at the same speed, no matter which track it is reading.

constant linear velocity (CLV)
> Videodisc technology in which the disc rotates at different speeds depending on which track is being read.

cross-platform compatibility
> Permits an application to be run on more than one platform, such as Windows and Mac.

DAC
> *see digital-to-analog converter*

digital signal processor (DSP)
> Integrated chip which quickly processes complex sound, graphics and video.

digital-to-analog converter (DAC)
> Used to convert digital sound to analog sound.

direct memory access (DMA)
> Technology that allows for data transfer directly between memory and hardware peripherals, thus bypassing the microprocessor.

DMA
> *see direct memory access*

DSP
> *see digital signal processor*

edutainment
> Multimedia software that provides educational material in an entertaining way.

EISA
> *see Extended Industry Standard Architecture*

Extended Industry Standard Architecture (EISA)
> Architecture used by most PC-compatible computers with 386 and 486 CPUs; evolved from ISA (Industry Standard Architecture).

Green Book specification
> An extension of the Red and Yellow Book specifications that allows for real time video and audio playback.

graphical user interface (GUI)
> Graphical environment used by Macintosh and Windows that displays windows, icons, and other graphical objects.

hyperfiction
> Interactive software that presents a fictional story that may be read in many different ways, and which contains hyperlinks to provide additional information where requested.

hypertext
> Text linked to additional information.

icon-based authoring software
> Authoring software that provides a set of icons, each associated with a series of commands that tell the computer what to do.

Industry Standard Architecture (ISA)
Early architecture used with IBM-PC computers with 8086 and 286 CPUs; eventually evolved into the Extended Industry Standard Architecture (EISA).

ISA
see Industry Standard Architecture

Joint Photographic Experts Group (JPEG)
Hardware-based codec in which every frame in the video is compressed.

JPEG
see Joint Photographic Experts Group

magneto-optical disks
High-density optical storage medium that uses a laser technology to rewrite data to the disk.

MCA
see Micro Channel Architecture

Micro Channel Architecture (MCA)
Architecture used by newer models of IBM PS/2 microcomputers.

MIDI
see Musical Instrument Digital Interface

model
Three-dimensional object that is drawn in several views according to coordinates along axes x, y, and z for use in 3-D animation.

morphing
A technique in which two or more images are blended to give the illusion that the first image is changing into the last one.

Motion Picture Experts Group (MPEG)
Hardware-based codec that compresses only key frames and the changes that occur between those frames; results in higher quality and greater compression than a JPEG codec.

MPEG

> *see Motion Picture Experts Group*

multimedia

> The use of more than one medium to convey information, such as text, sound, graphics and video.

multimedia database

> Software that stores information about the various multimedia files used for application development.

Multimedia PC (MPC) Standard

> Standard established by the Multimedia PC Marketing Council to ensure compatibility among hardware devices and software running under Windows.

multisession

> Technology that allows one to write to different parts of an optical disc in multiple sessions.

Musical Instrument Digital Interface (MIDI)

> International standard that allows electronic musical instruments to interface with digital computers.

Orange Book specification

> Standard used for CD-R that allows for multisession recording of data.

Optical Character Recognition (OCR) software

> Software that translates graphical representations of letters into textual characters.

patent

> Provides protection for technological innovations or inventions.

Photo CD

> Compact disc used to store photographic images to be viewed on a television screen.

presentation software
> Software that allows the user to easily create slide presentations with accompanying animation and sound.

raster graphics
> Bitmapped graphics used in most multimedia titles on the PC; store a pixel-by-pixel representation of an image.

Red Book specification
> Standard used for CD audio disc requiring 16-bit stereo with a sampling rate of 44.1 MHz.

reentrant
> A feature that allows a process with high priority to interrupt one with lower priority.

removable cartridge
> A magnetic storage medium that may be removed from the drive containing the electronics and the read/write heads.

rendering
> A process used in creating 3-D animation in which the model, background and other elements of the image are blended to make the image to appear more realistic, and to allow for cohesive frame transitions.

resolution
> Determines the detail of an image that may be displayed, or the quality of sound that is recorded and played back.

sampling rate
> Refers to the speed (or number of sound samples per second) at which the sound is recorded.

sampling size
> Refers to the amount of information, or the range of sound adjustment, made during the recording.

script-based authoring software
> Authoring software that requires that the developer enter lines of code called a scripting language.

U.S. Copyright Act
> Provides protection for intellectual property that falls into the category of creative art (vs. technological inventions).

vector graphics
> Store images as a set of instructions for recreating the image as an object consisting of geometric elements such as lines, circles, arcs and angles.

videodisc
> Optical medium involving the use of a laser beam to read pits and lands on the surface of a disc to decode data.

Yellow Book specification
> Standard used for CD-ROMs; requires special methods for encoding, organizing and accessing data on a disc.

Index

Numerics
11th Hour   172
2-D animation   251
3-D animation   251
7th Guest   41, 172

A
A.D.A.M.   86
A.D.A.M. Software   90
A.D.A.M. The Inside Story   89
adaptive differential code pulse modulation
    (ADCPM)   28, 251
ADC   251
ADCPM   251
Amiga   13, 15, 173
analog-to-digital converter (ADC)   42, 251
animation   40, 65, 251
    2-D   40
    3-D   41
    3D   40
    cast-based   40
    frame-based   40
    morphing   41
Arthur's Birthday   188
Arthur's Teacher Trouble   188, 193
artificial intelligence (AI)   3, 69, 224, 251
authoring software   10, 13, 47, 49, 50, 51,
    55, 71, 104, 252
auto hypertext   35

B
Bernoulli drive   24
book adaptation   8, 15, 187, 206
Brøderbund Software   188, 190

Buried in Time
    The Journeyman Project 2   159, 165
Byron Preiss Multimedia   77, 198, 200

C
CAV   252
CD-DA   27, 252
CD-I   13, 27, 28, 252
CD-R   27, 29, 252
CD-ROM   27, 28, 252
CD-ROM Extended Architecture (CD-ROM
    XA)   27, 28
CD-ROM XA   27, 28, 252
CLV   252
codec   46, 178, 252
compact disc   252
compact disc-digital audio (CD-DA)   27, 252
compact disc-interactive (CD-I)   27, 28, 253
compact disc-read only memory (CD-ROM)
    253
compact disc-read only memory extended ar-
    chitecture (CD-ROM XA)   253
compact disc-recordable (CD-R)   27, 29, 253
compact discs   26
    CD-DA   27
    CD-I   195
    CD-I   28
    CD-R   29
    CD-ROM   28
    CD-ROM XA   28
    Photo CD   29
constant angular velocity (CAV)   30, 253
constant linear velocity (CLV)   30, 253
consulting   210

copyright
    copyright infringement   18
    copyright protection
        exceptions   19
    infringement   20, 31
    protection   21, 31
cross-platform compatibility   27, 52, 253

D
DAC   253
digital multimedia   215
digital signal processor (DSP)   9, 253
digital-to-analog converter (DAC)   43, 253
Dinosaurs   34, 74
direct memory access (DMA)   13, 254
DMA   254
DSP   254

E
education   15, 31, 45, 58, 86, 97, 98, 122,
        123, 190, 193
edutainment   15, 59, 74, 198, 254
EISA   254
Electronic Business Card   136
Encarta   113
entertainment   4, 6, 8, 15, 27, 34, 41, 181,
        188, 190
Essential Frankenstein   197, 198, 200, 203
Extended Industry Standard Architecture (EI-
        SA)   254

F
Fermilab   60
file size   23, 37, 38, 39, 40, 52
fixed hard disk   23
floppy disk   25, 134, 135, 136, 141, 142
Friends of Fermilab   60

G
games   8, 14, 62, 156, 157, 191, 212
graphical user interface (GUI)   9, 254
graphics
    bitmapped   10, 37

    raster   37
    vector   10, 37
Green Book specification   27, 254
Grow with Hawaii into the Pacific Century
        147

H
hyperfiction   8, 187, 254
hyperlinks   5
hypertext   4, 35, 161, 254

I
IBM PS/2   10, 12, 15
icon   51
icon-based authoring software   254
icon-based programming   51
Imagix Productions   212, 218
Industry Standard Architecture (ISA)   255
information access   7, 8, 15, 34, 55, 112,
        113, 124, 129
integration   18, 47
interactive fiction   157, 187, 204
interactive television (ITV)   157
interactivity   4, 6, 47, 48, 51, 59, 67, 112,
        113, 135, 180, 187
ISA   255
ISO 9660 format   28

J
Joint Photographic Experts Group (JPEG)
        255
Journeyman Project   41, 158
Journeyman Project 2   158
JPEG   46
Just Grandma and Me   188, 189, 192, 194,
        195, 196

L
laserdisc   30, 45, 62
legal issues   18
Living Books (company)   196, 197
Living Books (series)   188, 189, 190, 191,
        192, 193, 194, 195, 197

M

Macintosh   9, 10, 11, 15, 62, 65, 158, 160, 161, 164, 180
magneto-optical disks   25, 255
Mark Twain   188, 200, 203
marketing   7, 15, 74, 80, 94, 122, 133, 134, 136, 147, 148, 207, 220, 228, 230
Mary Chapin Carpenter   136
MCA   255
Micro Channel Architecture (MCA)   15, 151, 255
Microsoft Corporation   75, 120, 122, 183, 207
MIDI   11, 12, 44, 55, 178, 255
model   40, 41, 82, 164, 255
morphing   5, 40, 41, 42, 43, 226, 255
Motion Picture Experts Group (MPEG)   255
MPC standard   11, 43
MPEG   46, 178, 256
multi session   12
multimedia   2, 256
    desktop multimedia   2
    digital multimedia   2
    growth   2, 11, 14, 15
    interactive multimedia   2
    platforms   9, 53
    sales   14
multimedia database   51, 52, 53, 54, 55, 256
Multimedia Hazmat   99
Multimedia PC (MPC) Standard   256
multisession   11, 27, 256
Musical Instrument Digital Interface (MIDI)   256

O

optical character recognition (OCR) software   35, 256
Orange Book specification   27, 256

P

Particles and Prairies   60
patents   21, 22, 31, 256
    Compton's patent claim   22, 32

Photo CD   27, 29, 256
platforms   13, 15, 52
presentation software   7, 47, 48, 135, 257
Presto Studios   157
production software   47, 49

R

raster graphics   257
real-time operating system (RTOS)   27
Red Book specification   27, 257
reentrant   257
removable cartridges   24, 257
rendering   41, 257
resolution   11, 22, 38, 46, 47, 257
RJM Multimedia   99, 100, 103

S

sales   7, 15, 34, 74, 80, 127, 134, 147, 165, 172
sampling rate   27, 43, 257
sampling size   43, 44, 257
Sapphire Pacific   221
script-based authoring software   258
Slaughterhouse Five   188, 200, 203
software
    2-D animation   40
    3-D animation   41
    authoring   49
    morphing   41
    optical character recognition (OCR)   35
    presentation   48
    production   49
    sound   44
sound   9, 10, 11, 12, 13, 15, 19, 21, 22, 27, 28, 42, 43, 44, 52, 53, 55, 137, 140, 144, 180, 181
    software   44
storage
    Bernouilli drive   24
    fixed hard disk   23
    floppy disks   25
    magneto-optical disks   25
    removable cartridges   24

T
text   4, 15, 23, 26, 34
Tom Coffman Multimedia   148, 149, 150,
    153
Tortoise and the Hare   189, 196
training   7, 30, 31, 34, 45, 84, 160, 212
Trilobyte   172, 173, 175, 183

U
U.S. Copyright Act   18, 31, 258
U.S. Patent and Trademark Office   22
Ultimedia   13, 135, 148, 150

V
vector graphics   258
video
    analog   2, 30, 45
    digital   2, 20, 45
Video Linguist   69
videodisc   30, 34, 45, 52, 61, 63, 84, 258
virtual reality   8, 40, 158

W
West End Post Interactive   136, 137, 138,
    142, 144, 146

Y
Yellow Book specification   27, 258

EXHIBIT C

ADOBE SYSTEMS INCORPORATED
MINIMUM TERMS OF END USER AGREEMENTS

(1)   Licensor grants Licensee a non-exclusive sublicense to use the Adobe software ("Software ")
and the related written materials ("Documentation") provided by Adobe Systems Incorporated
("Adobe") to Licensor as set forth below. Licensee may install and use the Software on one computer.

(2)   The Software is owned by Adobe and its suppliers and its structure, organization and code are
the valuable trade secrets of Adobe and its suppliers. Licensee agrees not to modify, adapt, translate,
reverse engineer decompile, disassemble or otherwise attempt to discover the source code of the
Software. Licensee agrees not to attempt to increase the functionality of the Software in any manner.
Licensee agrees that any permitted copies of the Software shall contain the same copyright and
other proprietary notices which appear on the and in the Software.

(3)   Except as stated above, this Agreement does not grant the Licensee any right (whether by license,
ownership or otherwise in or to intellectual property with respect to the Software.

(4)   Licensee will not export or re-export the Software Programs without the appropriate United
States or foreign government licenses.

(5)   Trademarks, if used by Licensee shall be used in accordance with accepted trademark
practice, including identification of the trademarks owner's name. Trademarks can only be used to
identify printed output produced by the Software. The use of any trademark as herein authorized
does not give Licensee rights of ownership in that trademark.

(6)   LICENSEE ACKNOWLEDGES THAT THE SOFTWARE IS A 'TRY OUT' VERSION OF AN
ADOBE PRODUCT, CONTAINING LIMITED FUNCTIONALITY. ADOBE IS LICENSING THE
SOFTWARE ON AN 'AS-IS BASIS' BASIS, AND ADOBE AND ITS SUPPLIERS MAKE NO
WARRANTIES EXPRESS OR IMPLIED, INCLUDING, WITHOUT LIMITATION, AS TO
NON-INFRINGEMENT OF THIRD PARTY RIGHTS, MERCHANTABILITY, OR FITNESS FOR ANY
PARTICULAR PURPOSE. IN NO EVENT WILL ADOBE OR ITS SUPPLIERS BE LIABLE TO
LICENSEE FOR ANY CONSEQUENTIAL, INCIDENTAL OR SPECIAL DAMAGES, INCLUDING
ANY LOST PROFITS OR LOST SAVINGS, EVEN IF REPRESENTATIVES OF SUCH PARTIES
HAVE BEEN ADVISED OF THE POSSIBILITY OF SUCH DAMAGES, OR FOR ANY CLAIM BY
ANY THIRD PARTY.

IF A SHRINKWRAP LICENSEE IS USED [some states or jurisdictions do not allow the exclusion or
limitation of incidental, consequential, or special damages, so the above limitation or exclusion may
not apply to Licensee. Also some states or jurisdictions do not allow the exclusion of implied
warranties or limitations on how long an implied warranty may last, so the above limitations may
not apply to Licensee. To the extent permissible, any implied warranties are limited to ninety (90)
days. This warranty gives Licensee specific legal rights. License may have other rights which
vary from state to state or jurisdiction.]

(7)   Notice to Government End Users: If this product is acquired under the terms of a: GSA
contract: Use, reproduction or disclosure is subject to the restrictions set forth in the applicable ADP
Schedule contract. DoD contract: Use, duplication or disclosure by the Government is subject to
restrictions set forth in subparagraph (c) (1) of 252.227-7013. Civilian Agency contract: Use,
reproduction, or disclosure is subject to 52.227-19 (a) through (d) and restrictions set forth in the
accompanying end user agreement. Unpublished- rights reserved under the copyright laws of the
United States.

Linda Tway
Multimedia in Action!

About the CD-ROM

The Windows-based CD-ROM contains demo versions of eleven of the multimedia titles profiled in the book, including "Dinosaurs," "A.D.A.M.," "Encarta," "The Journeyman Project," "Buried in Time," "The Tortoise and the Hare," and "Harry and the Haunted House." Also included are the various interactive and non-interactive demos of software products used to develop multimedia titles, such as "Photoshop," "Morph," "Photomorph," "Wave for Windows," "1000 of the World's Greatest Sound Effects," "250 of the World's Greatest Music Clips," "HSC Interactive," and "Animation Works Interactive."

System Requirements:

Minimum 386-33 MHz PC-compatible system, 4MB RAM, SVGA graphics capability, CD-ROM drive (dual speed), 8-bit sound card (SoundBlaster compatible), Mouse (Microsoft compatible), Windows 3.x.

Preferred 486-50 MHz (or faster) PC-compatible system, 8MB RAM, CD-ROM drive (triple - or quad-speed), 16-bit sound card.

Although most programs on this CD-ROM will run with the minimum requirements, a few will not produce sound without a 16-bit sound card.

Installation Instructions:

To install the program, insert the CD-ROM. Select "File" and "Run" from Window's Program Manager and enter:

> d:\install.exe (assuming that "d" is the specification of your CD-ROM drive)

This will install a Program Group and icons that allow you to run the program and read information about the program.

Note: You should print out the README.TXT file on the CD-ROM for other important information.

Troubleshooting:

If you encounter problems with the installation, you may still run the program from the Program Manager by selecting to run the file "kpwinrun.exe" and then selecting "mmaction.ckb."

If you encounter other problems, you may contact the author at one of the following e-mail addresses:

> CompuServe ID: 76066,2256
> ltway@ucsd.edu